Published

Thomas P. Adler	Tennessee Williams: *A Streetcar Named Desire/Cat on a Hot Tin Roof*
Pascale Aebischer	Jacobean Drama
Lucie Armitt	George Eliot: *Adam Bede/The Mill on the Floss/Middlemarch*
Simon Avery	Thomas Hardy: *The Mayor of Casterbridge/Jude the Obscure*
Paul Baines	Daniel Defoe: *Robinson Crusoe/Moll Flanders*
Brian Baker	Science Fiction
Annika Bautz	Jane Austen: *Sense and Sensibility/Pride and Prejudice/Emma*
Matthew Beedham	The Novels of Kazuo Ishiguro
Richard Beynon	D. H. Lawrence: *The Rainbow/Women in Love*
Peter Boxall	Samuel Beckett: *Waiting for Godot/Endgame*
Claire Brennan	The Poetry of Sylvia Plath
Susan Bruce	Shakespeare: *King Lear*
Sandie Byrne	Jane Austen: *Mansfield Park*
Sandie Byrne	The Poetry of Ted Hughes
Alison Chapman	Elizabeth Gaskell: *Mary Barton/North and South*
Peter Childs	The Fiction of Ian McEwan
Christine Clegg	Vladimir Nabokov: *Lolita*
John Coyle	James Joyce: *Ulysses/A Portrait of the Artist as a Young Man*
Martin Coyle	Shakespeare: *Richard II*
Sarah Davison	Modernist Literatures
Sarah Dewar-Watson	Tragedy
Justin D. Edwards	Postcolonial Literature
Michael Faherty	The Poetry of W. B. Yeats
Sarah Gamble	The Fiction of Angela Carter
Jodi-Anne George	*Beowulf*
Jodi-Anne George	Chaucer: The General Prologue to *The Canterbury Tales*
Jane Goldman	Virginia Woolf: *To the Lighthouse/The Waves*
Huw Griffiths	Shakespeare: *Hamlet*
Vanessa Guignery	The Fiction of Julian Barnes
Louisa Hadley	The Fiction of A. S. Byatt
Sarah Haggarty and Jon Mee	William Blake: *Songs of Innocence and Experience*
Geoffrey Harvey	Thomas Hardy: *Tess of the d'Urbervilles*
Paul Hendon	The Poetry of W. H. Auden
Terry Hodgson	The Plays of Tom Stoppard for Stage, Radio, TV and Film
William Hughes	Bram Stoker: *Dracula*
Stuart Hutchinson	Mark Twa
Stuart Hutchinson	Edith Wh~ the Cou
Betty Jay	E. M. For:
Aaron Kelly	Twentieth
Elmer Kennedy-Andrews	Nathaniel
Elmer Kennedy-Andrews	The Poetr,
Daniel Lea	George Orwell: *Animal Farm/Nineteen Eighty-Four*
Rachel Lister	Alice Walker: *The Color Purple*
Sara Lodge	Charlotte Brontë: *Jane Eyre*
Philippa Lyon	Twentieth-Century War Poetry
Merja Makinen	The Novels of Jeanette Winterson

Matt McGuire	Contemporary Scottish Literature
Timothy Milnes	Wordsworth: *The Prelude*
Jago Morrison	The Fiction of Chinua Achebe
Merritt Moseley	The Fiction of Pat Barker
Carl Plasa	Toni Morrison: *Beloved*
Carl Plasa	Jean Rhys: *Wide Sargasso Sea*
Nicholas Potter	Shakespeare: *Antony and Cleopatra*
Nicholas Potter	Shakespeare: *Othello*
Nicholas Potter	Shakespeare's Late Plays: *Pericles/Cymbeline/ The Winter's Tale/ The Tempest*
Steven Price	The Plays, Screenplays and Films of David Mamet
Berthold Schoene-Harwood	Mary Shelley: *Frankenstein*
Nicholas Seager	The Rise of the Novel
Nick Selby	T. S. Eliot: *The Waste Land*
Nick Selby	Herman Melville: *Moby Dick*
Nick Selby	The Poetry of Walt Whitman
David Smale	Salman Rushdie: *Midnight's Children/The Satanic Verses*
Patsy Stoneman	Emily Brontë: *Wuthering Heights*
Susie Thomas	Hanif Kureishi
Nicolas Tredell	Joseph Conrad: *Heart of Darkness*
Nicolas Tredell	Charles Dickens: *Great Expectations*
Nicolas Tredell	William Faulkner: *The Sound and the Fury/As I Lay Dying*
Nicolas Tredell	F. Scott Fitzgerald: *The Great Gatsby*
Nicolas Tredell	Shakespeare: *A Midsummer Night's Dream*
Nicolas Tredell	Shakespeare: *Macbeth*
Nicolas Tredell	Shakespeare: The Tragedies
Nicolas Tredell	The Fiction of Martin Amis
David Wheatley	Contemporary British Poetry
Martin Willis	Literature and Science
Matthew Woodcock	Shakespeare: *Henry V*
Gillian Woods	Shakespeare: *Romeo and Juliet*
Angela Wright	Gothic Fiction

Forthcoming

Nick Bentley	Contemporary British Fiction
Alan Gibbs	Jewish-American Literature since 1945
Keith Hughes	African-American Literature
Wendy Knepper	Caribbean Literature
Britta Martens	The Poetry of Robert Browning
Pat Pinsent and Clare Walsh	Children's Literature
Jane Poyner	The Fiction of J. M. Coetzee
Kate Watson	Crime and Detective Fiction
Andrew Wylie	The Plays of Harold Pinter

Readers' Guides to Essential Criticism
Series Standing Order ISBN 978–1–4039–0108–8
(*outside North America only*)

You can receive future titles in this series as they are published by placing a standing order. Please contact your bookseller or, in the case of difficulty, write to us at the address below with your name and address, the title of the series and the ISBN quoted above.

Customer Services Department, Macmillan Distribution Ltd, Houndmills, Basingstoke, Hampshire, RG21 6XS, UK

Shakespeare
The Tragedies

NICOLAS TREDELL

Consultant Editor: Nicolas Tredell

First published 2015 by
PALGRAVE

Palgrave in the UK is an imprint of Macmillan Publishers Limited, registered in England, company number 785998, of 4 Crinan Street, London N1 9XW.

Palgrave Macmillan in the US is a division of St Martin's Press LLC, 175 Fifth Avenue, New York, NY 10010.

Palgrave is a global imprint of the above companies and is represented throughout the world.

Palgrave® and Macmillan® are registered trademarks in the United States, the United Kingdom, Europe and other countries.

ISBN 978–1–137–40489–3   hardback
ISBN 978–1–137–40488–6   paperback

This book is printed on paper suitable for recycling and made from fully managed and sustained forest sources. Logging, pulping and manufacturing processes are expected to conform to the environmental regulations of the country of origin.

A catalogue record for this book is available from the British Library.

A catalog record for this book is available from the Library of Congress.

Typeset by MPS Limit

Printed in China

For Angela

CONTENTS

ACKNOWLEDGEMENTS   xi

NOTES ON TEXT AND REFERENCES   xii

INTRODUCTION   1

Discusses key questions in studying Shakespeare's tragedies: variant texts; co-authorship; classifications; definitions. Outlines the main chapters of the Guide.

CHAPTER ONE   9

The Augustans

Focuses on the uneasy and sometimes hostile response to Shakespeare's tragedies in the later seventeenth and eighteenth centuries, exemplified by Thomas Rymer's attack on *Othello* and the qualified praise of John Dryden, John Dennis and Samuel Johnson.

CHAPTER TWO   17

The Romantics

Discusses the Romantics' warmer welcome to Shakespeare's tragedies, in August von Schlegel's *Lectures on Dramatic Art and Literature* (1809); William Hazlitt's *Characters of Shakespeare's Plays* (1817); and Samuel Taylor Coleridge's observations on Shakespeare, posthumously published in 1836.

CHAPTER THREE   26

The Victorians

Examines three accounts of Shakespeare's tragedies, one from Ireland and two from Europe, which especially influenced the Victorian era: Edward Dowden's *Shakespere* [*sic*] (1875); G. G. Gervinus' *Shakespeare*

Commentaries (1877); and George Brandes' *William Shakespeare* (1898).

CHAPTER FOUR   30

Character and Correlative

Considers A. C. Bradley's magisterial *Shakespearean Tragedy* (1904), the first attempt to offer a systematic account of its subject, and T. S. Eliot's 'Hamlet and His Problems' (1919), which deploys the influential idea of the 'objective correlative'.

CHAPTER FIVE   40

Psychoanalysis and Desire

Explores key psychoanalytical readings of Shakespeare's tragedies in Sigmund Freud's accounts of *Hamlet* (1900) and *Macbeth* (1924); Ernest Jones's *Hamlet and Oedipus* (1949); and Jacques Lacan's 'Seven Lessons on *Hamlet*' (1959).

CHAPTER SIX   51

Imagery and Form

Traces the increasing focus on imagery and form in 1930s and 1940s Shakespeare criticism, discussing G. Wilson's Knight's *The Wheel of Fire* (1930); L. C. Knights' essay 'How Many Children Had Lady Macbeth?' (1933); Caroline Spurgeon's *Shakespeare's Imagery and What It Tells Us* (1935); and Cleanth Brooks' 'The Naked Babe and the Cloak of Manliness' (1946).

CHAPTER SEVEN   68

Archetype and Absurdity

Investigates major attempts to relate Shakespeare's tragedies to fundamental patterns of human thought and behaviour, in Northrop Frye's *Fools of Time* (1967); Jan Kott's *Shakespeare Our Contemporary* (1967); René Girard's *A Theatre of Envy* (1991); and Naomi Conn Liebler's *Shakespeare's Festive Tragedy* (1995).

CHAPTER EIGHT   83

History and Subjectivity

Surveys innovative New Historicist, cultural materialist and British post-structuralist work produced during the 1980s, looking at Stephen Greenblatt's *Shakespearean Negotiations* (1967); Leonard Tennenhouse's *Power on Display* (1986); Jonathan Dollimore's *Radical Tragedy* (1984); and Catherine Belsey's *The Subject of Tragedy* (1985).

CHAPTER NINE   101

Gender and Sexuality

Considers key analyses of gender and sexuality in Shakespeare's tragedies in Janet Adelman's *Suffocating Mothers* (1992); Philippa Berry's *Shakespeare's Feminine Endings* (1999); Coppélia Kahn's *Roman Shakespeare: Warriors, Wounds and Women* (1997); and Jason Edwards' account of *Coriolanus* in Madhavi Menon's *Shakesqueer* (2011).

CHAPTER TEN   120

Ethnicity and Ecology

Engages with crucial critical explorations of Shakespeare's tragedies in ethnic and ecological perspectives, examining Barbara Everett's '"Spanish" Othello: The Making of Shakespeare's Moor' (1982); Ania Loomba's *Shakespeare, Race, and Colonialism* (2002); Gabriel Egan's *Green Shakespeare* (2006); and Simon C. Estok's *Ecocriticism and Shakespeare* (2011).

CHAPTER ELEVEN   137

Philosophy and Ethics

Explores key philosophical readings of Shakespeare's tragedies in Stanley Cavell's *Disowning Knowledge in Seven Plays of Shakespeare* (2003); Jacques Derrida's *Specters of Marx* (1993); A. D. Nuttall's *Shakespeare the Thinker* (2007); and Donald R. Wehrs' 'Moral Physiology, Ethical Prototypes and the Denaturing of Sense in Shakespearean Tragedy' (2006).

CHAPTER TWELVE   155

Religions and Reformations

Examines accounts of the confluence and clash of religions in Shakespeare's tragedies, in Julia Reinhard Lupton's *Citizen-Saints: Shakespeare and Political Theology* (2005), and of the multiple impacts of the Reformation, in Stephen Greenblatt's *Hamlet in Purgatory* (2001) and Gillian Woods' *Shakespeare's Unreformed Fictions* (2013).

CONCLUSION   168

Adumbrates four possible future directions for the study of Shakespeare's tragedies, in terms of spirituality, science, domesticity and social media, citing Ewan Fernie's *Spiritual Shakespeares* (2005); Valerie Traub's 'The Nature of Norms in Early Modern England: Anatomy, Cartography, *King Lear*' (2009); Geraldo U. de Sousa's *At Home in Shakespeare's Tragedies* (2010); and Tom Standage's *Writing on the Wall* (2013).

NOTES   171

SELECT BIBLIOGRAPHY   188

INDEX   194

Acknowledgements

As ever, my deepest thanks go to my dear wife Angela, with whom I have watched and discussed Shakespeare's tragedies for 40 years and who has been an unfailing source of love and support during the writing of this book.

I am also most grateful to Sonya Barker, formerly Senior Humanities Editor at Palgrave and now embarked on a new life, for commissioning and encouraging the book; to Felicity Noble, Palgrave's recently retired Humanities Secretary, for her friendly and efficient assistance at key stages of the project; to the anonymous reviewers of the original proposal and completed draft for their many constructive comments; to Caroline Richards for her prompt and perceptive editing; and to Lucy Knight at Palgrave for overseeing the production process.

Notes on Text and References

All Shakespeare quotations are from The RSC Shakespeare, edited by Jonathan Bate and Eric Rasmussen (Palgrave Macmillan, 2007), and glosses, in square brackets and single quotation marks after the word or phrase, are also from this source unless otherwise noted.

Act, scene and line references are given in Arabic rather than Roman numerals, e.g., *Hamlet*, 'A little more than kin and less than kind' (1.2.64).

References to the Second Quartos of *Lear* and *Hamlet* are indicated by the abbreviation Q2.

In older texts, such as those of Samuel Johnson, capitalization, italicization and punctuation have been silently modernized, unless the older form seems especially significant.

Italics in quotations are in the original text cited unless otherwise stated.

Dates have been supplied for critics and other figures wherever possible, but in some cases these were not available.

Introduction

Shakespeare's tragedies engage, in incomparably resourceful language, with questions of meaning, being, life, death, love, hate, history, politics, sexuality, gender, ethnicity and ecology – and probably with other matters that have yet to be defined and discussed. The critical response to the tragedies is itself, in microcosm, a history of global culture, given their undeniable capacity to spread across and speak to the world. This Guide aims to select what seems essential from the Anglo-American strand of that response. Of course, the volume and variety of criticism that the tragedies have provoked means that readers may want to challenge, alter or augment this selection, and that is all to the good: the reader of this Guide is invited to work actively with its choices, testing them against one another, against alternatives that have not been included but may have a claim to essentialness, and, above all, against Shakespeare's texts.

There have been important developments, especially in recent years, in approaches that explore Shakespeare in relation to theatre, performance and film, the history of the book, and biography. All these are fascinating and fruitful, but, given the intensity and intricacy of Shakespeare's language, the primary focus of this Guide is on critical encounters with the texts of Shakespeare's tragedies – since it is the texts, after all, which are the fundamental reason for the extent and depth of our interest in other aspects of Shakespeare. Recent criticism and scholarship have, however, sharpened our awareness that 'Shakespeare's texts' are not the solid empirical entity they were once held to be. *King Lear* is the most famous example. The first printed version, known as the First Quarto (Q1), came out in 1608, while the second version, which seems to have undergone significant revision, appeared in the First Folio (F1) in 1623. Q1 has about 300 lines that are absent from F1, F1 includes 100 lines not found in Q1, and there are also lots of individual variants within lines. Until the late twentieth century, most critics and teachers worked with a conflated text of *Lear* – that is, a text that combined the versions in Q1 and F1, usually correcting the former against the latter. But Stanley Wells (b.1930) and Gary Taylor (b.1953), the general editors of the 1988 Oxford Shakespeare, rejected the idea of a conflated text and printed two separate texts in succession: the Quarto Text, under the title *The History of King Lear*, and the Folio Text, under the title *The Tragedy of King Lear*.[1] Faced with this, *Lear*'s readers and critics might echo Edmund's words in the play when both Goneril and Regan were avid for his favours: 'Which of them shall I take? / Both? One? Or neither?' (5.1.54–5).

The 'Tragedies' volume of the 1988 Norton Shakespeare, under the general editorship of Stephen Greenblatt (b.1943), followed the Oxford text in printing two versions, arranged as a parallel text, but then added a third, conflated version.[2] Given that there are other, different, conflated versions extant, we can no longer suppose we have a stable text of *Lear*. The texts of *Hamlet* and *Othello* are more stable but even so there are significant discrepancies. For example, the 1623 Folio version of *Hamlet* omits the final soliloquy starting 'How all occasions do inform against me / And spur my dull revenge!', which only appears in the second Quarto; but this soliloquy has often been seen as an important part of the play, and analysed by critics as such. The 1622 Quarto version of *Othello* does not include Desdemona's willow song but the 1623 Folio version does (4.3.42–59) and it is a significant and poignant precursor of her death. No text of *Macbeth* prior to the 1623 First Folio is extant but the unusual shortness of this version, and its inclusion of elements that may not be Shakespeare's, suggests the Folio version is an adaptation by another hand, possibly that of Thomas Middleton (c.1580–1627).

The mention of Middleton raises the issue of co-authorship, the idea that Shakespeare should be seen less as a unique genius working alone and more as a dramatist (and actor and shareholder) collaborating with others to produce his plays. Middleton, it seems, contributed to and perhaps cut and shaped *Macbeth*; Sir Brian Vickers (b.1937) has made a closely argued case, in his book *Shakespeare, Co-Author* (2004), for the co-authorship of Middleton in *Timon of Athens* and George Peele (1558–96) in *Titus Andronicus*. *Hamlet* is often thought to be a revision of an earlier Elizabethan text – often referred to as the *Ur-Hamlet* – which was probably not by Shakespeare.

Issues of text and authorship are compounded by the question of which plays by Shakespeare (individually or co-authored) should be included under the heading of 'Tragedy'. The 'Catalogue', or contents page, of the First Folio of 1623 places 11 plays under this rubric, although only three of these include the term 'tragedy' in their individual title. They are, in order of appearance: *The Tragedy of Coriolanus*; *Titus Andronicus*; *Romeo and Juliet*; *Timon of Athens*; *The Life and Death of Julius Caesar*; *The Tragedy of Macbeth*; *The Tragedy of Hamlet*; *King Lear*; *Othello, the Moor of Venice*; *Antony and Cleopatra*; *Cymbeline, King of Britain*. *Troilus and Cressida* does not appear under the 'Tragedies' heading or anywhere else in the First Folio contents page – apparently copy for the play only appeared at the eleventh hour, after the preliminary pages had been printed – but the text of the play was incorporated into the volume in between the histories and tragedies, a marker of its generic ambiguity.

In the classifications subsequently developed by editors, scholars and critics, *Cymbeline* has been grouped with the 'late romances' alongside *The Winter's Tale*, *Pericles* and *The Tempest*, while *Troilus and Cressida* has been assigned to the 'problem plays' with *All's Well that Ends Well* and *Measure for Measure*. These categories are not hard-and-fast – for instance, *The Winter's Tale* can also be seen as a problem play – but it is reasonable to say that it would seem eccentric to regard *Cymbeline* as a tragedy today and questionable to see *Troilus* in such a light. If the most evident criterion for a dramatic tragedy is invoked – the death of the protagonist(s) in the last act – then neither play qualifies.

The ten titles that remain in the tragic zone once *Cymbeline* and *Troilus* have been set aside have also been subdivided by critics in various ways. There are the 'big four', sometimes also called the 'Bradley four', after A(ndrew) C(ecil) Bradley (1851–1935), who focused on these in his seminal *Shakespearean Tragedy* (1904): *Hamlet*, *Macbeth*, *Othello* and *Lear*. There can be no doubt that these plays have attracted the greatest volume of critical commentary, with *Hamlet* taking the palm for the most-discussed title. Then there are *Titus Andronicus*, *Timon of Athens*, *Antony and Cleopatra* and *Coriolanus*, which have come to be known as the Roman plays, a term apparently first coined by the Scots-born, Australian-based critic Sir Mungo William MacCallum (1854–1942) in his book *Shakespeare's Roman Plays and Their Background* (1910). A further possible category, cutting across the two previous ones, is that of 'tragedies of love', which most obviously includes *Romeo and Juliet* but can also embrace at least one of the big four, *Othello*, and one of the Roman plays, *Antony and Cleopatra*, as well as sometimes extending to other less likely plays such as *Lear* and *Macbeth* (as in the book *Shakespeare's Tragedies of Love* [1970] by H. A. Mason [1911–93]). The mention of *Romeo and Juliet* brings in another classification, that of 'early' and 'mature' tragedies. *Titus Andronicus* and *Romeo and Juliet* fall under the 'early' (and sometimes, implicitly, 'immature') rubric and the big four under the 'mature' one (as in *Shakespeare's Mature Tragedies* [1986] by Bernard McElroy [1937–91]). Such classifications are not merely abstract; they carry with them a weight of implied and sometimes explicit assumptions that help to shape interpretations of individual tragedies and are, in turn, modified by those interpretations.

In talking of individual tragedies, another issue arises: whether it is legitimate to talk of 'Shakespearean tragedy' or preferable to think in terms of 'tragedies by Shakespeare'. In other words, is it possible and useful to try to generate a coherent conceptual model of Shakespearean tragedy that will accommodate and illuminate all the Shakespeare plays that might fall within its compass, or is it is more feasible and fruitful to think in terms of individual plays that might be defined as tragedies and attributed to the same author (or co-authors)? The idea of a total theory of Shakespearean tragedy (even if it is not put in quite those terms) has been a recurrent critical aspiration since Bradley (1904), and we shall encounter it in various forms in this Guide. While it fell out of favour in the wake of the post-modernist critiques of totality that emerged in the late twentieth century, it could well revive in the twenty-first, as postmodernism fades and an interest in apprehending and exploring holistic categories redevelops. But opposition to a total theory of Shakespearean tragedy originally came from the empiricist camp and was famously encapsulated by the distinguished critic and scholar Kenneth Muir (1907–96) when he declared, in *Shakespeare's Tragic Sequence* (1972): '[t]here is no such thing as Shakespearian [*sic*] Tragedy; there are only Shakespearian tragedies'.[3] An indication of the continued resonance of Muir's declaration at the start of the twenty-first century is its citation in the first sentence of Tom McAlindon's 'What Is a Shakespearean Tragedy?',[4] the opening essay in the first edition of the *Cambridge Companion to Shakespearean Tragedy* (2002) (though dropped from the 2013 second edition in favour of an essay by Colin Burrow under the same title[5]). McAlindon contends that more general ideas of Shakespearean tragedy are difficult to avoid and that Muir himself fails to do so. Clearly there is a range of positions between the two polarities, and the position a critic takes (which may not be explicit) is likely to affect (and, reciprocally, to be affected by) their procedures for interpreting tragedies by Shakespeare. This should be borne in mind throughout the Guide in considering specific critical readings and the construction of Shakespeare's tragedies as a genre.

There is also the question of the relationship between Shakespeare's tragedies – or Shakespearean tragedy – and the more general consideration of tragedy that begins, in extant written form, with the *Poetics* of the ancient Greek philosopher Aristotle (384–322 BCE), continues through the *Aesthetics* (1835–8) of the German philosopher G(eorg) W(ilhelm) F(riedrich) Hegel (1770–1831) and *The Birth of Tragedy* (1872) by the German philosopher and poet Friedrich Nietzsche (1844–1900), and still goes on in the twenty-first century. The consideration of tragedy as a general issue includes such matters as: what is the nature of tragedy? What is its history? What is the relationship between the literary and everyday uses of the term? Why do we get pleasure from tragedy and what kind of pleasure is it? What is the relationship between Shakespeare's tragedies and ancient tragedy, especially that of Greece? What is the relationship between Shakespearean and modern tragedy? What is the relationship between tragedy in drama and tragedy in the novel? These questions are expertly explored in another volume in this series, Sarah Dewar-Watson's Palgrave Macmillan Reader's Guide to the Essential Criticism of *Tragedy*, and those interested in the more general implications of the idea of tragedy should read that volume.[6] In this Guide, the topic will be addressed as it arises. For example, critics in the late seventeenth and the eighteenth centuries, such as Thomas Rymer (1642/3–1713), John Dryden (1631–1700), John Dennis (1658–1734) and Samuel Johnson (1709–84), addressed, in their respective ways, the problem – for so it was then seen – of Shakespeare's departure from the presumed conventions of classical tragedy. In the mid-twentieth century, the Polish critic Jan Kott (1914–2001) gave an extra charge to his interpretation of *Lear* by joining it to what might be seen as an ulti-mate modern tragedy, *Endgame* (first performed 1958; orig. *Fin de Partie* [1957] by Samuel Beckett [1906–89]).

This Guide is divided into 12 chapters, which cover a period from 1693 to 2013. The first three chapters proceed chronologically from the late Restoration period to the end of the Victorian era. The subsequent nine chapters are organized primarily in terms of topics but retain a certain measure of chronological structure. Chapter 1 focuses on the hostility and unease that Shakespeare's tragedies could arouse in the later seventeenth and the eighteenth centuries by their divergence from notions of tragedy derived from ancient Greece and by their apparent lack of linguistic clar-ity. The critics this chapter considers are Thomas Rymer, whose attack on *Othello* resonated into the twentieth century, and John Dryden, John Dennis and Samuel Johnson, all of whom praised Shakespeare highly but not wholly, finding themselves uneasy with certain aspects of his work that breached neoclassical decorum.

The second chapter explores the Romantic era, whose critics responded much more warmly to Shakespeare's tragedies, even if they appropriated them to suit their own predilections. The chapter starts with the potent observations on the tragedies in the *Lectures on Dramatic Art and Litera-ture* (1808) of the German critic August von Schlegel (1767–1845), who had a major influence on the next two critics we discuss: William Hazlitt (1778–1830), whose *Characters of Shakespeare's Plays* (1817) is a classic of Shakespearean criticism, and Samuel Taylor Coleridge (1772–1834), whose 'Poetry, the Drama and Shakespeare' and his insightful observations on individual tragedies, especially *Hamlet*, appeared posthumously in 1836.

Chapter 3 examines the observations on Shakespeare's tragedies by the Irish critic Edward Dowden (1843–1913) in *Shakspere [sic]: A Critical Study of His Mind and Art* (1875), and the accounts of Shakespeare tragedies in books by two critics, one German and one Danish, whose work proved influential in English translation: *Shakespeare Commentaries* (1877) by G(eorg) G(ottfried) Gervinus (1805–71) and *William Shakespeare* (1898) by George Brandes (1842–1927).

The fourth chapter concentrates on A. C. Bradley's *Shakespearean Tragedy* (1904), the first attempt to offer a systematic account of the 'big four' – *Hamlet, Othello, King Lear, Macbeth*. It also examines the shift in Shakespeare studies adumbrated, perhaps inaugurated, by T. S. Eliot (1888–1965) in his essay 'Hamlet and His Problems' (1919), which is notable both for its iconoclastic anti-bardolatry and its use of a loose but potent concept that would prove highly influential in Shakespeare criticism and indeed in Anglo-American literary criticism in general: that of the 'objective correlative'.

Chapter 5 considers early psychoanalytical approaches to Shakespeare's tragedies, which echoed and extended Bradley in regarding Shakespeare's protagonists as characters equipped with a past but extended this to provide them with an unconscious in which childhood memories could be repressed and reactivated. First, the chapter explores the account in *The Interpretation of Dreams*, published at the turn of the century, in which Sigmund Freud (1856–1939) finds the explanation of Hamlet's reluctance to kill Claudius in the prince's repressed infant desire to kill his father and marry his mother – which is exactly what Claudius, in adulthood, has done. Although Freud's reading of *Hamlet* is his best known interpretation of a Shakespeare tragedy, he also offered, in 'Some Character-Types Met With in Psychoanalytical Work' (1924), an analysis of *Macbeth* in terms of a contrast between sterility and fertility, and the chapter will consider this next. It then moves on to the book *Hamlet and Oedipus* (1949) by Ernest Jones (1879–1958), which amplifies Freud's interpretation of the play and engages substantially with literary critics and scholars. Finally, this chapter explores the 'Seven Lessons on *Hamlet*' (1959) of the revisionist French psychoanalyst Jacques Lacan (1901–81).

The sixth chapter considers the critical work which, in the 1930s and 1940s, moves decisively away from Bradley to focus not on character, but on imagery and form. First, it discusses *The Wheel of Fire: Interpretations of Shakespearean Tragedy* (1930) by G(eorge) (Richard) Wilson Knight (1897–1985), which introduces the idea of 'spatial form' in the study of Shakespeare. It then examines the famous essay by L(ionel) C(harles) Knights (1906–97), 'How Many Children Had Lady Macbeth?' (1933) – the title parodying a Bradleyan character-based approach – and Knights' claim that Shakespeare's plays must be seen as 'dramatic poems'. The chapter moves on to explore *Shakespeare's Imagery and What It Tells Us* (1935) by Caroline Spurgeon (1869–1942), with its significant tracing of image patterns in Shakespeare, such as that of ill-fitting clothes in *Macbeth*. Lastly, it discusses a classic example of American 'New Criticism' as applied to Shakespearean tragedy, the essay 'The Naked Babe and the Cloak of Manliness' (1946) by Cleanth Brooks (1906–94).

Chapter 7 focuses on key attempts to relate Shakespearean tragedy to supposedly fundamental patterns of human thought and behaviour, as represented in myth, philosophy, desire and ritual. The chapter starts with *Fools of Time: Studies in Shakespearean Tragedy* (1967) by the Canadian critic Northrop Frye (1912–91), which outlines three types of tragedy: the 'tragedy of order', the 'tragedy of passion' and the 'tragedy of isolation'. It next considers *Shakespeare Our Contemporary* (trans. 1964; 2nd rev. edn, 1967) by Jan Kott, a wild card that affronts traditional critics and brings Shakespeare powerfully into the mid-twentieth-century present. Then the chapter examines *A Theatre of Envy: William Shakespeare* (1991) by René Girard (b.1923), which analyses Shakespeare's tragedies in terms of his theory of mimetic desire – schematically, that one desires something because someone else desires it – and of the scapegoat. Finally, Chapter 7 explores Naomi Conn Liebler's *Shakespeare's Festive Tragedy: The Ritual Foundation of Genre* (1995), which draws upon cultural anthropology, drama studies and deconstruction to offer, 90 years after Bradley, a total theory of Shakespeare's tragedies.

The eighth chapter considers criticism of Shakespeare's tragedies produced during the dramatic changes in Anglo-American literary criticism in the 1980s provoked by French literary, cultural and psychoanalytical theory. The chapter starts by examining *Shakespearean Negotiations: The Circulation of Social Energy in the Renaissance* (1967) by the leading New Historicist critic Stephen Greenblatt (b. 1943). It moves on to *Power on Display: The Politics of Shakespeare's Genres* (1986) by Leonard Tennenhouse (b.1942), another classic New Historicist Shakespeare study that proposes a fascinating theory of the difference between *Hamlet*, as an Elizabethan tragedy, and *Othello, Lear, Macbeth* and *Antony and Cleopatra* as Jacobean tragedies. The chapter then discusses the powerful and pioneering *Radical Tragedy: Religion, Ideology and Power in the Drama of Shakespeare and his Contemporaries* (1984) by Jonathan Dollimore (b.1948), which stresses, contra New Historicism, how Jacobean tragedy can contest as well as echo a dominant ideology. Lastly, it focuses on *The Subject of Tragedy* (1985) by Catherine Belsey (b.1943), which explores the construction of male subjectivity, and the marginalization of woman, in early modern tragedy.

Chapter 9 addresses gender and sexuality. First, it discusses *Suffocating Mothers: Fantasies of Maternal Origin in Shakespeare's Plays* (1992) by Janet Adelman (1941–2010), which draws on a mixture of feminism, psychoanalysis and close reading to explore masculinity and the figure of the mother in Shakespearean tragedy. It moves on to Philippa Berry's *Shakespeare's Feminine Endings* (1999), which analyses in detail the way dying in Shakespearean tragedy is complicated by being evoked in feminine imagery. The chapter next considers Coppélia Kahn's *Roman Shakespeare: Warriors, Wounds and Women* (1997), which examines constructions of masculinity in the Roman plays, and ends by discussing Madhavi Menon's volume *Shakesqueer* (2010), looking particularly at Jason Edwards' reading of *Coriolanus*.

The tenth chapter engages with critical explorations of Shakespearean tragedy in ethnic and ecological perspectives. It begins with Barbara Everett's pioneering, pre-postcolonial-studies essay 'Spanish Othello: The

Making of Shakespeare's Moor' (1982) and goes on to examine Ania Loomba's reading of *Titus Andronicus* in her *Shakespeare, Race and Colonialism* (2002). The chapter then discusses Gabriel Egan's *Green Shakespeare: From Ecopolitics to Ecocriticism* (2006) and concludes with a consideration of Simon C. Estok's *Ecocriticism and Shakespeare: Reading Ecophobia in Shakespeare's Plays* (2011).

Chapter 11 explores key philosophical readings of Shakespearean tragedy. It starts with *Disowning Knowledge in Seven Plays of Shakespeare* (updated edn, 2003) by the American philosopher Stanley Cavell (b.1926), which interprets the tragedies as anticipatory dramatizations of the intellectual and emotional consequences of philosophical scepticism. Next the chapter considers *Specters of Marx: The State of the Debt, the Work of Mourning & the New International* (1993) by the French deconstructionist thinker Jacques Derrida (1930–2004), which attends closely, and from unusual angles, to the elusive ghost on the Elsinore battlements in *Hamlet*. The chapter moves on to *Shakespeare the Thinker* (2007) by A(nthony) D(avid) Nuttall (1937–2007), which argues that there are significant dramatic engagements with philosophy in Shakespeare's plays, for example in their criticisms of Stoicism. Finally, the chapter gives an account of Donald R. Wehrs' essay, 'Moral Physiology, Ethical Prototypes and the Denaturing of Sense in Shakespearean Tragedy' (2006), which links early modern moral physiology and twenty-first-century neuroscience.

The twelfth and last chapter examines analyses of religion in Shakespeare's tragedies. It first discusses Julia Reinhard Lupton's *Citizen-Saints: Shakespeare and Political Theology* (2005), which considers the combination of theology and politics in the early modern era and in Shakespeare's plays. Next the chapter explores Stephen Greenblatt's *Hamlet in Purgatory* (2002), with its focus on the survival of the Catholic idea of purgatory in a play written in a post-Reformation society. Lastly, it examines Gillian Woods' *Shakespeare's Unreformed Fictions* (2013), which concentrates on those elements in Shakespeare's plays that are neither Catholic in the orthodox sense nor fully reshaped by the Reformation. A conclusion sums up the Guide and indicates possible future developments in the criticism of Shakespeare's tragedies.

We have, then, a fascinating journey to make, crossing challenging territory and exploring intricate edifices on the way. To start it we must travel back in time, to the seventeenth and eighteenth centuries.

CHAPTER ONE

The Augustans

In this chapter, we will trace the development of critical thought about Shakespeare's tragedies from the later seventeenth to the later eighteenth century. We start in the Restoration period, which runs from the restoration of the monarchy in 1660, when Charles II (1630–85) comes to the throne, to around 1700. We move on to the Augustan era, which we have taken to run from around the accession of Queen Anne (1665–1714) in 1702 to the deaths in the mid-1740s of the poet and translator Alexander Pope (1688–1744) and the poet, pamphleteer and proto-novelist Jonathan Swift (1667–1745). We finally come to the later eighteenth century and the era of Samuel Johnson.

From the Restoration period to the later eighteenth century, it was open to question whether any of Shakespeare's plays qualified as tragedies in the classical sense – or, with some critics, in any sense at all. In this era, critical comment on the tragedies, and on Shakespeare's plays more generally, tended to take a fragmentary form, though it was not necessarily less insightful for that and on occasion could acquire an aphoristic force. It might appear in pamphlets, essays, and introductions to Shakespeare's works by prominent editors of the period.

The dominant critical ethos of the Restoration period and of the later Augustan age was antipathetic to the drama of Shakespeare in several ways. That ethos stressed order, unity and decorum in the language and structure of poetry and drama, and respect for ancient Greek and Roman models. Shakespeare's plays could often seem disordered, fragmented and indecorous and he seemed to lack learning, especially in the ancient Greek and Latin languages and texts that were regarded, at the time, as the basis of a proper education. In his elegy for Shakespeare published in the First Folio (1623), his fellow playwright Ben Jonson (1572–1637) had already famously observed that Shakespeare had 'small Latin and less Greek' (l. 30), an alleged failing of which late seventeenth- and eighteenth-century critics were strongly conscious.[1] While Shakespeare's poetic power was difficult to deny, it was attributed more to nature than learning. The poet John Milton (1608–74) summed up this idea in his poem 'L'Allegro' (written 1631?) which describes various sources of pleasure, including going to see a play:

■ Then to the well-trod stage anon,
  If Jonson's learned sock be on.
  Or sweetest Shakespeare fancy's child,
  Warbles his native wood-notes wild (ll. 131–4)[2] □

Not all critics were willing to exculpate Shakespeare on the grounds of his naturalness, however: the most notorious exception was Thomas Rymer (1642/3–1713).

Thomas Rymer

In *A Short View of Tragedy* (1693), Thomas Rymer launched an all-out attack on Shakespeare as a tragedian. Rymer likens Shakespeare to the sixteenth-century French players who employed 'carpenters, cobblers and illiterate fellows' when presenting scenes of Christ's passion, or from the Acts of the Apostles or the Old Testament; these rude mechanicals 'interlarded' 'drolls, and fooleries' which drew in 'the rabble' and lengthened the number of days it took to present the plays, thus bringing in more money. Rymer asserts ironically that Shakespeare was 'doubtless […] a great master in this craft', but, he implies, it was a low craft. 'These carpenters and cobblers were the guides he followed'.[3] So it is 'no wonder that we find so much farce and apocryphal matters in his tragedies'.[4] Shakespeare therefore unhallows the theatre, turning it into an unconsecrated place; profanes 'the name of tragedy'; and, 'instead of representing man and manners', turns 'all morality, good sense, and humanity into mockery and derision'.[5]

Rymer singles out *Othello* for ridicule, focusing on the handkerchief that provides Othello with the supposed 'ocular proof' of Desdemona's infidelity:

■ So much ado, so much stress, so much passion and repetition about a handkerchief! Why was this not called the *Tragedy of the Handkerchief*? […] Had it been *Desdemona*'s garter, the sagacious Moor might have smelt a rat: but the handkerchief is so remote a trifle, no booby, on this side Mauritania, could make any consequence from it.[6] □

Rymer's objections to *Othello* were to find support from one of the most influential Shakespeare critics of the twentieth century, T. S. Eliot (1888–1965), who, in a footnote to his essay on Hamlet (1919), an essay we shall discuss in Chapter 4 of this Guide, remarked that he had never 'seen a cogent refutation of Rymer's objections to *Othello*'.[7]

John Dryden

The leading Restoration poet, dramatist and critic John Dryden (1631–1700), took a more positive, though by no means wholly approving, view of Shakespeare's tragedies. In 'The Grounds of Criticism in Tragedy' (1679), which formed part of the introduction to Dryden's supposedly improved version of *Troilus and Cressida*, he acknowledges that Shakespeare 'understood the nature of the passions' and that this enabled him to create distinct characters, because 'confused passions make undistinguishable characters'. His 'failings', however, lie 'in his manner of expression: he often obscures his meaning by his words, and sometimes makes it unintelligible'. While Dryden demurs to claim that such a great poet could not distinguish between 'the blown puffy style' and 'true sublimity'[8] – though, like a good lawyer, Dryden, by this disclaimer, plants a suspicion in the reader's mind that what is disclaimed may be true – he 'venture[s] to maintain that the fury of his fancy often transported him beyond the bounds of judgment, either in coining of new words and phrases, or racking words which were in use into the violence of a catachresis [a supposedly misapplied word]'.[9] Dryden would not eliminate 'the use of metaphors from passion' since he thinks they are needed to arouse passion, following the authority of the ancient Greek critic Longinus – or, more precisely, the seminal work of critical theory *On the Sublime* (?first century AD), which is doubtfully attributed to Longinus. Dryden does not directly quote *On the Sublime* on metaphor and passion but one example that would support his case is its claim that 'in poetry its [imagery's] aim is to work on the feelings';[10] Dryden fears, however, that to use metaphors 'at every word, to say nothing without a metaphor, a simile, an image, or description' is 'to smell a little too strongly of the buskin'[11] – to seem artificial and theatrical.

John Dennis

In 'On the Genius and Writings of Shakespeare' (1712), an essay that takes the form of three letters, the critic and dramatist John Dennis (1658–1734) affirms that 'Shakespeare was one of the greatest geniuses that the world ever saw for the tragic stage'[12] and that although he 'succeeded very well in comedy, yet his principal talent and his chief delight was tragedy'[13] (a view that, as we shall see, was the reverse of that of one of the most prominent eighteenth-century men of letters, Samuel Johnson). Dennis asserts that Shakespeare's lack of learning disadvantaged him more than any subsequent playwright, but that he possessed 'greater and more genuine beauties than the best and greatest of them'.[14] Like Dryden, Dennis praises Shakespeare's grasp of the passions: '[h]e had so fine a talent for touching the passions, and they are so lively in him, and so truly in nature, that they often touch us more without their due preparations, than those of other tragic poets, who have all the beauty of design and all the advantage of incidents'.[15]

Dennis identifies Shakespeare's 'master-passion' as 'Terror' – it seems appropriate to retain the original capital 'T' here – and asserts that his capacity to arouse this was so powerful and wonderful that, if he had enjoyed 'the advantage of art and learning', he 'would have surpassed the very best and strongest of the Ancients'. His representations 'are often so beautiful and so lively, so graceful and so powerful, especially when he uses them in order to move Terror, that there is nothing perhaps more accomplished in our English poetry'. Moreover, Shakespeare's 'sentiments for the most part in his best tragedies, are noble, generous, easy and natural, and adapted to the persons who use them'. Dennis is less critical of Shakespeare's language than Dryden: his 'expression is in many places good and pure after a hundred years; simple though elevated, graceful though bold, and easy though strong'.[16]

Dennis further suggests that Shakespeare 'seems to have been the very Original of our English tragical harmony; that is the harmony of blank verse, diversified often' by endings of two or three syllables. It is this 'diversity' that 'distinguishes it from heroic harmony', and, bringing it closer to common usage, 'makes it more proper to gain attention, and more fit for action and dialogue'. It is the kind of verse 'we make when we are writing prose' and 'in common conversation'.[17]

But while nature had endowed Shakespeare with 'these great qualities', Dennis holds that his 'happy [...] genius' nonetheless lacked 'learning and the poetical art'. He sometimes makes 'gross mistakes in the characters which he has drawn from history' – in *Coriolanus*, for example, he has perpetrated a 'great absurdity' in portraying Menenius as 'an errant buffoon'[18] and Aufidius, the Volscian general, as 'a base and profligate Villain'. He presents Coriolanus himself as 'so open, so frank, so violent, and so magnanimous' in the first part of the tragedy but later seems to promote Aufidius' view of him as 'a flattering, fawning, cringing, insinuating traitor'.[19]

Moreover, lacking 'poetical art', Shakespeare has put elements in his tragedies that diminish the dignity of that noble genre, such as the 'rabble' in *Julius Caesar* and *Coriolanus*. Their appearance in the latter, Dennis contends, also offends against 'the truth of history', 'the customs of ancient Rome' and 'the majesty of the Roman people'.[20]

A further fault in most of Shakespeare's 'best tragedies' is his failure to dispense proper 'poetical justice'[21] – a term (now usually shortened to 'poetic justice') Thomas Rymer coined in *The Tragedies of the Last Age Considered* (1678) to mean a form of justice that metes out reward to the good characters and punishment to the bad, unlike what Rymer called 'historical justice', the actual practice of justice in human history that sometimes rewards the guilty and punishes the innocent.[22] In Shakespeare, Dennis feels, 'the guilty and the innocent perish promiscuously' – for example, Duncan, Banquo and Lady Macduff and her children in *Macbeth*; Desdemona in *Othello*; Cordelia, Kent, and the old king himself, in *Lear*; Brutus and Portia in *Julius Caesar*; and the title character in *Hamlet*. Dennis recognizes the objection that Hamlet deserves death because of his plan to kill his uncle, but discounts it because 'no less than a call from heaven, and raising one up from the dead to urge him to it' justify Hamlet's plan. Given the promiscuous perishing of the good and the bad in the best Shakespeare tragedies, 'they can offer little or nothing in the way of instruction' and indeed, Dennis suggests, may be harmful in encouraging religious doubt and loose behaviour; such events 'call the Government of Providence into Question' and 'sceptics and libertines' see them as evidence of the operations of chance.[23]

Dennis's desire for proper poetical justice in Shakespeare's tragedies was widely shared in the eighteenth century; this is evident in the popularity on stage of the revised version of *Lear* (1681) by the poet, playwright and translator Nahum Tate (1652–1715), in which, at the end, Lear and Cordelia survive and she is assigned to marry Edgar. This version dominated productions of *Lear* from its first appearance in 1781 until the late 1830s, and the next critic we consider, Samuel Johnson (1709–84), approved of its happy ending, finding the death of Cordelia too painful to tolerate.

Samuel Johnson

Perhaps the most influential eighteenth-century English man of letters, the Shakespeare editor, dictionary maker, critic, poet, biographer, novelist and dramatist Samuel Johnson argued, in his Preface to 'The Plays of William Shakespeare' (1765), that Shakespeare's plays 'are not in the rigorous and critical sense either tragedies or comedies, but compositions of a distinct kind' that, in effect, show what life is really like – a mixture of 'good and evil, joy and sorrow' – and express 'the course of the world, in which the loss of one is the gain of another'. The ancient Greek and Roman dramatists chose to focus, on the one hand, on crimes, the changes of fortune for the worse, and fear and distress and, on the other, on human absurdities, light-hearted events and cheerful prosperity. It was from these choices, Johnson contends, that there arose 'the two modes of imitation, known by the names of tragedy and comedy'.[24] These aimed 'to promote different ends by contrary means' and were 'so little allied' that, Johnson claims, no ancient Greek or Roman writer tried to produce both.[25]

Shakespeare, by contrast, 'has united the powers of exciting laughter and sorrow not only in one mind, but in one composition'. 'Almost all his plays are divided between serious and ludicrous characters, and, in the successive evolutions of the design, sometimes produce seriousness and sorrow, and sometimes levity and laughter.' Johnson acknowledges that this 'practice' is 'contrary to the rules of criticism' but asserts that we can always 'appeal [...] from criticism to nature'. Affirming that the 'end of writing is to instruct' and 'the end of poetry is to instruct by pleasing', Johnson contends that what he calls 'the mingled drama' may 'convey all the instruction of tragedy or comedy', because it shows both alternately and is thus more lifelike than either, since it demonstrates 'how great machinations and slender designs may promote or obviate one another, and the high and the low co-operate in the general system by unavoidable concatenation'.[26]

Johnson considers the objection that this mingling of tragedy and comedy interrupts the 'progression of the passions' and, by insufficient preparation and build-up, robs 'the principal event' of that 'power to move, which constitutes the perfection of dramatic poetry'. But he dismisses this cavil as 'false to experience' and asserts that the 'interchanges of mingled scenes seldom fail to produce the intended vicissitudes of passion'.[27]

The actors who, in their edition, divided Shakespeare's work into comedies, histories and tragedies do not seem, in Johnson's view, 'to have distinguished the three kinds, by any very exact or definite ideas'. They did not see tragedy, as Johnson claims his own age does, as 'a poem of more general dignity or elevation than comedy'; it needed only 'a calamitous conclusion'. '[P]lays were written, which, by changing the catastrophe, were tragedies today and comedies to-morrow.'[28]

If the line between Shakespeare's comedies and tragedies is, in a positive sense, more honoured in the breach than the observance for Johnson, the line between tragedy and history also fails to hold. *Antony and Cleopatra* does not have much more unity of action than *Richard II*. But Johnson does hint at a possible distinction between tragedy and history: while a history can continue through many plays, a tragedy is end-stopped.

Through tragedy, comedy and history, Shakespeare always delivers 'an interchange of seriousness and merriment' that at different times softens or exhilarates the mind. But he always attains his end: 'as he commands us, we laugh or mourn, or sit silent with quiet expectation, in tranquillity without indifference'.[29]

For Johnson, a proper understanding of this hybrid aspect of Shakespeare dissolves the criticisms of Rymer or the leading French Enlightenment writer Voltaire (pseud. of François-Marie Arouet, 1694–1778), who had begun as a supporter of Shakespeare but later attacked him strongly, for instance calling *Hamlet* 'a vulgar and barbarous play' that seemed like 'the inspiration of a drunken savage'.[30] Johnson, however, affirms that '*Hamlet* is opened, without impropriety, by two sentinels', that 'the character of Polonius is seasonable and useful', and that 'the Gravediggers themselves may be heard with applause', while in *Othello* 'Iago bellows at Brabantio's window, without injury to the scheme of the play'.[31]

Johnson does concur with Rymer, however, in feeling that Shakespeare's 'natural disposition', unchecked by proper learning, sound public judgement, classical models and authoritative critics, was for comedy rather than tragedy. This is the reverse of John Dennis's view, discussed above, that although Shakespeare 'succeeded very well in comedy, yet his principal talent and his chief delight was tragedy'. Johnson develops the contrast between Shakespeare as a comic and tragic writer in a series of antitheses:

> ■ In tragedy he often writes with great appearance of toil and study, what is written at last with little felicity; but in his comic scenes, he seems to produce without labour what no labour can improve. In tragedy he is always struggling after some occasion to be comic, but in comedy he seems to repose, or to luxuriate, as in a mode of thinking congenial to his nature. In his tragic scenes there is always something wanting, but his comedy often surpasses expectation or desire. His comedy pleases by the thoughts and the language, and his tragedy for the greater part by incident or action. His tragedy seems to be skill, his comedy to be instinct.[32] □

Johnson later enlarges the point about Shakespeare labouring over language in tragedy to negligible or negative effect. He asserts that, in tragedy, Shakespeare's writing worsens in proportion to the effort he makes: 'whenever he solicits his invention, or strains his faculties, the offspring of his throes is tumour, meanness, tediousness, and obscurity'. Johnson finds his 'declamations or set speeches [...] commonly cold and weak' and explains this by reiterating that Shakespeare's 'power was the power of nature': 'when he endeavoured, like other tragic writers, to catch opportunities of amplification, and instead of inquiring what the occasion demanded, to show how much his stores of knowledge could supply, he seldom escapes without the pity and resentment of his reader'.[33]

Now and then, Johnson finds, Shakespeare gets 'entangled with an unwieldy sentiment, which he cannot well express, and will not reject; he struggles with it a while, and if it continues stubborn, comprises it in words such as occur, and leaves it to be disentangled and evolved by those who have more leisure to bestow upon it'. Literary critics and scholars of the twentieth and twenty-first centuries have, of course, been keen to disentangle Shakespeare and to demonstrate that what seems unclear conveys profound meaning, even if (as in a post-structuralist perspective) that meaning is the lack of stable meaning; but Johnson questions the relationship between Shakespearean difficulty and the quality of meaning it yields. Where 'the language is intricate', 'the thought' sometimes lacks subtlety; 'where the line is bulky', the image is not always 'great'.[34] There is a frequent disproportion between Shakespeare's language and the things – concepts – that it denotes: 'the equality of words to things is very often neglected, and trivial sentiments and vulgar ideas disappoint the attention, to which they are recommended by sonorous epithets and swelling figures'.[35]

Johnson goes on to make his famous denunciation of Shakespeare's fondness for letting a 'quibble' – in its now archaic sense of a pun, a play on words – lead him astray:

> ■ A quibble is the golden apple for which he will always turn aside from his career [path], or stoop from his elevation. A quibble, poor and barren as it is, gave him such delight that he was content to purchase it by the sacrifice of reason, propriety and truth. A quibble was to him the fatal Cleopatra for which he lost the world, and was content to lose it.[36] □

In that last image, Johnson figures Shakespeare as an Antony led astray by language that takes the form of the seductive, feminine Cleopatra (it opens up the fascinating possibility of reading *Antony and Cleopatra* as a play about writing, about the allure of language). In denouncing Shakespeare's wordplay, Johnson denounces an aspect of Shakespeare's work, in the tragedies and elsewhere, that would prove peculiarly fascinating for a range of later twentieth-century critics – which does not mean, of course, that Johnson is wrong, but that he is approaching the issue from a different, eighteenth-century perspective in which clarity of language and the correspondence of word to meaning was more highly valued than ambiguity and slippery signifiers. However, as the eighteenth century drew to a close, that perspective was already about to change.

CHAPTER TWO

The Romantics

Towards the end of the eighteenth century, cultural and literary values, in England and across Europe, began to undergo a wide-ranging transformation that marked the start of the Romantic era. This period was also marked by major historical events: the American War of Independence (1775–83); the French Revolution (1789–99); the Napoleonic Wars (1803–15). No simple summary can convey the range and complexity of the changes in this epoch – or the extent to which older eighteenth-century Augustan attitudes may have persisted within it in modified or differently clothed forms: the novels of Jane Austen (1775–1817) are heirs to the eighteenth century in their ordered structure and style even as they affirm the value of personal self-determination in matters of the heart (for example in *Pride and Prejudice* [1813], when Elizabeth Bennet defies Lady Catherine de Bourgh and proceeds with her marriage to Mr Darcy); Lord Byron (George Gordon (1788–1824), at the start of his 'epic satire' *Don Juan* (1819–24), exalts John Milton, John Dryden and Alexander Pope as models of poetry rather than William Wordsworth (1770–1850), Samuel Taylor Coleridge (1772–1834) or Robert Southey (1774–1843): 'Thou shalt believe in Milton, Dryden, Pope; / Thou shalt not set up Wordsworth, Coleridge, Southey' (1.205.1–2),[1] even as he generates a poetry of racy and ingenious rhyme, rhythm and diction that breaks free of Augustan poetic decorum.

But there were clearly large changes of emphasis across the whole of the arts: feeling came to seem more important than reason, energy than order, mobility rather than stasis, the marginal extremes rather than the middle ground, sensibility than sense, originality rather than the improved reiteration of the familiar (Pope's 'what oft was thought / But ne'er so well expressed' in his poetic *Essay on Criticism* [1711]). In literature, it was the era of the Romantic poets: William Blake (1757–1827), Wordsworth, Coleridge, Percy Bysshe Shelley (1792–1822); of Gothic fiction such as *The Castle of Otranto* (1764) by Horace Walpole (1717–97) and *The Mysteries of Udolpho* (1794) by Ann Radcliffe (1764–1823); of the rich historical novels of Sir Walter Scott (1771–1832) alongside Jane Austen; of the prose of Thomas De Quincey (1785–1859) in *Confessions of an English Opium Eater* (1821/22) and *On Murder Considered as One of the Fine Arts* (1827); and of William Hazlitt (1778–1830) in *Lectures on the Spirit of the Age* (1825). Inevitably these striking shifts in contemporary literature involved a reshaping of attitudes to the literary and dramatic work of the past, especially that of Shakespeare, given his national and international importance. As Henry Crawford remarks in chapter 34 of Jane Austen's *Mansfield Park*, 'Shakespeare one gets acquainted with without knowing how. It is a part of an Englishman's constitution.'[2] But if that constitution, in its cultural form, was changing, one's acquaintance with Shakespeare would change too. One of the most prominent Romantic poets and the major British contemporary theorist of Romanticism, Coleridge, and one of its leading essayists, Hazlitt, were also notable Shakespeare critics. But both Coleridge and Hazlitt were influenced by the German poet, critic and scholar August Wilhelm von Schlegel (1767–1845) (although Coleridge vigorously denied charges that his account of *Hamlet* had plagiarized Schlegel[3]). For Shakespeare was not only part of an Englishman's constitution; he was also becoming part of a European's constitution, and this assimilation was furthered by Schlegel's translation, with his countryman Ludwig Tieck (1773–1853), of Shakespeare's plays into German (1797–1810), and Schlegel's consideration of Shakespeare in his *Lectures on Dramatic Art and Literature* (1809; trans. 1815). It is Schlegel's remarks on Shakespeare's tragedies in these lectures that fed back into English criticism, and which we shall now consider before moving on to Coleridge and Hazlitt.

August von Schlegel

In chapter 23 of his *Lectures on Dramatic Art and Literature*, Schlegel takes issue with Samuel Johnson's assertion, which we saw above, that 'Shakespeare had a greater talent for comedy than tragedy' and affirms that it would only need 'a few of [the] less celebrated scenes from the tragedies', not even the whole of 'the great tragical compositions themselves', to refute this.[4] He does, however, consider further Johnson's objections to Shakespeare's plays upon words and appeals to the idea of 'original nature' as a justification for it; children and 'nations of simple manners' like and practise wordplay.[5] Schlegel hails Shakespeare as 'this tragical Titan, who storms the heavens and threatens to tear the world from off its hinges, who, more terrible than Aeschylus, makes our hair to stand on end, [but who] possessed at the same time the insinuating loveliness of the sweetest poesy. [...] He unites in his soul the utmost elevation and the utmost depth; and the most opposite and even apparently irreconcilable properties subsist in him peaceably together.'[6]

This is far more lavish praise of Shakespeare as a tragedian than the eighteenth century could offer.

Chapter 25 of Schlegel's *Lectures* is specifically devoted to 'Criticisms on Shakespeare's Tragedies'. Schlegel starts with *Romeo and Juliet*,[7] praising its 'excellent dramatic arrangement, the significance of every character in its place, the judicious selection of all the circumstances, even the most minute'.[8] The nature of this praise implies an important general idea that will come to be applied much more widely to Shakespeare's plays in the 1930s: that each element of a Shakespeare play, even the smallest, contributes to its overall significance. Contrasting *Romeo and Juliet* with *Othello*, Schlegel calls the latter 'a strongly shaded picture', 'a tragical Rembrandt'. He then goes on to employ what is, in the twenty-first century, a racist stereotype, praising Shakespeare for making Othello 'every inch a negro' in whom we recognize 'the wild nature of that glowing zone which generates the most ravenous beasts of prey and the most deadly poisons'. Othello both seems and is 'noble, frank, confiding, grateful for the love shown him' and he is, moreover, 'a hero who spurns at danger, a worthy leader of an army, a faithful servant of the state'. But blood will out: 'the mere physical force of passion puts to flight in one moment all his acquired and mere habitual virtues, and gives the upper hand to the savage over the moral man [...] [Othello] suffers as a double man; at once in the higher and the lower sphere into which his being was divided'.[9] But the 'double man' idea is interesting: if one translates it from the spheres of race and hierarchy ('higher and lower') into that of culture and sees Othello's doubleness as a product of being divided between two cultures, it offers a potential for analysis drawing on postcolonial theory (for instance, the idea of the 'mimic man', the colonized subject who adopts the modes of the colonizer and thereby calls them into question). Schlegel also stresses the public dimension of the play: 'The public events of the first two acts show us Othello in his most glorious aspect, as the support of Venice and the terror of the Turks: they serve to withdraw the story from the mere domestic circle', as the Montague/Capulet division in *Romeo and Juliet* places the love story in a wider public sphere.[10] Schlegel concludes by stressing 'the overwhelming force of the catastrophe in *Othello*, – the pressure of feelings which measure out in a moment the abysses of eternity'.[11]

Schlegel finds *Hamlet* 'singular in its kind' and defines it as 'a tragedy of thought inspired by continual and never-satisfied meditation on human destiny and the dark perplexity of the events of this world' which is 'calculated' to arouse the same meditation in its audience. He draws a mathematical analogy: this 'enigmatical work resembles those irrational equations in which a fraction of unknown magnitude always remains, that will in no way admit of solution'.[12] Thus Schlegel does not align himself either with those who see *Hamlet* as a problem that can be wholly solved, or with those, such as T. S. Eliot, who attribute its enigmatic quality to failings on Shakespeare's part. He does, however, offer a summary of the main import of the whole play: it is 'intended to show that a calculating consideration, which exhausts all the relations and possible consequences of a deed must cripple the power of acting'.[13]

Schlegel then turns to Hamlet's character and dissents from the favourable view of it offered by his older compatriot, the poet, playwright, novelist and all-round writer Johann Wolfgang von Goethe (1749–1832). While he acknowledges some virtues in Hamlet, he contends that 'in the resolutions which he so often embraces and always leaves unexecuted, his weakness is too apparent'.[14] It is not simply necessity that impels him 'to artifice and dissimulation'; 'he has a natural inclination for crooked ways'. He is 'a hypocrite towards himself; his far-fetched scruples are often mere pretexts to cover his want of determination'. He is 'too much overwhelmed with his own sorrow to have any compassion to spare for others'; he shows 'a malicious joy, when he has succeeded in getting rid of his enemies, more through necessity and accident, which alone are able to impel him to quick and decisive measures, than by the merit of his own courage'. Hamlet, Schlegel continues, 'has no firm belief either in himself or anything else; from expressions of religious confidence he passes over to sceptical doubts; he believes in the ghost of his father as long as he sees it, but as soon as it has disappeared, it appears to him almost in the light of a deception'.[15] Schlegel deploys this last point when he addresses, in a footnote, the charge that there is a contradiction between Hamlet's claim, in the 'To be, or not to be' soliloquy, that death is an 'undiscovered country / From whose bourn no traveller returns' and the fact that he has actually seen and spoken with a returnee from the dead in the shape of his father's ghost. Shakespeare, Schlegel asserts, 'purposely wished to show that Hamlet could not fix himself in any conviction of any kind whatever'.[16]

Schlegel does not, in this context, use the term 'poetical justice', but makes it clear that *Hamlet* lacks it:

■ [T]he criminals are at last punished, but, as it were, by an accidental blow, and not in the solemn way requisite to convey to the world a warning example of justice; irresolute foresight, cunning treachery, and impetuous rage, hurry on to a common destruction; the less guilty and the innocent are equally involved in the general ruin. The destiny of humanity is there exhibited as a gigantic Sphinx, which threatens to precipitate into the abyss of scepticism all who are unable to solve her dreadful enigmas.[17] □

It is notable here that Schlegel shifts the emphasis from Hamlet's character to the more general import of the play's conclusion, which is seen to present human destiny as a fearsome Sphinx-like puzzle that will consign those who cannot solve it to the depths of scepticism.

Schlegel praises *Macbeth* as a 'sublime work', the most 'grand and terrible' since the *Eumenides* (458 BCE), the last play of the *Oresteia* trilogy by the ancient Greek tragedian Aeschylus (c.525/4–456 BCE). Such praise is a sign that, in the Romantic era, Shakespeare's tragedies are coming to be seen, not as inferior to those of the Greek classical tragedians, but their equal. Schlegel at once acknowledges that *Macbeth*'s witches are not 'divine Eumenides' – the term means 'Well-Wishers' and is often translated as 'The Kindly Ones' – but 'the ignoble and vulgar instruments of hell'.[18] In this, however, they are fit for purpose. 'These repulsive things, from which the imagination shrinks, are here emblems of the hostile powers which operate in nature'. Macbeth himself, in Schlegel's eyes, does rather better than Hamlet: '[h]owever much we may abhor his actions, we cannot altogether refuse to compassionate the state of his mind; we lament the ruin of so many noble qualities'.[19] Schlegel also contrasts the pace of the two tragedies: '[i]n the progress of the action', *Macbeth* 'is altogether the reverse of *Hamlet*: it strides forward with amazing rapidity, from the first catastrophe [Duncan's murder] to the last'.[20]

In *Lear*, the 'principal characters […] are not those who act, but those who suffer'.[21] We have 'a fall from the highest elevation into the deepest abyss of misery, where humanity is stripped of all external and internal advantages, and given up a prey to naked helplessness'.[22] Schlegel defends the function of the Gloucester subplot and the 'ingenuity and skill' with which 'the two main parts of the composition' have been 'dovetailed into one another'. But he goes further, affirming that 'it is the very combination' of these two parts 'which constitutes the sublime beauty' of *Lear*. While the cases of Lear and Gloucester broadly resemble each other and their stories 'make a correspondent impression on the heart', 'all the circumstances are so different' that they 'form a complete contrast for the imagination'. They become more than two tales of personal ill fortune: 'two such unheard-of examples taking place at the same time have the appearance of a great commotion in the moral world: the picture becomes gigantic, and fills us with such alarm as we should entertain at the idea that the heavenly bodies might one day fall from their appointed orbits'.[23] Here, Schlegel is not focusing on character, but on the structure and plots of *Lear* and how they contribute to a sense of an ethical upheaval that produces fear of the same kind as cosmic disorder might.

When Schlegel does consider a specific character, Cordelia, he lauds her 'heavenly beauty of soul' and elevates her to the same topmost status as the protagonist of the ancient Greek drama *Antigone* (performed 442/441 BCE) by Sophocles (c.496–406 BCE) – like the earlier comparison between *Macbeth* and the *Eumenides* of Aeschylus, this serves to ratchet up Shakespeare's own reputation as a tragedian so that it is equal rather than inferior to that of the ancient Greek dramatists.

Schlegel would be cited in William Hazlitt's 'Preface' to his *Characters of Shakespeare's Plays* as an important corrective to Samuel Johnson's criticisms of Shakespeare. It is Hazlitt to whom we turn next.

William Hazlitt

In *Characters of Shakespeare's Plays* (1817), Hazlitt has chapters that discuss, among the tragedies, the big four, *Macbeth*, *Othello*, *Hamlet* and *Lear*; *Romeo and Juliet*; and the Roman Plays, *Julius Caesar*, *Antony and Cleopatra*, *Coriolanus* and *Timon of Athens*. Comparing the big four at the start of his *Macbeth* chapter, he contends that:

> ■ *Lear* stands first for the profound intensity of the passion; *Macbeth* for the wildness of the imagination and the rapidity of the action; *Othello* for the progressive interest and powerful alternations of feeling; *Hamlet* for the refined development of thought and sentiment.[24] □

Hazlitt goes on to propose further specific characteristics of these four tragedies. *Macbeth* is structured upon 'a stronger and more systematic principle of contrast than any of Shakespeare's other plays'. It is 'a constant struggle between life and death'; the 'action is desperate and the reaction is dreadful.'[25]

Othello, Hazlitt feels, 'excites our sympathy in an extraordinary degree' and conveys a moral that is more closely applicable to 'the concerns of human life' than in any of Shakespeare's other plays. While 'the pathos' in *Lear* is 'more dreadful and overpowering', it is 'less natural', less of an everyday occurrence. The passions in *Macbeth* do not arouse our sympathy to the extent that those in *Othello* do, and the 'interest in *Hamlet* is more remote and reflex'. In *Othello*, it is 'at once equally profound and affecting'.[26]

Hazlitt affirms that if '*Lear* shows the greatest depth of passion, *Hamlet* is the most remarkable for the ingenuity, originality, and unstudied development of character'.[27] Hamlet himself is 'the prince of philosophical speculators', and a perfectionist: 'because he cannot have his revenge perfect, according to the most refined idea his wish can form, he misses it altogether'.[28]

In discussing *Othello*, Hazlitt offers an especially interesting account of Iago, challenging the idea – which would later be memorably formulated by Coleridge, as we shall see later in this chapter – that 'his villa[i]ny is *without a sufficient motive*'[29] and offering his own memorable observation, which A. C. Bradley would cite soon after the start of the twentieth century (as Chapter 4 will show):

> ■ [Iago] is an amateur of tragedy in real life; and instead of employing his invention on imaginary characters, or long-forgotten incidents, he takes the bolder and more desperate course of getting up his plot at home, casts the principal parts among his nearest friends and connexions, and rehearses it in downright earnest, with steady nerves and unabated resolution.[30] □

Lear, for Hazlitt, is 'the best of all Shakespeare's plays, for it is the one in which he was the most in earnest'.[31] Hazlitt agrees with the view that *Lear*'s first three acts, and the third act of *Othello*, are 'Shakespeare's great masterpieces in the logic of passion' and 'contain the highest examples not only of the force of individual passion, but of its dramatic vicissitudes and striking effects arising from the different circumstances and characters of the persons speaking'.[32] Like Schlegel, Hazlitt praises the way in which the Lear and Gloucester plots are interwoven but sees this as the product of 'art' in contrast to 'the carrying on of the tide of passion' which is driven by the force of 'nature'.[33]

Hazlitt strongly objects to the happy ending of Nahum Tate's revised *Lear*, which Samuel Johnson approved and Schlegel denounced but which still dominated English stage productions of the play in the earlier nineteenth century. Here Hazlitt quotes his contemporary, the essayist and poet Charles Lamb (1775–1834), in the essay 'On the Tragedies of Shakespeare' (1811): 'A happy ending! – as if the living martyrdom that Lear had gone through, – the flaying of his feelings alive, did not make a fair dismissal from the stage of life the only decorous thing for him […] as if at his years, and with his experience, any thing was left but to die.'[34] Hazlitt concludes his account of *Lear* with a reflection, generated by reading the play, on why tragedy gives pleasure: 'the circumstance which balances the pleasure against the pain in tragedy is, that in proportion to the greatness of the evil, is our sense and desire of the opposite good excited'.[35]

Samuel Taylor Coleridge

In addition to Schlegel and Hazlitt, the other great Shakespearean critic of the Romantic era was Coleridge. But his 'Lectures upon Shakespeare and other Dramatists', though delivered in 1810, were only published posthumously, along with his 'Notes' on Shakespeare, in his *Literary Remains* (1836). In his account of *Hamlet*, Coleridge makes an interesting general point about the titles of Shakespeare's tragedies as an index of their structure and effect. In the comedies, such as *A Midsummer Night's Dream*, or the romances, like *The Winter's Tale*, 'the total effect is produced by a co-ordination of the characters, as in a wreath of flowers'. In the plays whose titles name one or two characters – for instance, *Coriolanus*, *Lear*, *Romeo and Juliet*, *Hamlet*, *Othello* – 'the effect arises from the subordination of all to one, either as the prominent person, or the principal object'.[36]

In his lectures on *Hamlet* and on *Macbeth*, Coleridge draws a number of contrasts between the two plays that serve to illuminate each of them. Whereas *Hamlet* opens with 'the easy language of common life', *Macbeth* starts with 'direful music and wild wayward rhythm and abrupt lyrics'.[37] The ghost in *Hamlet* is 'a superstition connected with the most mysterious truths of revealed religion' and thus Shakespeare treats it reverently, in contrast to 'the foul earthly witcheries and wild language in *Macbeth*'.[38] In the latter play, 'the poet's object was to raise the mind at once to the high tragic tone' to prepare the audience for 'the precipitate consummation of guilt in the early part of the play'.[39] Hamlet's first utterance is a play on words – 'A little more than kin and less than kind' (1.2.64) – but a 'complete absence' of wordplay 'characterizes *Macbeth*' throughout[40] – except for what Coleridge calls the 'disgusting' scene with the Porter (2.3) and dismisses as an interpolation by the actors. Take out this scene and *Macbeth* shows 'an entire absence of comedy' and 'even of irony and philosophical contemplation' – 'the play being wholly and purely tragic'.[41]

In his lecture on *Othello*, Coleridge is concerned to establish that Othello is a Moor rather than a 'negro': for an early nineteenth-century audience, and certainly for an early seventeenth-century one, 'it would be something monstrous to conceive this beautiful Venetian girl falling in love with a veritable negro'.[42] The issue of Othello's ethnic identity will be pursued further in this Guide, especially in Chapter 10, 'Ethnicity and Ecology'.

Coleridge sees Iago's speech on 'Virtue' (1.3.333–41) as conveying his 'passionless character': '[i]t is all will in intellect; and therefore he is here a bold partisan of a truth, but yet of a truth converted into a falsehood by the absence of all the necessary modifications caused by the frail nature of man.'[43] In Iago's soliloquy at the end of the same scene (2.1.372–93), he declares 'I hate the Moor' but can give as a reason only the rumour, of whose truth he admits he is uncertain, that Othello has made love to his wife. Coleridge sees this as 'the motive-hunting of a motiveless malignity', and that last phrase, 'motiveless malignity', has become famous in Shakespeare criticism.[44] It is Iago's plotting, stemming from his seemingly unmotivated hatred, which helps to create the peculiar nature of Othello's murder of Desdemona: 'Othello does not kill Desdemona in jealousy, but in a conviction forced upon him by the almost superhuman art of Iago'.[45] Othello 'had no life but in Desdemona' and 'the belief that she, his angel, had fallen from the heaven of her native innocence, wrought a civil war in his heart'.[46]

Coleridge opens his lecture on *Lear* by declaring that, while *Macbeth* is the 'most rapid' and *Hamlet* the 'slowest, in movement', *Lear* 'combines length with rapidity'.[47] In the portrayal of Lear, 'old age is itself a character – its natural imperfections being increased by life-long habits' of being instantly obeyed: '[a]ny addition of individuality would have been unnecessary and painful: for the relations of others to him, of wondrous fidelity and of frightful ingratitude, alone sufficiently distinguish him.'[48] Here, Coleridge moves away from the idea of individualized character to see Lear as an embodiment of a phase of life, old age, and as constituted by the relationships of others to him. This opens another possible approach to Shakespeare's tragedies. But it would be the emphasis on character that would persist throughout the nineteenth century and the Victorian era. It is to three influential later nineteenth-century critics that we now turn.

CHAPTER THREE

The Victorians

Victorian critics of Shakespeare tended to conserve – and sometimes dilute – the insights of their Romantic forebears. In an era of relative stability and prosperity, Shakespeare became even more a part of an Englishman's constitution, a national treasure that gave further proof of the superiority of the British way of life. The poet Algernon Charles Swinburne (1837–1909) was in some ways a rebel against Victorian conventions and an *aficionado* of Shakespeare, deeply read in both classical and Elizabethan drama; but his critical writings – for example, in *A Study of Shakespeare* (1880) – lack the close reference to quoted passages from Shakespeare's texts that was increasingly expected in serious criticism.[1] It is perhaps significant that the three most influential Shakespeare critics of this period all came from outside mainland Britain: Edward Dowden was Irish, born in Cork and educated at Queen's College and Trinity College, Dublin, where he became Professor of English Studies in 1867; G. G. Gervinus was German and taught at universities in Göttingen and Heidelberg; and George Brandes was Danish, born of non-Orthodox Jewish parents, and the leader of Denmark's radical intellectuals. We shall first discuss Dowden.

Edward Dowden

Edward Dowden (1843–1913) was the author of *Shakspere* [Dowden's preferred spelling]: *A Critical Study of His Mind and Art*, a book first published in 1875 that proved popular and went through several editions. Dowden sets Shakespeare's tragedies in a developmental account of his career as a dramatist. In this perspective, *Romeo and Juliet* is 'the work of the artist's adolescence', while *Hamlet* shows that 'he had become adult, and in this supreme department [i.e., tragedy] master of his craft'.[2] *Romeo and Juliet* is 'steeped in passion', *Hamlet* 'in meditation'.[3] Like Schlegel, Dowden affirms that *Hamlet* is 'never wholly explicable'.[4]

Dowden finds a pattern in several Shakespeare tragedies: '[T]he tragic disturbance is caused by the subjection of the chief person of the drama to some dominant passion, essentially antipathetic to his nature, though proceeding from some inherent weakness or imperfection, – a passion from which the victim cannot deliver himself, and which finally works out his destruction.'[5] Dowden gives a number of examples. Othello's 'nature is instinctively trustful and confiding' but he is 'inoculated [a word that seems inadvertently to pun on Othello's demand for 'the ocular proof' (3.3.398)] with the poison of jealousy and suspicion', which 'maddens and destroys him'. Macbeth is 'made for subordination' but becomes 'the victim of a terrible and unnatural ambition'. Lear, who is 'ignorant of true love' but has 'a supreme need of loving and of being loved', is 'compelled to hatred' and shuts out the one person, Cordelia, who might have satisfied his need. Taking issue with the emphasis of Schlegel and Coleridge upon the intellectual aspect of Hamlet and the way this inhibits action, Dowden stresses that the emotional side of Hamlet is equally important and impaired: 'his malady is as deep-seated in his sensibilities and in his heart as it is in the brain'.[6]

Dowden's disagreements with Schlegel showed how the influence of the latter persisted in the Victorian era. A second German influence on Victorian ideas of Shakespearean tragedy would emerge about the same time as Dowden's book: *Shakespeare* (1849) by the literary historian G(eorg) G(ottfried) Gervinus (1805–71), which was translated by F(anny) E(lizabeth) Bunnètt as *Shakespeare Commentaries* (1st edn 1862).

G. G. Gervinus

In *Shakespeare Commentaries*, Gervinus asserts that tragedy, in a general sense, 'exhibits men everywhere at issue with fate'. But in Shakespearean tragedy, fate is 'no mere blind external force, to which man falls sacrifice as an involuntary tool', but 'nothing else than man's own nature'. With Othello, Hamlet and Macbeth, the 'passions of these men wove the web of their own fate'. We see Shakespeare, in his tragedies, 'continually advancing in his description of those fearful trials, delusions and excesses' to which his noble protagonists are subject through their passions. In *Lear*, Gervinus claims, 'this advance seems ever on the increase, in proportion as the theme is more comprehensive and vast'.[7] In *Hamlet*, *Macbeth* and *Othello* – and also, for Gervinus, in *Timon of Athens* – 'everything turns on one principal character'[8] and 'one single passion and its development were essentially treated'. But in *Lear* – which Gervinus couples at this point with *Cymbeline* – Shakespeare 'takes a much wider subject': 'whole ages and races are, as it were, represented':

■ We are not here confined especially to individual characters [...] Twofold or still more manifold actions are united; characters equally important and fascinating move in greater number, in mutual relation; the actual matter gains greatly thereby in richness, extent and compressed fullness; [...] a mass of facts in well-connected order lies almost concealed even in the subordinate parts, though at first glance it may be overlooked in the abundance of matter. [...] This very extension of the events is the cause why these plays are less rich than others in explanatory sentences, why the actions themselves are left to explain the essential point of the whole, and why the accurate consideration of events is as important here as the psychological development of character.[9] □

Like Coleridge, Gervinus shifts the focus away from character as far as *Lear* is concerned, calling into question the value of a character-centred approach, at least for this tragedy.

A third important influence on approaches to Shakespeare in the Victorian era was the Danish literary critic George Brandes (1842–1927), whose *William Shakespeare* (1895; first trans. 1898), in translation, became a best-seller in Britain.

George Brandes

Like Dowden's *Shakspere*, Brandes' *William Shakespeare* interweaves scholarly and critical commentary on the plays with biographical and historical material. In regard to *Hamlet*, Brandes contends that 'the great fundamental difficulty [for the prince] is an inward one' and 'the real scene of the tragedy lies in the hero's soul'.[10] Considering *Macbeth*, Brandes offers a series of contrasts between its protagonist and Hamlet. Hamlet's 'nature is passionate, but refined and thoughtful', but 'he never betrays the slightest remorse for a murder once committed'. (This is not quite true, since Hamlet does say, after he has killed Polonius, 'For this same lord, / I do repent' (3.4.170–1), but the mood of repentance, if it exists, is not sustained.) Macbeth, by contrast, is 'the rough, blunt soldier, the man of action', who, after his initial hesitations, kills Duncan decisively, but is immediately afterwards 'attacked' by visual and aural 'hallucinations' and 'hounded on, wild and vacillating and frenzied, from crime to crime'. Hamlet is 'the dreamer', Macbeth 'the captain [in the military sense], "Bellona's bridegroom" [1.3.59]', married to the Roman goddess of war. Hamlet has 'a superabundance of culture and of intellectual power'. 'His strength is of the kind that wears a mask; he is a master in the art of dissimulation'. Macbeth, however, is 'unsophisticated to the point of clumsiness, betraying himself when he tries to deceive'.[11] Whereas Hamlet is 'the born aristocrat', Macbeth sees 'a wreath on the head, a crown on the brow' as 'greatness'.

Nonetheless, Macbeth and Hamlet are alike in some ways. In his first soliloquy, Macbeth has 'Hamlet-like misgivings' (1.7.1–28) like those of the

Prince in his 'To be, or not to be' soliloquy (3.1.61–94). Like Hamlet, 'he has imagination, but of a more timorous and visionary cast'; Hamlet needs 'no peculiar faculty' to see his father's ghost (at least in the opening scenes) since it has been, and is, visible to others, while Macbeth 'sees apparitions', and hears voices unperceived by anyone else.[12] But there is a further 'kinship between the Danish and the Scottish tragedy': these are the only plays of the big four in which the dead reappear. Neither *Othello* nor *Lear* has any supernatural element. This does not mean the ghosts in *Hamlet* or *Macbeth*, or the witches in the latter, evidence a suprahuman force intervening in human affairs; but they are not mere illusions or hallucinations.

In contrast to Rymer, with whom we began Chapter 1, Brandes finds *Othello* 'flawless'. But he suggests a limitation: it 'is the only one of Shakespeare's tragedies which does not treat of national events, but is a family tragedy – what was later known as *tragédie domestique* or *bourgeoise*'. But for Brandes, 'the treatment is anything but bourgeois; the style is of the very grandest'.[13] He then goes on, however, to suggest a further limitation: *Othello* is a 'great work' but 'a monograph' that 'lacks the breadth which Shakespeare's plays as a rule possess'. It is 'a sharply limited study of a single and very special form of passion' that 'becomes monumental only by the grandeur of its treatment'.

Shakespeare's next tragedy, however, is 'least of all a monograph'; it is 'nothing less than the universal tragedy – all the great woes of human life concentrated into one universal symbol'.[14] In *Lear*, Brandes contends, Shakespeare presents 'horrors' that had not featured in his work since *Titus Andronicus*, 'not even shrinking from the tearing out of Glo[u]cester's eyes'. 'He means to show pitilessly what life is: "[y]ou see how the world goes," says Lear in the play [4.5.150–1].' In his stress on *Lear*'s relentless exposure of reality, Brandes anticipates the later twentieth-century view of the play, for example in Jan Kott's work. Brandes also defends the original ending, which had been restored to Victorian stage productions in the late 1830s, though here, sounding rather more nineteenth-century in tone, he generalizes it into an image of life itself that figures loss in the image of a woman: 'The loss of a Cordelia – that is the great catastrophe. We all lose, or live under the dread of losing, our Cordelia. The loss of the dearest and the best, of that which alone makes life worth living – that is the tragedy of life.'[15]

Brandes, in the last decade of the nineteenth century, as the Victorian era in England was drawing to a close, adds to the now substantial weight of commentary on Shakespeare's tragedies. Like Dowden and Gervinus, he does so within a more general, book-length account of Shakespeare's life and work that pulls together, dissents from and develops the more compressed or fragmentary accounts of earlier critics and scholars. But the task of focusing on Shakespeare's tragedies in a book lay ahead; this would be undertaken, early in the twentieth century, by A. C. Bradley.

CHAPTER FOUR

Character and Correlative

Three major forces helped to create a new kind of criticism of Shakespeare's tragedies in the early twentieth century: the explosion, across the arts, of Modernist innovations; the First World War; and the development of English Literature as an academic discipline. The complex of literary practices that we now call Modernist – represented by, among many others, Luigi Pirandello (1867–1936) in drama, T. S. Eliot (1888–1965) and Ezra Pound (1885–1972) in poetry, James Joyce (1882–1941) and Virginia Woolf (1882–1941) in fiction – placed a premium on difficulty: it challenged nineteenth-century preconceptions of literary form and subject matter and, in effect, asked its audiences to work at interpretation. This benefited the study of Shakespeare, especially of his tragedies, which offered many interpretative challenges; he could be seen as a Modernist artist *avant la lettre*. It is no accident that the most influential anglophone Shakespeare critic in the early twentieth century was also a major – perhaps *the* major – Modernist poet: T. S. Eliot.

The relationship of the First World War to Modernism and to the development of English as an academic discipline is complicated and no simple cause-and-effect model can be applied. Harbingers of Modernist literature appeared well before the outbreak of war – for example, in the play *Ubu Roi* [*Ubu the King*] (1896) by the French writer Alfred Jarry (1873–1907), or in the novella 'Heart of Darkness' (1899) and the novel *The Secret Agent* (1907) by the British-based Polish novelist Joseph Conrad (1857–1924). Significant Modernist innovation in visual art and music – for example, the painting known as *Les Demoiselles d'Avignon* (1908) by the Spanish painter Pablo Picasso (1881–1973) and the ballet score *Le Sacre du Printemps* [*Rite of Spring*] (1913) by the Russian composer Igor Stravinsky (1882–1971) – preceded the outbreak of war but could be seen as registering the strains and tensions that led up to it. It was after the war that the major Modernist literary texts appeared – Joyce's *Ulysses* and Eliot's *The Waste Land*, both in 1922, Woolf's *Mrs Dalloway* (1925). But it is possible to suggest that the cataclysmic death toll and break-up of older social and political structures that occurred in the war related to the break-up of older artistic structures. More directly, the assault, especially from some of the English 'War Poets' who were also serving officers, such as Wilfred Owen (1893–1918) and Siegfried Sassoon (1886–1967), on the heroic ideas of war that might be derived from a partial reading of Shakespeare's plays, especially *Henry V*, was a further force which made it seem that the interpretation of Shakespeare needed to change.

English Literature, as a fledgling discipline competing with the long-established study of the ancient Greek and Roman classics, the foundation of a gentleman's education, had begun to develop in the later nineteenth century and had to prove itself. In this task, its greatest asset was the national dramatist, Shakespeare. It was necessary to appropriate and exploit his work, but it had to be done in ways that looked different from the critical discourse of the nineteenth century which had been produced by men and women of letters in extra-academic modes, venues and publications. It had to seem more systematic and professional. In this respect A. C. Bradley's *Shakespearean Tragedy* (1904), however nineteenth-century it might now appear in some respects, offered a synthesis and elaboration of ideas about Shakespearean tragedy that had previously been scattered, fragmentary, or barely articulated. We shall consider this book first.

A. C. Bradley

A. C. Bradley's *Shakespearean Tragedy* is a massive, influential, much-challenged but still durable study. Bradley's own philosophical sources are the *Poetics* of the ancient Greek philosopher Aristotle (384–322 BCE)[1] and what Bradley calls 'certainly the most important theory of tragedy [since Aristotle's]', that of the German philosopher G[eorg] W[ilhelm] F[riedrich] Hegel (1770–1831), though each of them is only mentioned directly twice in his book.[2] Bradley starts by posing a question: 'What is the substance of a Shakespearean tragedy, taken in abstraction both from its form and from the differences in point of substance between one tragedy and another?'[3] This at once pitches the book on to an abstract, philosophical plane that breaks away from an empirical, piecemeal approach to Shakespeare's tragedies, although later in the text Bradley will offer many empirical examples. But his readiness to engage with his topic in a theoretical way may be one of the elements that has helped *Shakespearean Tragedy* to survive through the heyday of literary theory in the 1980s and 1990s and beyond it into the twenty-first century.

Bradley goes on to outline his 'idea of Shakespearean Tragedy'. While a Shakespeare tragedy has many characters, 'it is pre-eminently the story of one person, the "hero" [who, in *Julius Caesar*, is not Caesar but Brutus], or at most of two, the "hero" and "heroine"', in *Romeo and Juliet* and *Antony and Cleopatra*.[4] 'The rest, including *Macbeth*, are single stars'[5] (and, we might add today, male). For Bradley, the tragic story is 'essentially a tale of suffering and calamity' that leads to death: 'no play at the end of which the hero remains alive is, in the full Shakespearean sense, a tragedy' (as Bradley acknowledges, this excludes *Troilus and Cressida* and *Cymbeline*).[6] In Shakespearean tragedy, such 'suffering and calamity' are 'exceptional'; they 'befall a conspicuous person', are 'themselves of some striking kind' and are usually 'unexpected' and contrast with 'some previous happiness or glory'. They also usually extend 'far and wide beyond the hero', making 'the whole scene a scene of woe'.[7]

There is an important further element in Shakespearean tragedy, however: its calamities 'do not simply happen, nor are they sent; they proceed mainly from [...] the actions of men'. These acts, or omissions, are 'thoroughly expressive of the doer, – characteristic deeds. The centre of the tragedy, therefore, may be said with equal truth to lie in action issuing from character, or in character issuing in action'. While Shakespeare's 'main interest lay here', it would be quite wrong to say that 'it lay in *mere* character, or was a psychological interest', since 'he was dramatic to the tips of his fingers'.[8] This statement is a significant corrective to those who later criticized Bradley's preoccupation with character and his supposed lack of interest in Shakespeare on stage.

Shakespeare admits into his tragedies 'abnormal conditions of mind' such as 'insanity', 'somnambulism, hallucinations'. But these are not used as 'the origin of deeds' of any dramatic significance. He also employs the supernatural, which cannot be explained in rational terms, but always places it 'in the closest relation with character'. Moreover, he lets 'chance' or 'accident' play a role, but 'chance' or 'accident' is a 'prominent fact [...] of human life', so it would be false '[t]o exclude it *wholly* from tragedy. Moreover, it is 'a *tragic* fact' that 'men may start a course of events but can neither calculate nor control it' and accident in a drama, provided it is moderate, can highlight this.[9]

Shakespearean tragedy is not the kind in which the hero opposes 'an undivided soul' to 'a hostile force'. The struggle is both within and without. Bradley suggests that 'spiritual force' is a more 'definite' concept than 'conflict'. By 'spiritual force' he means 'whatever forces act in the human spirit, whether good or evil, whether personal passion or impersonal principle; doubts, desires, scruples, ideas – whatever can animate, shake, possess and drive a man's soul'. A Shakespearean tragedy shows 'such forces [...] in conflict'.

Almost all Shakespeare's tragic characters exhibit 'the fundamental tragic trait': 'a marked one-sidedness, a predisposition in some particular direction'; 'a total incapacity, in certain circumstances, of resisting the force which draws in this direction'; and 'a fatal tendency to identify the whole being with one interest, object, passion, or habit of mind'.[10] But they must be on a larger scale than the general run of human beings, have 'so much of greatness that in [their] error and fall we may be vividly conscious of the possibilities of human nature'.[11] This greatness is, for Bradley, linked with 'the centre of the tragic impression' – 'the impression of waste'. In Shakespearean tragedy, pity and fear 'seem to unite with, and even to merge in, a profound sense of sadness and mystery' that is 'a type of the mystery of the whole world, the tragic fact which extends far beyond the limits of tragedy'.[12] Tragedy confronts us with 'the inexplicable fact, or [...] appearance, of a world travailing [undergoing painful or laborious effort] for perfection, but bringing to birth, together with glorious good, an evil which it is able to overcome only by self-torture and self-waste'.[13] Thus Bradley elevates Shakespearean tragedy to the highest level: it is an image of the substance of human life.

We can now explore examples of Bradley's approach to the big four Shakespeare tragedies on which he focuses. With *Hamlet*, he declares that 'the whole story turns on the peculiar character of the hero', and without him it would seem 'sensational and horrible'.[14] The 'direct cause' of Hamlet's irresolution, Bradley proposes, was 'a state of profound melancholy', 'induced by special circumstances'.[15] But this would merely be a 'pathological condition' were it not linked to Hamlet's 'speculative genius'. It is the link between Hamlet's 'melancholy' and his 'speculative genius' that gives 'his story its peculiar fascination and makes it appear [...] as the symbol of a tragic mystery inherent in human nature'.[16] If on one level Bradley treats Hamlet as a character with a past – for example, '[d]oubtless in happier days he was a close and constant observer of men and manners'[17] – on another level, as is evident here, he sees Hamlet's story as symbolic of a widespread truth.

In his account of *Othello*, Bradley calls it 'the most painfully exciting and the most terrible' of all Shakespeare's tragedies,[18] but 'the comparative confinement of the imaginative atmosphere' means that it does not equal *Hamlet*, *Macbeth* and *Lear* in 'the power of dilating the imagination by vague suggestions of huge universal powers working in the world of individual fate and passion. It is, in a sense, less "symbolic"'[19] and 'leaves an impression that in *Othello* we are not in contact with the whole of Shakespeare'.[20] Bradley does address the issue of Othello's colour and asserts that it is 'nearly certain that [Shakespeare] imagined Othello as a black man, and not as a light-brown one'. He mocks what he sees as the 'horror of most American critics [...] at the idea of a black Othello' but points out that Coleridge anticipated them (as we saw in Chapter 2). For Bradley, a black Othello enhances the character of Desdemona; she 'had no theories about universal brotherhood', but 'when her soul came in sight of the noblest soul on earth, she made nothing of the shrinking of her senses, but followed her soul until her senses took part with it, and "loved him with the love which was her doom"' (the line, showing Bradley's Victorianism, is from *Lancelot and Elaine*, the seventh of the poem-sequence *Idylls of the King* (1872–3) by Alfred, Lord Tennyson [1809–92]).[21] While 'innocence, gentleness, sweetness, lovingness were the salient and, in a sense, the principal traits of Desdemona's character', her choice of the black Othello demonstrated 'a love not only full of romance' but 'showing a strange freedom and energy of spirit, and leading to a most unusual boldness of action' which was 'carried through with a confidence and decision worthy of Juliet or Cordelia'.[22] This is a character-centred comment but it does endow Desdemona with a degree of agency as a female character that she has not always been accorded.

Bradley's account of Iago is similarly character-centred but, like Hazlitt's, it has a metadramatic dimension in which Iago, a figure in a drama, figures as an image of the dramatist, even, Bradley hazards, of Shakespeare himself: '[Iago] is not simply a man of action; he is an artist. His action is a plot, the intricate plot of a drama, and in the conception and execution of it he experiences the tension and the joy of artistic creation.'[23] Bradley, however, demurs on the idea that Iago combines 'supreme intellect' with supreme wickedness,[24] arguing that such a combination is 'an impossible fiction' and that Iago displays the 'rare' but extant fusion of 'unusual intellect with extreme evil'.[25]

In his chapters on *Lear*, Bradley argues against the view of *Lear* as ultimately pessimistic and suggests that it could as well be called *The Redemption of King Lear* in which the old king attains 'through apparently hopeless failure the very end and aim of life'.[26] Bradley does not mean 'redemption' in a Christian sense (although it would be easy to adapt it to a Christian reading of the play); Lear is redeemed by being brought through suffering to a condition where he can humbly love. Bradley links the idea of redemption with Lear's words when a stirring feather seems to show that Cordelia is not dead after all:

■ she lives! If it be so,
   It is a chance which does redeem all sorrows
   That ever I have felt! (5.3.274–6) □

For Bradley, the possibility of redemption adumbrated here is realized in Lear's last words, which Bradley interprets as meaning that Lear believes that Cordelia does live:

■ Do you see this? Look on her, look, her lips,
   Look there, look there! (5.3.327–8) □

We may object that Lear is wrong and that this compounds the pessimistic interpretation of the play. Lear dies happy but only because he is deluding himself. Bradley, however, sees an awareness that Lear is mistaken as insufficient to annul the reality of his joy and redemption. But Bradley does not consider a possible alternative interpretation of Lear's last words: that Lear has recognized that Cordelia is indeed dead – that her lips are still – and that he is urging others to share his recognition of that reality. In light of this interpretation, Lear might still be seen as redeemed, brought through illusion to reality, but it would be much more difficult to see him as unequivocally joyful as Bradley would like him to be.

Bradley's account of *Lear* also contains passages that move, interestingly, towards an approach that anticipates the analysis of Shakespearean imagery conducted by critics such as G. Wilson Knight and Caroline Spurgeon, which we consider in Chapter 6 of this Guide. He points, for instance, to the 'idea of monstrosity – of beings, actions, states of mind, which appear abnormal but absolutely contrary to nature' that occurs throughout Shakespeare's work but unusually often in *Lear*. Among his examples are Lear's '[i]ngratitude, thou marble-hearted fiend, / More hideous when thou show'st thee in a child / Than the sea-monster' (1.4.205–7); Lear's '[f]ilial ingratitude! / Is it not as this mouth should tear this hand / For lifting food to't?' (3.4.16–18); Albany's altered view of Goneril: '[t]hou changèd and self-covered thing, for shame / Bemonster not thy feature' (Q, 4.2.164–5, RSC Shakespeare p. 2078);[27] and (although Bradley quotes this a little later[28]) his observation that '[h]umanity must perforce prey on itself, / Like monsters of the deep' (Q, 4.2.155–6, RSC Shakespeare p. 2078).

Bradley links this idea of monstrosity with a notable aspect of the language of Lear that is unparalleled except in *Timon* – the 'incessant reference' to what he calls 'the lower animals' and 'man's likeness to them'. There is Edgar's fictional description of his days as a 'servingman' when he was a 'hog in sloth, fox in stealth, wolf in greediness, dog in madness, lion in prey' (3.4.74, 79–80); Lear's attack on female sexuality – 'The fitchew [polecat/prostitute] nor the soilèd horse goes to't / With a more riotous appetite' (4.5.129–30); the bestial insults directed against Goneril that liken her to a 'kite' [bird of prey, scavenger] (1.4.209), a serpent (1.4.236–7; 2.2.336–7; 5.3.87), a wolf (1.4.257), a vulture (2.2.307) and a boar (3.7.61); the images of both daughters as dogs (Q, 223, RSC Shakespeare p. 2079), tigers (Q, 147, RSC Shakespeare p. 2078) and adders (5.2.53–4); and the descriptions of Oswald as a 'son and heir of a mongrel bitch' (2.2.17), a 'wagtail' ['tail-wagger, obsequious person/ womanizer'] (2.2.50) and a goose (2.2.66).[29] These passages demonstrate that Bradley was perfectly capable of collating images in the manner later adopted and developed by Wilson Knight and Spurgeon, but that the weight of his interest lay elsewhere.

In his account of *Macbeth*, Bradley puts forward another general rule for Shakespearean tragedy: such a tragedy usually 'has a special tone or atmosphere of its own, quite perceptible, however difficult to describe'.[30] 'Tone' and 'atmosphere' are vague terms in themselves, but Bradley does try to be more specific about the sources of the atmosphere of *Macbeth* and in this he once again shows his capacity for image collation. He asserts that '[d]arkness, we may even say blackness, broods over this tragedy'[31] and gives examples of the way in which its language contributes to this effect: 'black and deep desires' (1.5.56); 'darkness does the face of earth entomb' (2.4.10); 'night's black agents' (3.3.58); 'black and midnight hags' (4.1.47). But the blackness of the *Macbeth*-impression is sometimes broken by colour, especially that of blood: 'the image of blood is forced upon us continually, not merely by the events themselves, but by full descriptions, and even by reiteration of the word in unlikely parts of the dialogue'. Bradley does not specify these 'unlikely parts of the dialogue' but does give examples of the term occurring in contexts in the play where it might be expected: among these are, after the first battle, '[w]hat bloody [i.e. bleeding, bloodstained] man is that?' (1.2.1) and 'bloody execution' (1.2.20); Lady Macbeth's '[m]ake thick my blood' (1.5.41)[32] and '[y]et who would have thought the old man to have had so much blood in him?' (5.1.28–9);[33] the First Murderer with 'blood upon [his] face' (3.4.13) in the banquet scene and 'blood-boltered Banquo' in the witches' show of apparitions (4.1.132).[34]

Bradley goes on to point to the 'vividness, magnitude and violence of the imagery' that pervades almost all of *Macbeth*, instancing images such as 'the babe torn smiling from the breast and dashed to death' (1.7.58–62); 'pouring the sweet milk of concord into hell' (4.3.110); 'the earth shaking in fever' (2.3.54–5); 'the frame of things disjointed' (3.2.18); 'sorrows striking heaven on the face, so that it resounds and yells out like syllables of dolour' (4.3.6–9); 'the mind lying in restless ecstasy on a rack' (3.2.23–4); 'the mind full of scorpions' (3.3.40); and 'the tale told by an idiot, full of sound and fury' (5.5.26–7). All these, Bradley contends, 'keep the imagination moving "on a wild and violent sea"' (4.2.24) and rarely allow it, even momentarily, 'to dwell on thoughts of peace and beauty'.[35]

As Bradley had suggested, following Hazlitt, that Iago, in *Othello*, was a kind of artist, so he suggests that Macbeth, this 'bold ambitious man of action', has, 'within certain limits, the imagination of a poet' which is, on the one hand, 'extremely sensitive to impressions of a certain kind and, on the other, productive of violent disturbance both of mind and body'.[36] Bradley outlines what he sees as the limits to Macbeth's poetic imagination by contrasting him with two other tragic protagonists of Shakespeare: Macbeth lacks 'the universal meditative imagination of Hamlet', coming to share (presumably in the 'Tomorrow and tomorrow' soliloquy (5.5.19–28))

Hamlet's sporadic view of humanity as the 'quintessence of dust' (2.2.287), but unable to reflect as Hamlet does on 'man's noble reason and infinite faculty' (2.2.284–5) or to perceive 'this brave overhanging firmament, this majestical roof fretted with golden fire' (2.2.282). In Bradley's view, Macbeth also suffers by comparison with Othello, since he cannot feel 'the romance of war or the infinity of love'. Macbeth's 'imagination is excitable and intense, but narrow'. [37]

In regard to Macbeth's 'judg[e]ment on life' in the lines of the 'Tomorrow and tomorrow' speech that run from 'Out, out, brief can-dle!' to 'Signifying nothing' (5.5.23–8), Bradley is concerned to rebut the view that such a judgement, 'the despair of a man who has know-ingly made mortal war on his own soul', 'should be frequently quoted as Shakespeare's own judg[e]ment, and should even be adduced, in serious criticism, as a proof of [Shakespeare's] pessimism!'. Bradley does not give any examples of the 'serious criticism' which he mentions: but it is striking, in the perspective of the critical history of Shakespeare's tragedies, that his desire to close off the possibility that such a judge-ment might be the overall import of *Macbeth* is shared by two of his most prominent opponents in the 1930s, L. C. Knights (1906–97) and F. R. Leavis (1895–1978). Whatever their differences, Bradley, Knights and Leavis are at one in their rejection of a nihilistic *Macbeth*.

To mention Knights and Leavis is to anticipate how, as the twen-tieth century proceeds, Bradley will be – to use a 1930s metaphor for the toppling of literary reputations – dislodged (from his pedestal) as a critic of Shakespearean tragedy. This dislodgement did not only come from Leavis and his Cambridge followers like Knights but also from those examining Shakespearean tragedy in a history-of-ideas perspective such as Lily B. Campbell. There were six main areas of objection to Bradley; that he was a 'character-chaser' who focused on the characters of Shakespeare's tragedies and treated them as if they were real people – or at least characters in realist novels – about whose lives and psychology one could make a range of inferences; that he gave insufficient attention to the language of Shakespeare's plays; that he treated the tragedies as if they were novels to be read in the privacy of the study rather than watched on stage; that he ignored Elizabethan and Jacobean dramatic and theatrical conventions; that he played down the importance of Christianity in Shakespeare's times and in his tragedies; and that he took little account of the history of the Elizabethan and Jacobean periods. We shall consider these further in the course of this Guide. But a decisive shift away from the character-centred approach to Shakespearean tragedy came from outside the academy, with T. S. Eliot's essay 'Hamlet and His Problems', first published in the *Athenaeum* (26 Sept. 1919), and later collected in *The Sacred Wood* (1920).

T. S. Eliot

Eliot throws down the gauntlet right at the start of his essay by accusing most critics of being in denial about *Hamlet* in that they see the character, rather than the play, as 'the primary problem'. For Eliot, Hamlet the character seems especially attractive to what he calls 'that most dangerous type of critic', who has a mind 'which is naturally of the creative order but through some weakness in creative power exercises itself in criticism instead'. Such critics 'often find in Hamlet a vicarious existence for their own artistic realization'. His examples (bold put-downs, by a poet and critic who was then a young upstart, of major Romantic writers who are hardly mere 'critics') are Goethe, 'who made of Hamlet a Werther' (in his novel *Die Leiden des jungen Werthers* (1774), trans. as *The Sufferings of Young Werther*); and Coleridge, in the account we discussed in Chapter 2 of this Guide, 'who made of Hamlet a Coleridge'.[38] Citing J. M. Robertson (1856–1933) in support, Eliot asserts that '*Hamlet* is a stratification' that 'represents the efforts of a series of men, each making what he could out of the work of his predecessors'[39] and in which Shakespeare's work is 'superposed upon much cruder material which persists even in the final form'.[40] Shakespeare's '*Hamlet*' is 'a play dealing with the effect of a mother's guilt upon her son', but Shakespeare could not 'impose this motive successfully upon the "intractable" material of the old play'. This means that *Hamlet*, 'far from being Shakespeare's masterpiece', is 'most certainly an artistic failure'. 'In several ways, the play is puzzling, and disquieting as is none of the others'.[41] Eliot suggests that 'probably more people have thought *Hamlet* a work of art because they found it interesting, than have found it interesting because it is a work of art'. Eliot compares it to the famous painting of 1503–6 by the Italian artist Leonard da Vinci (1452–1519), which now hangs in the Louvre in Paris: '*Hamlet* is 'the "Mona Lisa" of literature'.[42] While 'the suspicion of Othello, the infatuation of Antony' and 'the pride of Coriolanus' each form the subject of a tragedy that is 'intelligible, self-complete, in the sunlight', *Hamlet*, like Shakespeare's sonnets, is 'full of some stuff that the writer could not drag to light, contemplate, or manipulate into art'. Eliot is unable to locate this 'stuff' precisely since it lies less in the play's action or any selected quotations than 'in an unmistakable tone which is unmistakably not in the earlier play'.[43]

It is at this point that Eliot proffers what was to become his famous description of the 'objective correlative'; the term had originally been used, in a different context, by the American painter Washington Allston (1779–1843) (a friend of Coleridge) in his posthumously published *Lectures on Art* (1850) and, according to John J. Duffy (1969), 'it was a Romantic commonplace in the vocabulary of artists, intellectuals and students of New England' in the 1830s.[44] But it was Eliot's formulation that was to have an enormous influence on the criticism of Shakespearean tragedy and on literary criticism more widely:

■ The only way of expressing emotion in the form of art is by finding an 'objective correlative'; in other words, a set of objects, a situation, a chain of events which shall be the formula of that *particular* emotion; such that when the external facts, which must terminate in sensory emotion, are given, the emotion is immediately evoked.[45] □

In Eliot's view, 'Shakespeare's more successful tragedies' exhibit 'this exact equivalence'. He gives two examples from *Macbeth*: Lady Macbeth's state of mind while sleepwalking is conveyed by 'a skilful accumulation of imagined sensory impressions'; when told of her death, Macbeth's words 'strike us as if, given the sequence of events', they 'were automatically released by the last event in the series'. The 'artistic "inevitability" lies in the complete adequacy of the external to the emotion' and this is exactly what *Hamlet* lacks: 'Hamlet (the man) is dominated by an emotion which is inexpressible, because it is in *excess* of the facts as they appear.'[46]

Eliot locates the problem in Hamlet's mother. While she occasions his disgust, she is 'not an adequate equivalent for it; his disgust envelops and exceeds her'. But to have 'heightened the criminality of Gertrude would have been to provide the formula for a totally different emotion in Hamlet; it is just *because* her character is so negative that she arouses in Hamlet the feeling she is incapable of representing'.[47]

According to Eliot, Shakespeare could not solve this problem and we cannot grasp why he tried to, because of a dearth of biographical evidence and, above all, because of the way in which any experience Shakespeare might have undergone that prompted him to tackle *Hamlet* would itself have exceeded the facts that would have accompanied the experience. To understand why Shakespeare tried to write *Hamlet*, we 'should have to understand things which Shakespeare did not understand himself'.[48]

For Eliot, understanding things which Shakespeare did not understand was an impossibility; all we could do was to understand that Shakespeare did not understand. But an attempt to understand things Shakespeare did not understand – or at least did not formulate explicitly – was to be made by the field of enquiry that specialized in making the supposedly unconscious conscious and that emerged slightly before Bradley and made a widespread impact in the twentieth century: psychoanalysis. It is the psychoanalytic interpretations of Shakespearean tragedy – of *Hamlet* above all, but also of *Macbeth* – which we explore in the next chapter.

CHAPTER FIVE

Psychoanalysis and Desire

Four years before Bradley's *Shakespearean Tragedy*, at the very turn of the nineteenth century, a book had appeared that would have far-reaching cultural effects: *The Interpretation of Dreams* (dated 1900; in fact issued 1899) by a then obscure Viennese Jewish doctor called Sigmund Freud (1856–1939). Shakespearean tragedy was only one concern of this multifarious work; but Freud's footnote on *Hamlet*, later promoted to the main text, was to prove fruitful, especially when Freud's disciple, Ernest Jones (1879–1958), developed the ideas expressed there in an essay and then a book, *Hamlet and Oedipus* (1949). The French revisionist psychoanalyst Jacques Lacan (1901–81) later explored *Hamlet* in his 'Sept Leçons sur *Hamlet*' ['Seven Lessons on *Hamlet*'] (1958–9) and although Lacan's impact on Shakespeare studies, and on literary studies, was to be delayed, it was considerable when it came.

We start with Freud, considering first his interpretation of *Hamlet* but then his less widely known reading of *Macbeth*.

Sigmund Freud

In *The Interpretation of Dreams*, Freud's account of *Hamlet* starts with a comparison to the ancient Greek legend of Oedipus and the dramas *Oedipus Tyrannos* (performed posthumously 401 BCE) and *Oedipus at Colonus* (?435–425 BCE) by Sophocles (496–406 BCE). The fundamental material of both, Freud contends, is the same: the desire of the boy-child to kill his father and marry his mother which, for Freud, is a universal experience in male infancy. In the Oedipus legend, this desire is inadvertently realized in young adulthood. Oedipus does not know his own parents; his father, Laïus, had cast him out to die as an infant because an oracle had warned him that his son by Jocasta would kill him. A shepherd had rescued the child and taken him to King Polybus in Corinth, where Polybus raised him as his son and heir. Warned by the oracle at Delphi that he would kill his father and marry his mother, he decides to escape his fate by not returning to Corinth. On the road to Thebes, he meets

Laïus and kills him after a quarrel, without of course knowing who he is. He goes on to Thebes, solves the riddle of the Sphinx, and then unknowingly marries his own mother, Jocasta, the widow of Laïus. Later a plague falls on Thebes and the oracle says this can only be lifted if the killer of Laïus is driven from the land. When Oedipus finds he is the killer, he blinds himself and later vanishes in a sacred grove. In *Hamlet*, Freud argues, the prince is unable to resolve to kill King Claudius because Claudius has done what Hamlet, as an infant, would have liked to do: murder Hamlet's father and marry his mother.

Freud attributes the different treatment of the same basic material in *Oedipus Rex* and *Hamlet* to a wider difference between 'the mental life of these two widely separated epochs of civilization', the classical and the early modern, a difference that indicates 'the secular advance of repression in the emotional life of mankind' from the early period to the later. In the Oedipus legend and Sophocles' plays, 'the child's wishful phantasy that underlies [them] is brought into the open and realized as it would be in a dream'. In *Hamlet*, the wishful fantasy stays repressed and, as with a neurosis, only manifests itself through 'its inhibiting consequences'.[1]

Freud observes that, strangely, 'the overwhelming effect' that *Hamlet* produces on its audiences and readers seems compatible with a complete failure to grasp its protagonist's character. The play, Freud stresses, is 'built up on Hamlet's hesitations' over fulfilling his assigned task of revenge; but the text does not adequately explain these hesitations and critical attempts to account for them have so far proved inconclusive. Freud cites the view, which he sees as still dominant, of Goethe (and, we might add, Coleridge): 'Hamlet represents the kind of man whose capacity to act is numbed by excessive intellectual development' – 'sicklied o'er with the pale cast of thought' (3.1.91). Another view Freud mentions is that Shakespeare has sought to represent a 'pathologically irresolute', 'neurasthenic' figure. But Freud rejects both those views by making the point (as Bradley would) that Hamlet is perfectly capable of taking action sometimes: when he kills Polonius and 'in a premeditated and even crafty fashion, when, with all the callousness of a Renaissance prince, he sends the two courtiers [Rosencrantz and Guildenstern] to the death that had been planned for himself'. If he can kill with such ease, why cannot he kill Claudius? This is Freud's answer:

■ it is the peculiar nature of the task. Hamlet is able to do anything – except take vengeance on the man who did away with his father and took that father's place with his mother, the man who shows him the repressed wishes of his own childhood realized. Thus the loathing which should drive him on to revenge is replaced in him by self-reproaches, by scruples of conscience, which remind him that he himself is literally no better than the sinner whom he is to punish.[2] □

Freud here claims that he is consciously expressing what is necessarily 'unconscious in Hamlet's mind' and he accepts that Hamlet might be called 'a hysteric'. Such a diagnosis could accommodate the 'distaste for sexuality in [Hamlet's] conversation with Ophelia' – a distaste that would reach 'its extreme expression' in *Timon of Athens*.

Freud's mention of Hamlet's 'mind' highlights that this approach treats Hamlet as if he were a real person, complete with analysable psyche, rather than as, say, a set of complexities produced by the unsuccessful superimposition of one kind of play upon another (as T. S. Eliot, following Robertson and Stoll, suggested in his 1919 essay 'Hamlet and His Problems', discussed in the previous chapter of this Guide). Freud then shifts, in fact, from Hamlet's mind to the inferred mind of Shakespeare: 'it can only be the poet's own mind which confronts us in Hamlet'. Like many others at the time, Freud had read George Brandes' then recently published book *William Shakespeare* (discussed in Chapter 3 of this Guide). He cites Brandes' statement that Shakespeare wrote *Hamlet* soon after his own father's death in 1601 and points out, as Brandes does, that this would have reawakened the son's feelings about the father.[3] Freud, also like Brandes, makes a further link to the death of Shakespeare's son, Hamnet, on 11 August 1596, and moves on from this to compare, briefly but suggestively, *Hamlet* and *Macbeth*: 'Just as *Hamlet* deals with the relation of a son to his parents, *Macbeth* [...] is concerned with the subject of childlessness'.[4]

Freud develops this view of *Macbeth* in 'Some Character-Types Met With in Psycho-Analytical Work' (1916). Here he proposes that the action of *Macbeth* turns on the contrast between 'the curse of unfruitfulness and the blessing of continuous generation'. Although Freud's approach is not primarily historical, he sets his interpretation in the context of Shakespeare's time: like Macbeth and his lady, Queen Elizabeth I of England (b.1533; reigned 1558–1603) had no children, and thus no direct descendant to continue her line, so it was James I (b.1556; King of Scotland, as James VI, from 1576; King of England, 1603–25) who took the throne – a son of Elizabeth's competitor for power, Mary Queen of Scots (1542–87), who had been executed on Elizabeth's warrant, as Banquo had been murdered on Macbeth's covert orders.

Freud argues that Macbeth wants to become not only a king, but also the father of kings, 'to found a dynasty'.[5] Quoting Macduff's words after hearing of the slaughter of his wife and family, 'He has no children' (4.3.249), Freud identifies the 'He' here as Macbeth, rather than Malcolm[6] and interprets the line to mean: 'Only because he himself is childless could he murder my children'. Freud then draws attention to a recurrent set of references to father–son and mother–son relationships in the play:

■ The murder of the kindly Duncan is little else than parricide [the murder of a father]; in Banquo's case, Macbeth kills the father while the son escapes him [3.3]; and in Macduff's, he kills the children because the father has fled from him [4.2]. A bloody child, and then a crowned one, are shown him by the witches in the apparition scene [4.1]; the armed [armoured] head which is seen earlier [in 4.1] is no doubt Macbeth himself. But in the background rises the sinister form of the avenger, Macduff, who is himself an exception to the laws of generation, since he was not born of his mother but ripp'd from her womb [5.7.53–4].[7] □

In Freud's perspective, Macbeth's lack of children also explains Lady Macbeth's psychological collapse: 'what was it that broke this character which had seemed forged from the toughest metal?'[8] One possible reason, Freud acknowledges, is that the 'concentration and high tension' she displays before Duncan's murder 'could not endure for long'. But Freud suggests that 'a deeper motivation' that would 'make her collapse more humanly intelligible' is her childlessness, which proves to her that she is helpless against the forces of nature and stops her giving Macbeth the children that would ensure the continuance of his line rather than Banquo's.[9]

There is, Freud admits, a problem with this idea: Lady Macbeth changes too quickly in Shakespeare's play. In Shakespeare's source, Holinshed, Macbeth, partly incited by his wife, kills Duncan, takes the crown and reigns effectively for ten years. It is only then that he begins to become a tyrant, for instance by having Banquo murdered. Holinshed, as Freud acknowledges, does not indicate that Macbeth's childlessness impels him towards tyranny; but the decade of comparatively competent rule would, Freud speculates, allow time for the Macbeths to undergo 'a long-drawn-out disappointment of their hopes of offspring' that would 'break the woman down and drive the man to defiant rage'. Freud recognizes, however, that Shakespeare's play cannot be stretched to support his explanation fully.

Near the end of his discussion of *Macbeth*, Freud considers another possible approach to explaining Lady Macbeth – and Macbeth himself – which does not focus on them as individual characters. Freud mentions an apparently unpublished paper by his fellow psychoanalyst Ludwig Jekels (1867–1954), which suggests that Shakespeare's plays often split a character into two figures which can only be fully understood if they are considered together. If this were true of Lady Macbeth and her husband, 'it would of course be pointless to regard her as an independent character and seek to discover the motives for her change, without considering the Macbeth who completes her'.[10] Freud goes on to provide a range of examples of the exchange of elements between Macbeth and his lady which demonstrates how they might be grasped, not as individual characters, but as two aspects of a larger entity:

■ [T]he germs of fear which break out in Macbeth on the night of the murder do not develop further in *him* but in *her*. It is he who has the hallucination of the dagger before the crime [2.1.40–56]; but it is she who afterwards falls ill of a mental disorder [5.1]. It is he who after the murder hears the cry in the house: 'Sleep no more!' ... 'Glamis [Macbeth] hath murdered sleep' and so 'Macbeth shall sleep no more' [2.2.42, 49–51]; but we never hear that *he* slept no more, while the Queen, as we see, rises from her bed and, talking in her sleep, betrays her guilt. It is he who stands helpless with bloody hands, lamenting that 'all great Neptune's ocean' will not wash them clean, while she comforts him 'A little water clears us of this deed' [2.2.71, 78]; but later it is she who washes her hands for a quarter of an hour and cannot get rid of the bloodstains: 'all the perfumes of Arabia will not sweeten this little hand' [5.1.20, 37–8]. Thus what he feared in his pangs of conscience is fulfilled in her; she becomes all remorse and he all defiance. Together they exhaust the possibilities of reaction to the crime, like two disunited parts of a single psychical individuality.[11] ☐

Here, as in his earlier discussion (quoted above) of father–son and mother–son relationships in *Macbeth*, Freud offers a perspective on the play that does not focus on (psycho-)analysing individual characters but involves identifying recurrent and related motifs that run across different characters and incidents. This can be linked to the pursuit of image patterns in the work of Caroline Spurgeon and G. Wilson Knight in the 1930s.

Fascinating though Freud's account of *Macbeth* is, it was his interpretation of *Hamlet* that would become perhaps the most famous reading of the play, and of any Shakespearean tragedy, in the twentieth century – influencing, for example, the 1948 *Hamlet* film adapted, directed by and starring Laurence Olivier (1907–89). It would be developed magisterially and lucidly in the book *Hamlet and Oedipus* by Ernest Jones, to which we turn next.

Ernest Jones

Ernest Jones's book is a further revision and extension of an essay that had originally appeared in 1910 and had subsequently been twice revised and extended. Jones is well aware of the objection that may be made to treating a character in a drama as if he were a real person, but contends that it is a necessary and inevitable fiction. 'No dramatic criticism of the personae in a play is possible except under the pretence that they are living people, and surely one is well aware of this pretence.'[12] He also asserts that, if one takes a character in a play as a living person, it follows that this person must 'have had a life before the action in the play began, since no one starts life as an adult'.[13] In light of these two assertions, Jones declares his intention to proceed on the pretence 'that

Hamlet was a living person' and 'inquire what measure of man such a person must have been to feel and act in certain situations in the way Shakespeare tells us he did'.[14]

Jones adapts a celebrated description of hysterical paralysis by the surgeon and pathologist Sir James Paget (1814–99) to sum up Hamlet's situation:[15] 'Hamlet's advocates say he cannot do his duty, his detractors say he will not, whereas the truth is that he cannot will.' His inability to will, however, is confined to one area: killing his uncle. We may call this, Jones suggests, a *specific aboulia* [absence of will power, indecisiveness (*OED*)]'.[16] Such an aboulia, Jones argues, is always due to 'some hidden reason' that a person will not admit to himself and of which he is hardly, if at all, conscious. Each of Hamlet's stated reasons for delay is plausible to some extent – otherwise they could hardly function as pretexts – but each collapses under close scrutiny.

Jones infers that Hamlet, in childhood, had had 'the warmest affection for his mother' which, as always with such affection in a Freudian perspective, 'had contained elements of a disguised erotic quality, still more so in infancy'. This inference is supported, Jones contends, by two aspects of the Queen – 'her markedly sensual nature and her passionate fondness for her son'. As an example of the latter, Jones quotes Claudius to Laertes: 'The queen his mother / Lives almost by his looks' (4.6.13–14). But Hamlet seems to have 'weaned himself' from his mother and taken Ophelia as his love-object,[17] perhaps because her 'naïve piety, her obedient resignation and her unreflecting simplicity sharply contrast with the Queen's character'. Jones suggests it may even be possible that Hamlet's relationship with Ophelia stemmed less from her attractiveness to him than from 'an unconscious desire to play her off against his mother'. As an illustration of such playing-off, Jones gives an example from the play scene when Gertrude says 'Come hither, my good Hamlet, sit by me' and her son replies 'No, good mother, here's metal more attractive' (3.2.90–1) and goes to Ophelia. Jones suggests that we can barely begin to account for Hamlet's 'coarse familiarity and bandying of ambiguous jests' (such as 'Do you think I meant c[o]untry matters?' (3.2.97)), unless we recognize that these are perpetrated in sight (and hearing) of Gertrude. As Jones puts it: 'It is as if [Hamlet's] unconscious were trying to convey to [his mother] the following thought: 'You give yourself to other men whom you prefer to me. Let me assure you that I can dispense with your favours and even prefer those of a woman whom I no longer love.'[18]

Hamlet's 'reaction against Ophelia' preceded the play scene and was a result of the reawakening of the Oedipal situation by the appearance of the ghost and its confirmation that Claudius had done what Hamlet had once wanted to do – murder his father and marry his mother – and that his mother was possessed of a sensuality that he had trained himself not to perceive since infancy.[19] This is the source of 'the bitter misogyny of his outburst against Ophelia, who is devastated at having to hear a reaction so wholly out of proportion to her own offence and has no idea that in reviling her Hamlet is really expressing his bitter resentment against his mother': 'I have heard of your paintings [cosmetics, make-up] too, well enough. God has given you one face and you make yourself another: you jig, you amble and you lisp, and nickname God's creatures, and make your wantonness your ignorance. Go to, I'll no more on't: it hath made me mad' (3.1.142–5).

Jones contends that Hamlet's 'similar tone and advice' to Ophelia and Gertrude demonstrates his close mental identification of the two women.[20] His two examples are, first, Hamlet to Ophelia: 'Get thee to a nunnery. Why wouldst thou be a breeder of sinners?' (3.1.125) – Jones makes the point that 'nunnery' could also mean 'brothel'.[21] Jones's second example is Hamlet to Gertrude: 'Refrain [i.e., from sex with Claudius] tonight, / And that shall lend a kind of easiness / To the next abstinence' (3.4.166–8). On the level of play-events rather than language, the Gertrude/Ophelia identification, Jones suggests, shows itself further in Hamlet's killing of the men, Claudius and Polonius, who block his way to these two women.

Jones argues that 'Hamlet's conception of his task differed somewhat from his father's'.[22] The ghost of old Hamlet, though sure his son should kill Claudius, urged him to protect his mother. Hamlet knew it was his duty to kill Claudius but it mattered more to him to stop the incestuous uncle–mother relationship and he was uncertain how to handle his mother and worried he might hurt – even perhaps kill – her. In his verbal assault on Ophelia, Hamlet says 'I could accuse me of such things that it were better my mother had not borne me' (3.1.126–7) and Jones highlights the distinction between 'had I never been born' and 'had my mother not borne me'. 'Need the mother be mentioned, and for whom would it have been better?' Hamlet goes on to say to Ophelia, 'those that are married already, all but one shall live' (3.1.145–6). Although 'one' is often taken to refer to Claudius, Jones asserts that since Hamlet is verbally attacking women at this stage, he might mean Gertrude, and his declaration that Gertrude will live could be a prophylactic against his own matricidal urges. Both Gertrude herself and Claudius are aware that Hamlet may be a threat to the Queen as to others: in the bedroom scene, Gertrude says to Hamlet, 'What wilt thou do? Thou wilt not murder me?' (3.4.24), and calls for help, thus provoking the movement behind the arras that results in Hamlet's killing of Polonius. When Claudius learns of the killing, he says, 'His [Hamlet's] liberty is full of threats to all' (4.1.221). Jones draws attention to 'the curious slip of the tongue'[23] when Hamlet is packed off to England with Rosencrantz and Guildenstern and says to Claudius 'Farewell, dear mother'. Jones takes this slip to show the similarity of Hamlet's feelings towards his mother and stepfather and he underlines how, after Claudius has seemingly corrected him – 'Thy loving father, Hamlet' – Hamlet explains the logic of his mode of address: 'Father and mother is man and wife: man and wife is one flesh, and so my mother' (4.2.51–2). Jones observes that, in psychoanalysis, 'this idea, common in infancy, is known by the somewhat portentous title of the "combined parent concept". It dates from the phantasy of the parents in coitus, i.e. "one flesh"'.[24]

Hamlet and Oedipus also has a significant discussion of another Shakespeare tragedy, *Julius Caesar*. This latter drama may appear to lack any sexual difficulty or motivation but, like *Hamlet*, it can be seen to derive from the Oedipus complex. Jones cites his fellow psychoanalyst Otto Rank (1884–1939), who argued that Caesar stands for the father and Brutus, Cassius and Antony for different aspects of his sons in the Oedipal formation. Jones points to the link to Julius Caesar through Polonius, who is, along with Claudius, one of the 'bad' father figures in *Hamlet*. When Hamlet asks Polonius what part he once enacted in a university production, Polonius replies: 'I did enact Julius Caesar: I was killed i'th'Capitol: Brutus killed me' (3.2.86). Following Rank's argument about the three different aspects of the 'son' in the characters of *Julius Caesar*, Jones suggests that Caesar represents the father, while three aspects of his 'son' are assigned to three different characters: Brutus, 'rebelliousness'; Cassius 'remorsefulness'; and Antony 'natural piety'.[25] By contrast, three different aspects of Hamlet's attitudes to the father are represented by three different father figures: his actual father ('love and piety'); the 'father-type' Polonius ('hatred and contempt'); and Claudius ('conscious detestation and unconscious sympathy and identification, one paralysing the other'). In *Hamlet*, the 'parricidal wish [...] is displaced from the actual father to the father-substitutes'.[26] In *Caesar*, there is no mention of any blood relation between Caesar and the main 'son' type, Brutus.

Here Jones points to a significant omission in *Julius Caesar*: Shakespeare's known source for the play, Plutarch, includes the rumour that Brutus was the illegitimate son of Caesar by Servilia;[27] but Shakespeare makes no mention of this. It is also the case, Jones acknowledges, that *Caesar* seems to leave out a crucial element that does figure strongly in *Hamlet*: 'the son's relation to the mother, the other side of the whole Oedipus complex'. But Jones finds a hint of this in *Caesar*, in Brutus's words to the citizens: 'not that I loved Caesar less, but that I loved Rome more' (3.2.19–20), given that, in Jones's psychoanalytical perspective, cities, like countries, are 'symbols of the mother' – so Brutus is acknowledging that he killed his 'father' (Caesar) to protect his 'mother' (Rome). The two plays also have in common the appearance of 'the ghost of the murdered ruler', in one case to one of his killers, in the other to a would-be killer in the shape of Hamlet: 'although dramatically the ghost is another being, psychologically it represents the remorseful conscience of the (would-be) murderer'.[28]

Ernest Jones's interpretation of *Hamlet* would be taken up and discussed in Jacques Lacan's 'Seven Lessons on *Hamlet*' (1959), which we shall now consider.

Jacques Lacan

In his 'Seven Lessons on *Hamlet*', Jacques Lacan pays his respects to Freud and Jones but develops an interpretation of his own within the context of his distinctive revision of psychoanalysis. Citing Jones's decision to treat Hamlet as though he were a real character, even while knowing full well he is not, Lacan offers a different way of looking at Hamlet as, not a character, but 'purely and simply the place of desire'.[29] Hamlet is 'neither a clinical case nor a real being'. He is, rather, 'like a hub [une plaque tournante] where a desire is situated and we can rediscover there all the traits of desire'.[30]

Lacan also reinterprets the nature of Hamlet's desire. In the perspective of Freud and Jones, the repressed desire that his father's murder and mother's remarriage reawakens, but which he cannot acknowledge, is for his mother. But for Lacan, Hamlet 'wrestles with, a desire that is far away from himself [...] the desire, not *for* his mother, but *of* his mother'.[31] The ghost's words to Hamlet raise this issue when he points to his wife's 'falling-off' and, just before he vanishes, tells his son: 'Taint not thy mind nor let thy soul contrive / Against thy mother aught' (1.5.52, 90–1) – an injunction that Hamlet finds almost as difficult to obey as the command to avenge his father. Hamlet has to confront a desire, evident in his mother, that is triply troubling: it is a desire that is not his own and that brings home the force of other people's desire and the ways in which this may threaten and thwart him; it is a desire that is intimately close to him, in that it inheres in his mother whom he has wanted to see as sexless; and it is a voracious, omnivorous, undiscriminating desire that 'does not choose between the eminent, idealized, exalted object' (Hamlet's father) and 'the disparaged, contemptible object' (Claudius, the 'crooked and adulterous brother').[32]

Lacan also highlights the extent to which Hamlet operates as the bearer of a certain kind of discourse. It is 'one of Hamlet's functions to make, all the time, plays on words, puns, double meanings, equivocations and ambiguities'.[33] Hamlet's anguish 'should not disguise the fact that, from a certain perspective, this tragedy promotes to the level of hero someone who is, literally, a madman, a clown, a punster'.[34] It is as if – though Lacan does not quite say this – Hamlet has assimilated the functions of the long-dead Yorick and anticipates those of Lear's Fool, in a court which no longer has a jester.

Ophelia is, for Lacan, 'one of the most fascinating creations ever offered to the human imagination'. Her drama and unhappiness incarnate what Lacan calls 'the drama of the feminine object, the drama of desire' that appears at the dawn of Western civilization in the form of Helen of Troy. It is possible, Lacan suggests, to hear in her name both 'o-phallus' and 'omphalos' ('navel' in ancient Greek).[35] In one of the quasi-algebraic formulae of which Lacan is fond, he locates Ophelia on the level of the 'little object *a*', the fantasy object that serves as the underlying support of desire, insofar as we can distinguish desire from demand (an insistent request for something we think we want) and need (an essential requirement, like food or drink). This fantasy object '*a*' can take many forms and in this play it assumes Ophelia's shape; she is 'a most intimate element of the Hamlet who has lost his way, the path of his desire'.[36]

In the play scene, after Hamlet has fallen out of love with her, Ophelia becomes for him no more than the bearer of children and breeder of sinners unless she goes to a nunnery (which may merely return her to that role, since, as we saw in our discussion of Ernest Jones above and as Lacan also observes, 'nunnery', in the English of Shakespeare's time, could mean 'brothel'). As Lacan puts it, Ophelia becomes, for Hamlet, 'purely and simply the support of a life which, in its essences, is now condemned'. According to Lacan, 'what happens at this moment is the destruction or loss of the object, which is reintegrated into its narcissistic frame'.[37] 'All the dialogue with Ophelia well shows that the woman is here conceived uniquely as the bearer of this vital swelling [turgescence] that is to be cursed and dried up [Lacan uses the French verb 'tarir'].'[38]

Considering the flowers with which Ophelia decks herself before drowning, Lacan homes in on the 'long purples / That liberal shepherds give a grosser name, / But our cold maids do dead men's fingers call them' (4.6.152–4). Lacan follows a line of scholars in identifying this plant as the 'orchis mascula' ['a type of purple orchid'][39] and, he suggests, it has some link with mandragora ['sedative made from the root of the [...] mandrake plant'], mentioned in *Othello* (3.3.366) and *Antony and Cleopatra* (1.5.4)),[40] and therefore with the phallic element. This reinforces his idea of Ophelia as a phallic object.

Lacan also focuses on the graveyard scene which presents 'a reintegration of the "little object *a*" and the possibility of looping the loop [boucler la boucle], of hurrying at last to his destiny'.[41] Laertes leaps into Ophelia's grave to embrace his sister's body and Hamlet jumps in after him. Hamlet throws himself on Laertes 'in a passionate embrace' and they fight; Hamlet then springs from the grave 'literally as another, with the cry': 'This is I, Hamlet the Dane' (5.1.210–11).[42] Laertes functions here, Lacan suggests, as an example and support for Hamlet. It is this moment which re-establishes Hamlet's relationship as a subject with Ophelia, the 'little object *a*' that has earlier been rejected, and which, for a brief instant, makes a man of him, who can fight and kill – and thus, soon afterwards, bring the play to an end.

Lacan, then, offers a psychoanalytical perspective on *Hamlet* that treats the characters, not as if they were real people, but as subject and object positions in the playing out of a primal drama of desire and death. The play itself becomes, as Lacan puts it, 'a kind of network, made of bird-catchers' thread' which captures human desire.[43] *Hamlet* does not simply repeat the Oedipal drama, or, as Freud would have it, rewrite it for an era that has experienced 'the secular advance of repression in the emotional life of mankind';[44] rather, it pushes that drama 'to such a point that it modifies the manner in which the fundamental structure of the eternal saga that one rediscovers from the dawn of time presents itself'.[45] Like any psychoanalytical approach, Lacan's is open to the general objection that its theories of human formation may not be true because they relate to regions of experience that are, by their very nature, not easily open to conscious exploration and certainly not to scientific testing; but Lacan's interpretation, like those of Freud and Jones, undoubtedly seems to fit, and to illuminate, certain aspects of this tragedy, even if it looks too schematic and reductive to provide a more comprehensive interpretation. It is notable that Lacan's reading of *Hamlet* mentions the work of the English critic John Dover Wilson (1881–1969), whom he seems to have discovered through Ernest Jones's book, but does not otherwise engage with twentieth-century Shakespeare criticism on *Hamlet*, or on Shakespearean tragedy more generally – and by 1959, when Lacan delivered his seminars, there was plenty of it. But to a large extent, Anglo-American literary criticism had developed separately from – if sometimes in concealed rivalry with – psychoanalysis, and it would not be until the 1980s that revived psychoanalytical approaches, often influenced by Lacan but also fuelled by feminism, would be applied to Shakespeare's tragedies. We shall consider this further in Chapter 9 of this Guide. But now we must explore that separate development in criticism up to the 1950s, and to do so, we must go back in time, to 1930 and the emergence and consolidation of a new approach to Shakespeare's tragedies in the work of G. Wilson Knight, L. C. Knights, Caroline Spurgeon and Cleanth Brooks.

CHAPTER SIX

Imagery and Form

In the 1930s, a major change came about in the study of Shakespeare. There was a repudiation, sometimes implicit, sometimes polemically explicit, of what was seen as the Bradley approach and its alleged tendency to focus on Shakespeare's characters and treat them as if they were real people. New approaches to the interpretation of Shakespeare's plays developed that focused on patterns of imagery and on the text as a whole. The pioneering book here is G. Wilson Knight's *The Wheel of Fire: Interpretations of Shakespearian Tragedy with Three New Essays*, published at the start of the decade, and we shall consider this first.

G. Wilson Knight

Like Bradley's *Shakespearean Tragedy*, *The Wheel of Fire* (1930) begins with what we might call a theoretical chapter. But Wilson Knight is more practically orientated than Bradley. Whereas Bradley sought to define the substance of Shakespearian tragedy, Wilson Knight considers 'the principles of Shakespeare Interpretation' and outlines, not only a concept of what Shakespeare's plays are, but also a methodology, a way of doing interpretation – and this was very useful for an academic discipline that was still establishing itself.

Wilson Knight starts by distinguishing between 'interpretation' and 'criticism'. 'Criticism' involves turning a literary work into a kind of object, comparing it with other works, particularly in terms of its supposed artistic quality, assessing its strengths and weaknesses, and predicting its durability. Under the name of 'discrimination', criticism, thus defined, was to become a keynote of the approach associated with F. R. Leavis and his followers. 'Interpretation', for Wilson Knight, involves accepting and blending with the 'poetic unit' that is the literary work, trying to grasp it in its own terms, suspending judgement on its merits, largely eschewing external considerations of other works or secondary material (e.g., scholarship, biography), and trying to express the nature of that unit in critical prose. Wilson Knight sums up the difference between the two modes thus: '[c]riticism is a judgement of vision; interpretation a reconstruction of vision'.[1]

Criticism and interpretation are in practice, Knight acknowledges, often mixed. But Shakespeare's work is so powerful that it overwhelms adverse criticism. 'Any profitable commentary on such work must necessarily tend towards a pure interpretation.'[2] The most fruitful approach is to try to 'interpret our original imaginative experience into the slower consciousness of logic and intellect'. We need first of all 'to receive the whole Shakespearean vision into the intellectual consciousness', but this 'demands a certain and very definite act of mind'. Such an act of mind entails 'seeing the whole play in space as well as in time'. While it is 'natural' to analyse a play in sequence, unfolding in the temporal dimension of beginning, middle and end, the spatial dimension of a Shakespeare play is at least equally important because there is throughout each play 'a set of correspondences which relate to each other independently of the time-sequence which is the story'. Two of Wilson Knight's examples are 'the death-theme in *Hamlet*' and 'the nightmare evil of *Macbeth*'. It is such sets of correspondences that create the play's 'atmosphere'. Once 'we see the whole play laid out, so to speak, as an area, being simultaneously aware of these thickly-scattered correspondences in a single view of the whole, we possess the unique quality of the play in a new sense'.[3] This spatial perspective makes the alleged faults of the plays, which may seem to obtrude in a temporal perspective, disappear.

Although Wilson Knight has earlier argued that the 'spatial' apprehension of a Shakespeare play demands a definite act of mind, he then suggests that it is always present to some extent in 'our imaginative pleasure' and that it is, 'probably, the ability to see larger and still larger areas of a great work spatially with a continual widening of vision that causes us to appreciate it more deeply, to own it with our minds more surely, on every reading'.[4]

Wilson Knight rejects three other approaches to Shakespearean tragedy: one via authorial intention, the second via sources, the third via character. Anticipating the American New Critics' rejection of what they called 'the intentional fallacy', though for different reasons, Wilson Knight contends that '[i]ntentions belong to the plane of intellect and memory'. A critic who talks about an author's 'intentions' 'has lost touch with the essentials of the work'. Similarly with the idea of 'sources' which, like 'intentions', constitutes an attempt 'to explain art in terms of causality'.[5] But, Wilson Knight argues, 'the work of Plutarch, Holinshed, V[i]rgil, Ovid, and the Bible'[6] cannot be a cause or 'source' in the sense of being the 'origin' of 'the poetic reality' of the text. For Wilson Knight, 'the source of poetry is rooted in the otherness of mental or spiritual reality', but these 'are a "nothing" until mated with earthly shapes. Creation is thus born of a union between "earth" and "heaven", the material and the spiritual'.[7] In this context, Wilson Knight cites Theseus' famous speech on the poetic imagination in *A Midsummer Night's Dream*: '[t]he poet's eye [...] / Doth glance from heaven to earth, from earth to heaven' and 'the poet's pen' turns the 'forms of things unknown' to 'shapes' and 'gives to airy nothing / A local habitation and a name' (5.1.12, 13, 15, 16–17).

In regard to 'character', Wilson Knight rejects it because it is always bound up with 'ethical' criticism of the kind that takes Shakespeare's tragedies primarily as demonstrations of the faults of their protagonists and the fatal consequences of those faults. Such criticism also always invokes the 'intention' approach in respect of the author – the idea that Shakespeare *intended* to show us how such faults lead to tragedy – and can moreover involve seeing characters in terms of intentions, as in what Wilson Knight calls 'the constant and fruitless search for "motives"', for instance to explain the behaviour of Macbeth and Iago.[8] It is not that ethical considerations in relation to Shakespeare's characters can or should be avoided; but these considerations will, at least while there is sufficient continuity between Shakespeare's world and ours, arise instinctively from the poetic matter of the play rather than being imposed from outside it. The 'delicate symbols of the poet's imagination' should not be subjected to 'the rough machinery of an ethical philosophy created to control the turbulences of actual life'. A critic who adopts 'the ethical attitude' is usually 'unconsciously lifting the object of his attention from his setting and regarding him as actually alive'. When a critic finds 'faults' in the 'character' of Timon or Macbeth or Lear, he is 'in effect saying that [they] would not be a success in real life'; but this, Wilson Knight asserts, is 'beside the point, since [Timon], and Macbeth, and Lear, are evidently dramatic successes'.[9]

Wilson Knight affirms that '[o]ur reaction to great literature is a positive and dynamic experience' and interpretation should aim, on a lower plane, to be similarly positive and dynamic. In pursuit of this aim, it should 'regard each play as a visionary whole, close-knit in personification, atmospheric suggestion, and direct poetic-symbolism'.[10]

Wilson Knight then offers four 'main principles of right Shakespearean interpretation'. We should 'regard each play as a visionary unit bound to obey none but its self-imposed laws'; we should 'recognize' both '"temporal" and "spatial" elements'[11] and see each play as 'an expanded metaphor'; we 'should analyse the use and meaning of direct poetic symbolism'; and we should regard the plays from *Julius Caesar* to *The Tempest* as 'a significant sequence'.[12] This last principle is a latecomer – the previous pages have not really prepared the reader for it – and Wilson Knight acknowledges that it needs careful application in order not to obscure the particularity of a specific play. To some extent, it is in tension with his first principle of regarding each play as a visionary unit.

Despite this difficulty, Wilson Knight's opening pages are packed with fruitful suggestions for a new critical approach which eschews ideas of intention, source, character and evaluation and focuses on the plays as poetic units to be apprehended in space as well as time. He breaks from Bradley and his nineteenth-century precursors while retaining and refurbishing Romantic, aesthetic and quasi-religious terms such as 'beauty' and 'mystery' and giving a solid methodological grounding to his metaphysical flights and intensities, such as 'a true philosophic and imaginative interpretation will aim at cutting below the surface to reveal that burning core of mental or spiritual reality from which each play derives its nature and meaning'.[13]

How do these principles function in Wilson Knight's practice? He by no means avoids talking of Shakespeare's protagonists in terms of character and their inferred inner psychological processes and pre-play histories: for example, '[t]here is a continual process of self-murder at work in Hamlet's mind'[14] and we 'can guess what he was like before'.[15] Wilson Knight also protests against the sentimentalization of Hamlet's 'personality'[16] – a term which, deliberately or not, enables Wilson Knight to avoid calling Hamlet a 'character' – and unashamedly concentrates on 'the unpleasant parts of the play',[17] in order, he asserts, to enhance our vision of 'the protagonist, the play as a whole, and its place in Shakespeare's work'.[18] The 'theme of *Hamlet*,' Wilson Knight insists, 'is death', which he sees lying over the whole play, in the multiple deaths which it invokes or portrays on-stage. But, he contends, the play hardly gives us 'that sense of blackness and the abysms of spiritual evil' conveyed by *Macbeth* or 'the universal gloom' of *Lear*. Wilson Knight attributes this partly to the way in which 'the predominating imaginative atmospheres' in the two latter plays reinforce and amplify the tumults voiced by their protagonists, whereas in *Hamlet* there is a disjunction between the protagonist as death-carrier and what Wilson Knight calls 'the *Hamlet* universe' which is, he claims, '[e]xcept for the original murder of Hamlet's father', one of 'healthy and robust life, good-nature, humour, romantic strength and welfare'.[19] For example, Claudius, as we see him, is quite an effective ruler and a 'typical kindly uncle'.[20] Wilson Knight judges that Hamlet is right to see what lies beneath the court's smooth surfaces but that he is inhuman, nihilistic, life-negating: 'the ambassador of death walking amid life'.[21] He 'is not tragic in the usual Shakespearean sense; there is no surge and swell of passion pressing onward through the play to leave us, as in *King Lear*, with the mighty crash and backwash of a tragic peace'. Rather, Hamlet is 'a dualized personality' – we may note again the use of the word 'personality' where other critics might have said 'character' – who wavers between 'grace and the hell of cynicism'. The plot of the play 'reflects this see-saw motion', 'lack[ing] direction' and 'pivoting on Hamlet's incertitude'. This explains 'the play's fascination', which includes the vertiginous sensation that analysing it produces, and 'its lack of unified and concise poetic statement'.[22]

In his discussion of *Othello*, Wilson Knight focuses on what he calls the '*Othello* music' which, he claims, is unique in Shakespeare's drama. *Othello* 'holds a rich music all its own, and possesses a unique solidity and precision of picturesque phrase or image, a peculiar chastity and serenity of thought'. It seems 'aloof' from the reader because of its 'inward separation of image from image, word from word', which makes its 'dominant quality [...] separation, not, as is more usual in Shakespeare, cohesion'. Wilson Knight gives two examples, both spoken by Othello after he has murdered Desdemona:

> ■ O heavy hour!
> Methinks it should be now a huge eclipse
> Of sun and moon and that th'affrighted globe
> Did yawn at alteration. (5.2.115–18) □

And:

> ■ It is the very error of the moon:
> She comes more nearer earth than she was wont,
> And makes men mad. (5.2.127–9) □

Wilson Knight admires the poetry in these lines but contends that we can remove them from their context with no great loss, in contrast to equally poetic passages in *Lear* and *Macbeth*, which depend on their context for their full vitality.

The 'detached' style of *Othello*, Wilson Knight argues, is very clear and stately, but lacks a certain degree of power. 'At moments of great tension, the *Othello* style fails of a supreme effect' and 'sinks sometimes to a studied artificiality, nerveless and without force'.[23] For example, Othello, in the speech that culminates in his suicide, speaks of himself as:

> ■ [O]ne whose subdued eyes,
> Albeit unused to the melting mood,
> Drops tears as fast as the Arabian trees
> Their medicinable gum. (5.2.391–4). □

Wilson Knight contrasts this with Macduff's words, in *Macbeth*, after he has learnt of the murder of his wife and children:

> ■ O, I could play the woman with mine eyes
> And braggart with my tongue! But, gentle heavens,
> Cut short all intermission. (4.3.264–5). □

Wilson Knight finds 'more force in [Macduff's] first line than all Othello's slightly over-strained phraseology of "subdued eyes" and "melting mood"'. The strength of this line comes from 'the compression of metaphor and the sudden heightened significance of a single, very commonplace word ("woman")', while the *Othello* style 'deliberately refuses power' in its monotonous, tediously lengthy similes, and 'searches always for the picturesque'.[24] The *Othello* style neither encompasses nor, for the most part, seeks the overwhelming, merging language of *Lear* or *Macbeth*; but 'apparent weakness' occurs at 'the most agonizing moments of Othello's story' and results in 'an exaggerated, false rhetoric'.[25]

Despite Wilson Knight's earlier eschewal of 'criticism', in the sense of fault-finding through comparison between one work and another, it is clear that we still have judgement here – that Wilson Knight is judging that the language of *Othello*, for all its grandeur, is inferior to that of *Macbeth* or *Lear*. But he is supporting his judgement by what came to be called 'close reading' – a careful, responsive scrutiny of the verbal detail and nuance of the texts in question – and by specific examples. In this kind of scrutiny and copious deployment of examples, Wilson Knight is setting a new standard in criticism that would provide the basis for all future literary study, whatever its theoretical or ideological perspective. If Shakespeare's tragedies were to be adequately discussed in the future, this would be likely to involve scrupulous and sensitive attention to the detail of the text as well as a sense of the way such detail might fit into the whole of the play and, perhaps, into the whole of Shakespeare's oeuvre. This attention to detail and totality, part and whole, can also be found, with different emphases, three years later in L. C. Knights' notable essay, 'How Many Children Had Lady Macbeth?' (1933).

L. C. Knights

The title of Knights' essay is famous but the subtitle less familiar: 'An Essay in the Theory and Practice of Shakespeare Criticism'. But the subtitle is important because it does emphasize that Knights was offering, in outline, a theoretical perspective (before theory – or 'philosophy' – was proscribed by F. R. Leavis[26]) and a demonstration of a methodology, in a form that was less extended than that of Wilson Knight in *The Wheel of Fire* but no less influential – perhaps more so, because of its compression. Looking back in 1945, Knights locates the essay in a time of change in Shakespeare criticism, a 'literary period [...] in which a new valuation of Shakespeare's greatness was in process'. He discerns in the first part of his essay 'a slight headiness springing from the exhilaration of attacking what was still the orthodox academic view of Shakespeare', and acknowledges, in its second part, 'an extensive indebtedness to the early work' of G. Wilson Knight, praising 'the genuine original insight contained, in good measure, in *The Wheel of Fire* [from which he has already quoted in the first part of his essay] and *The Imperial Theme* [1931]'. But he also quotes from a footnote originally appended to 'How Many Children … ' (though omitted from the reprint here), which is clearly an attack on Knight's generalizing tendencies: 'a preoccupation with imagery and symbols, unless minutely controlled by a sensitive intelligence directed upon the text, can lead to abstractions almost as dangerous as does a preoccupation with "character"'.[27]

It is, however, the 'preoccupation with "character"' that Knights assails in 'How Many Children …'. He calls 'the assumption that Shakespeare was pre-eminently a great "creator of characters"' the 'most fruitful of irrelevancies'[28] and finds 'the most illustrious example of this approach' to be Bradley's *Shakespearean Tragedy*, which, in Knights' view, assumes throughout its length that 'the most profitable discussion of Shakespeare's tragedies is in terms of the characters of which they are composed'.[29] But in making this assumption Bradley, for Knights, has a long lineage that runs from the late seventeenth to the early twentieth century and includes several of the critics discussed earlier in this book: Rymer (whose endorsement by T. S. Eliot, noted in Chapter 1 of this Guide, Knights challenges in a footnote), Dryden, Coleridge, Hazlitt and Dowden. Even Samuel Johnson, though not charged with character criticism, is faulted for censuring Shakespeare's language. Knights' account of late seventeenth- and eighteenth-century Shakespeare criticism reinforces a favourite Leavisian notion, derived from T. S. Eliot's essay 'The Metaphysical Poets' (1921): that there had occurred, in the seventeenth century, a 'dissociation of sensibility' (as Eliot called it), in which thought and emotion, language and experience, had become detached from one another.[30] In some sense, a Shakespeare play becomes an exemplar of, a portal to, an associated sensibility from which 'character' – 'like "plot", "rhythm", "construction" and all our other critical counters – is merely an abstraction':[31]

■ A Shakespeare play is a dramatic poem. It uses action, gesture, formal grouping and symbols, and it relies upon the general conventions governing Elizabethan plays. But [...] its end is to communicate a rich and controlled experience by means of words – words used in a way to which, without some training, we are no longer accustomed to respond.[32] □

By 'training' here Knights does not primarily mean the kind of scholarly, philological training that would enable one to know, by consulting an inner dictionary, what Shakespearean words and phrases meant in their own time; rather, he has in mind the kind of training which

Shakespeare's original audiences supposedly enjoyed. This training, provided 'by pamphlets, by sermons and by common conversation', enabled those audiences 'to listen or to read with an athleticism which we, in the era of the *Daily Mail* and the Best Seller, have consciously to acquire or do our best to acquire'.[33] The idea of criticism as a mental gymnasium and the depreciation of popular forms of writing by metonymy ('*Daily Mail*') and reification ('Best Seller'), were characteristic of the Leavisian approach and its appeal to what would become the stock responses of a self-appointed cultural elite; but the concept of the cultivation of a special form of attention to literary texts has continued to resonate through later critical movements.

In Part Two of the essay, Knights provides a specific reading of a Shakespeare play, *Macbeth*, as 'a precise particular experience, a poem' that must be apprehended with 'the razor-edge of sensibility'.[34] *Macbeth* is 'a statement of evil',[35] but 'it is a statement not of a philosophy but of ordered emotion'.[36] Its two 'main themes' are 'the reversal of value and of unnatural disorder', and a 'closely related [...] third theme' is 'that of the deceitful appearance and consequent doubt, uncertainty and confusion'.[37] Knights continues in this section, however, to formulate general maxims. He states, for instance, 'a general principle in the work of Shakespeare, and many of his contemporaries': 'that when A is made to describe X, a minor character or event, the description is not merely immediately applicable to X, it helps to determine the way in which our whole response shall develop'.[38] One example is the lines:

■ – Doubtful it stood,
   As two spent swimmers, that do cling together
   And choke their art. (1.2.9–11) □

This applies, Knights asserts, 'not only to the battle [that has just taken place] but to the ambiguity of Macbeth's future fortunes'.[39]

Knights is concerned to stress that in a Shakespeare play, every scene, every detail counts. 'A poem works by calling into play, directing, and integrating certain interests. If we really accept the suggestion, which then becomes revolutionary, that *Macbeth* is a poem, it is clear that the impulses aroused in [1.1. and 1.2] are part of the whole response, even if they are not all immediately relevant to the fortunes of the protagonist.'[40] In his concern to demonstrate that every aspect of a Shakespeare play contributes to its total effect, Knights offers an explanation of a scene that has often puzzled critics, the dialogue between Malcolm and Macduff in 4.3 in which Malcolm confesses to a range of vices that make him unsuitable to be king and then claims his confessions were false. The primary function of this scene, Knights contends, is 'choric commentary' in which, in 'alternating speeches, the evil that

Macbeth has caused is stated impersonally and without extenuation',[41] and where Malcolm, in his 'self-accusation' has 'ceased to be a person' and his 'lines repeat and magnify' Macbeth's evils and implicitly 'contrast [them] with the opposite virtues', 'As justice, verity, temp'rance, stableness' (4.3.104).[42]

Those 'opposite virtues' are very important for Knights. He stresses that the evil in the play is balanced by 'the positive values' Shakespeare has established by means of 'images of grace and of the holy supernatural'[43] (as distinct from the diabolically supernatural in the witches): '[f]ood and sleep, society and the political order [...], represented as supernaturally sanctioned';[44] 'images of health';[45] and the 'disorder' in the final act,[46] as Macbeth's defeat looms, which, despite its apparent use of the artificial, deceitful and unnatural (e.g., the moving trees) 'has a positive tendency, towards the good which Macbeth had attempted to destroy'.[47] Remarking on Macbeth's 'Tomorrow and tomorrow' speech, Knights, like Bradley, is concerned to correct what he sees as a dangerous tendency to take it as Shakespeare's own judgement on life: 'the poetry is so fine that we are almost bullied into accepting an essential ambiguity in the final statement of the play, as though Shakespeare were expressing his own "philosophy" in the lines'. But, Knights goes on, 'the lines are "placed" by the tendency of the last act' towards order and truth, a tendency which culminates in 'the recognition of the Witches' equivocation ('And be these juggling fiends no more believed' (5.7.57)), the death of Macbeth, and the last words of Siward, Macduff, and Malcolm (5.7.95–120)'.[48]

Knights' potent essay retains its forensic impact and analytic sharpness. But it is open to challenge on several counts. As Katherine Cooke points out in *A. C. Bradley and His Influence in Twentieth-Century Shakespeare Criticism* (1972), Bradley himself used Knights' central term, 'dramatic poem', in comparing *Macbeth* and *King Lear*,[49] and we can suggest that there is, more generally, greater continuity between the Bradleyan and Knightsian approach than Knights allows. Knights' focus on a Shakespeare play as a 'dramatic poem' also raises the question of where the drama comes in. There is an interesting slippage of focus from poem to performance, from page to stage, when Knights says, of the last act: 'If we merely read the play we are liable to overlook the importance of the sights and sounds which are obvious on the stage. The frequent stage directions should be observed – *Drum and Colours, Enter Malcolm ... and Soldiers Marching* – and there are continuous directions for *Alarums, Flourishes*, and fighting'.[50] The implication here is that 'merely' reading the play, focusing on the meanings of the words on the page, is not enough in itself but must be supplemented by imagining what the play would look like on the stage. And in what sense do stage directions – which Shakespeare may not have put there – form part of a 'dramatic poem', since they are not incorporated into the verse or prose of the play?

Perhaps the most central objection to Knights' approach, however, especially in the context of this Guide, is that he gives no account of why *Macbeth* might be called a tragedy; indeed, he rather avoids the word. There is, however, one occasion on which he does use it that is significant. The last act of *Macbeth*, he suggests, provides 'a vantage point from which the whole course of the drama may be surveyed in retrospect' but asserts that '[t]here is no formula that will describe this final effect'. It is, he continues, 'no use saying that we are "quietened", "purged", or "exalted" at the end of *Macbeth* or any other tragedy' or 'taking one step nearer the play and saying we are purged, etc., because we see the downfall of a wicked man or because we realize the justice of Macbeth's doom whilst retaining enough sympathy for him or admiration of his potential qualities to be filled with a sense of "waste"'. Indeed, 'it is no use discussing the effect in abstract terms at all' and we 'can only discuss it in terms of the poet's concrete realization of certain emotions and attitudes'.[51] The insistent anaphora here – the repetition of 'it is no use' – begs the question of why it serves no practical purpose to engage in such discussions of the effect of tragedy, which have been a topic of exploration since Aristotle. Knights here anticipates the Leavisian rejection of 'philosophy'.

Knights in fact offers little reason why we should see *Macbeth* as a tragedy. He makes it sound more like a poetically intensified morality play that shows how 'evil' is defeated by 'good' – and given that 'good' wins out, where do we locate the tragedy, except in the collateral damage along the way (Duncan, the two grooms, Banquo, Lady Macduff, her children, Young Siward, Lady Macbeth, Macbeth, the anonymous victims of Macbeth's tyranny and of the battle to remove him)? But these corpses, or some other ones, are surely necessary, in Knights' perspective, to reinforce the play's 'statement of evil' and it is not clear how they differ in their effect from the deaths that might occur in a history play.

Knights' emphasis on 'placing' is significant here: if the destructive, negative forces in a play or any other literary text are 'placed', checked by other elements in the text which are finally triumphant, then tragedy vanishes in a broader, more optimistic perspective. In a sense, Knights turns *Macbeth* into a model of how the literary text, in a Leavisian perspective, should work: it should be poetically dense, it should be a poetic whole and it should show how the negative impulses it invokes are finally 'placed' by positive ones. But where is the tragedy here?

Seven years later, in his essay 'Prince Hamlet' (1940), Knights modifies his anti-character stance and stresses that '"Shakespearian Tragedy" is not all of one kind'. Thus (glancing back, implicitly, to his "How Many Children ... " essay), 'the speeches of the protagonists [in *Macbeth*] refer not merely inwards to a hypothetical "character" behind them, but outward to the pattern of the play as a whole in which "character" is subordinate and often irrelevant.' In *Othello*, by contrast, the character of the protagonist – 'in so far as we are intended to be aware of it, and we are aware of it only through the poetry – emerges from the pattern and interest is centred there'. But *Hamlet* seems to ask us, 'more explicitly and continuously than in *Macbeth*, or *Lear*, or *Antony and Cleopatra*, to be aware of, and therefore to assess, a particular state of mind and feeling embodied in the dramatic figure of the hero'.[52] This seems a rather circumlocutory way of saying that he is going to focus on *Hamlet* as a character and this is indeed what he does, for example deploying the word 'character' as he judges him by a favourite Leavisian criterion: maturity. 'The desire to escape from the complexities of adult living is central to Hamlet's character.'[53] Knights locates Hamlet's appeal here, in a language that seems partly influenced by psychoanalysis (he quotes Ernest Jones in the essay and has a favourable footnote on Jones' work which praises its explanatory value). The tendency to over-identify with the hero is due to 'the strength of our own regressive impulses and unconscious confusions'.[54] Knights then switches into a Leavisian moral register: *Hamlet* can provide an indulgence for 'some of our most cherished weaknesses' but cannot lead us far 'towards maturity and self-knowledge'.[55] We need to see how the play builds in its criticism of its central character and we can then see it justly 'in relation to the supreme achievement – the achieved maturity – of the later plays'.[56] It is clear that Knights is still concerned that a Shakespeare tragedy should engage in a moral 'placing' of its negative elements, but here this seems tantamount to 'placing' Hamlet as a character. Like 'How Many Children …', however, 'Prince Hamlet' offers no account of why *Hamlet* is a tragedy.

It is also interesting that, in 'Prince Hamlet', Knights seems open to the idea that the play is partly autobiographical: 'there does seem to be some ground for believing that Hamlet, in his recoil from the grossness of physical existence and his desire for death, expresses feelings that were personal to Shakespeare'.[57] In this respect, he starts to enter into the kind of ungrounded speculation about Shakespeare's life and personality that Caroline Spurgeon would pursue much more widely in *Shakespeare's Imagery and What It Tells Us* (1935). For Spurgeon, it tells us quite a lot about Shakespeare himself, and that is, unashamedly, one of her key interests; but it also tells us quite a lot about his plays, including his tragedies, and it is this aspect of her work that we will now consider.

Caroline Spurgeon

Caroline Spurgeon's study of Shakespeare's imagery collects, collates and categorizes a huge range of images and uses them in two main ways. The first is to make questionable and unsupportable inferences about Shakespeare himself; the second is to trace image patterns in Shakespeare's plays. It is the latter aspect of her book that has endured and that concerns us here. Spurgeon acknowledges that her definition of an 'image' is a loose one, covering 'simile, metaphor, personification, metonymy, synecdoche and the like'[58] – anything that serves 'the purposes of analogy'.[59] She wants to rid the term 'image' of its purely visual associations and to see it as applicable to everything from a single word to a recurrent motif running through a scene or play.

Chapter 15 of her book focuses on 'Leading Motives in the Tragedies'. She contends that 'the part played by recurrent images in raising, developing, sustaining and repeating emotion in the tragedies has not, as far as I know, ever yet been noticed' – though they had, of course, begun to be noticed by Wilson Knight and L. C. Knights, and indeed Spurgeon was aware of *The Wheel of Fire* because she both commends and challenges its reading of *Timon of Athens* in this chapter.[60] But then, parts of Spurgeon's book had been given as lectures in 1930 and 1931 and Wilson Knight refers to her work in *The Imperial Theme*,[61] so the questions of influence and priority between Knight and Spurgeon are complex. For Spurgeon the recurrent images 'reveal the dominant picture or sensation – and for Shakespeare the two are identical – in terms of which he sees and feels the main problem or theme of the play'.[62] On one level, then, the image pattern gives direct access to Shakespeare's mind, and this aspect of Spurgeon's approach seems doubtful; on the other hand, the image patterns are, to a considerable extent, there in the plays, backed up by Spurgeon's copious quotation, and can be used and modified by subsequent scholars and critics without assenting to any of Spurgeon's inferences about Shakespeare's perceptions and intentions in his writing.

In *Romeo and Juliet*, the 'dominating image is *light*, every form and manifestation of it'.[63] But *Hamlet* has 'an entirely different atmosphere', which is 'partly due to the number of images of sickness, disease or blemish of the body' and the 'dominating' idea of 'an ulcer or tumour' which conveys the bad moral condition of Denmark. In the Queen's bedroom scene, for example, Hamlet calls his mother's remarriage to Claudius 'a blister' on 'the fair forehead of an innocent love' (3.4.50, 49) and, as in *Lear*, 'the emotion is so strong and the picture so vivid, that the metaphor overflows into the verbs and adjectives': 'thought-sick' (3.4.57); 'mildewed ear / Blasting his wholesome brother' (3.4.71–2); 'apoplexed', 'sickly' (Q2, 3.4.54, 60, RSC Shakespeare p. 2001).[64] Spurgeon also sees a 'marked contrast' between *Lear* and *Hamlet*, however. *Hamlet* stresses 'bodily disease' but has few references to 'bodily action and strain'.[65] In *Lear*, such references 'intensify the feeling of mental anguish', but in *Hamlet* 'anguish' is not 'the dominating thought' but '*rottenness*, disease, corruption'.[66] This leads Spurgeon to a reformulation of what makes *Hamlet* a tragedy:

> ■ [T]he problem in *Hamlet* is not predominantly that of will and reason, of a mind too philosophic or a nature temperamentally unfitted to act quickly; [Shakespeare] sees it pictorially *not as the problem of an individual at all*, but as something greater and even more mysterious, as a *condition* for which the individual himself is apparently not responsible, any more than the sick man is to blame for the infection which strikes and devours him but which nevertheless, in its course and development, impartially and relentlessly, annihilates him and others, innocent and guilty alike. That is the tragedy of *Hamlet*, as it is perhaps the chief tragic mystery of life.[67] □

Whereas L. C. Knights' interpretation of *Hamlet*, as we saw above, moves back from the image-based approach of 'How Many Children ... ' to a moral-psychological focus on Hamlet's character, in which he is condemned as immature, Spurgeon, in her overall view of the play, follows out what she sees as the implications of the 'disease' imagery and produces what is, in a sense, a more radical reading, in which the play focuses on an aspect of the human condition rather than an individual. It is not a politically radical reading in that it does not see the rottenness in the state of Denmark as the result of remediable political circumstances; but it moves away from the focus on a specific protagonist to a more general malaise.

With *Othello*, Spurgeon stresses not the noble and aloof aspect of its verse identified by Wilson Knight, but the imagery of 'animals in action, preying upon one another, mischievous, lascivious, cruel or suffering'. This main strand of imagery increases and sustains 'the general sense of pain and unpleasantness'.[68] Spurgeon contrasts the animal imagery in *Othello* and *Lear*. In *Othello*, the imagery relates to animals who are, in Spurgeon's perspective, 'a low type of life', not especially cruel but acting according to their nature when they torment and kill other animals. For Spurgeon, this 'reflects and repeats the spectacle of the wanton torture of one human being by another, which we witness in the tragedy'.[69]

Lear, by contrast, fills our imagination 'with the accumulated pictures of active ferocity, of wolf, tiger, wild boar, vulture, serpent and sea-monster, all animals of a certain dignity and grandeur' even though shown in *Lear* at their most savage.[70] *Lear* is dominated, however, by 'one overpowering [...] image' that runs throughout the play. This is what Spurgeon calls a 'general "floating" image' sustained mainly by verbs, but also by metaphor, 'of a human body in anguished movement, tugged, wrenched, beaten, pierced, stung, scourged, dislocated, flayed, gashed, scalded, tortured and finally broken on the rack'.[71]

Spurgeon's most durable reading, however, is that of the 'clothes' imagery in *Macbeth*. As she puts it, '[t]he idea constantly recurs that Macbeth's new honours sit ill upon him, like a loose and badly fitting garment, belonging to someone else'.[72] When Ross hails Macbeth as Thane of Cawdor, Macbeth says: '[t]he Thane of Cawdor lives: / Why do you dress me / In borrowed robes?' (1.3.13–14). Soon after, Banquo observes of Macbeth: '[n]ew honours come upon him, / Like our strange garments, cleave not to their mould / But with the aid of use' (1.3.156–8). Back at his castle, Macbeth tells his wife that he would like to enjoy his current high reputation rather than murder Duncan: 'I have bought / Golden opinions from all sorts of people, / Which would be worn now in their newest gloss, / Not cast aside so soon' (1.7.33–6) and Lady Macbeth replies scathingly: '[w]as the hope drunk / Wherein you dressed yourself?' (1.7.37–8). As Ross departs for Scone to see Macbeth crowned, Macduff observes: '[w]ell, may you see things well done there. Adieu, / Lest our old robes sit easier than our new!' (3.1.47–8). In Act 5, as Macbeth's power crumbles, Caithness remarks: '[h]e cannot buckle his distempered cause / Within the belt of rule' (5.2.17–18) and Angus comments: 'now he does feel his title / Hang loose about him, like a giant's robe / Upon a dwarfish thief' (5.2.23–5). This leads Spurgeon to challenge Macbeth's stature: '[u]ndoubtedly Macbeth is built on great lines and in heroic proportions, with great possibilities – there could be no tragedy else'. But he cannot compare with, for example, Hamlet or Othello in 'nobility of nature' and 'there *is* an aspect in which he is but a poor, vain, cruel, treacherous creature'.[73]

This, then, is a rather different view of tragedy from that which Spurgeon takes in regard to *Hamlet*. With *Hamlet*, the tragedy lay, as we saw above, not solely in Hamlet himself, but in a sickness of the human condition, akin to that which can show itself in actual life, which pervaded the whole play. With *Macbeth*, it is necessary that Macbeth should be a great, heroic man in order that the play be a tragedy, but the 'clothes' imagery that is applied to him reduces his stature and thus makes the play, implicitly, lesser than *Othello* or *Hamlet*.

Spurgeon's general interpretations, and her specific readings of particular image patterns, are open to question in a range of ways. Moreover, in her work, as in Wilson Knight's, there is an underlying and sometimes explicit mysticism, linked to a sense of mystery, that would not play well in the secular and materialist Shakespeare criticism of the later twentieth century, or even in the Christian kind of the mid-twentieth. But the technique that Spurgeon developed, of selecting and collating images through close study of Shakespeare's texts, and of then drawing conclusions about the plays (rather than 'Shakespeare the man') from them, was and remains a valuable interpretative methodology, even if subsequent critics' conclusions are likely to differ from Spurgeon's, or at least to be expressed in a different critical idiom. We move on to Cleanth

Brooks' classic New Critical essay on *Macbeth*, which cites and takes issue with Spurgeon.

Cleanth Brooks

Cleanth Brooks was the leading figure in American New Criticism, which developed in the 1930s and became dominant in the US academy after the Second World War from the 1950s to the 1970s. While English literary criticism of this period, such as that of Knights and Leavis, is now sometimes placed under the New Critical rubric, and while they both focused on 'close reading' as a methodology, they were really separate developments, though with key overlaps and common concerns. New Criticism's model text was the short lyric poem – for example by John Donne (c.1572–1631) – which created, through its style and imagery, a distinctive artefact in which ambiguities, ironies and affirmations were held in tension in an organic unity. Using New Criticism to analyse Shakespeare's plays – especially his tragedies – thus posed a challenge. An example of how it might be done had been offered, in the UK, by L. C. Knights in 'How Many Children … ' and the work of Wilson Knight and Spurgeon, with its pursuit of patterns of imagery, could also hold useful pointers. But it was Brooks' essay 'The Naked Babe and the Cloak of Manliness', first published in 1946 and collected in Brooks' *The Well Wrought Urn* (1947), which showed that a New Critic could do it – and although Brooks does not mention Knights, his chosen play, like Knights', is *Macbeth*.

Brooks does mention Spurgeon and the clothes imagery she locates in *Macbeth*, but charges that she has failed to realize 'the full implications of her discovery'.[74] He points out that although Caithness and Angus use the clothes imagery to demean Macbeth, there is no reason to suppose Shakespeare concurs with their view. He also contends that the 'crucial point' of the comparison is not the mismatch in size between man and robes but the fact that the robes are not his – they are stolen. Brooks further argues that, 'if we free ourselves of Miss Spurgeon's rather mechanical scheme of classification', we find 'a series of masking and cloaking images' that are variants of the usurped clothes motif.[75] He thus aims to operate with a wider, more flexible idea of what might constitute 'clothes' imagery, with 'clothes' expanding into 'cloaks'. Among the most potent 'cloaking images', Brooks maintains, are those in Lady Macbeth's lines at the end of her 'unsex me here' speech:

■ Come, thick night,
And pall thee in the dunnest smoke of hell,
That my keen knife see not the wound it makes,

Nor heaven peep through the blanket of the dark,
To cry, 'Hold, hold!' (1.5.48–52) □

Brooks suggests that her 'keen knife' here may be Macbeth himself and that she is asking night to 'blanket the deed from the hesitant doer'.[76] Brooks also argues that the lines in which Macbeth describes the daggers of Duncan's alleged killers as '[u]nmannerly breeched [RSC: 'covered, as if wearing breeches'] with gore' (2.3.120) belong to this 'cloaking' imagery. The daggers 'have been carefully "clothed" [with blood] to play a part' and are not 'honorably naked in readiness to guard the king, or, "mannerly", clothed in their own sheaths'. But 'the disguise [the daggers] will wear will enable Macbeth to assume the robes of Duncan', to which he is not entitled.[77] So here 'cloaking' and 'clothes' imagery are linked.

The other dominant motif is that of babes, which appears on several levels: for instance, as an image, in the simile of 'pity / like a naked new-born babe striding the blast'; as a character, in Macduff's child (perhaps rather old for a babe); as a symbol in the shape of the crowned and bloody babe the witches show Macbeth (4.1, in between lines 82 and 83, 92 and 93; RSC has 'a bloody child' and 'a crowned child' rather than 'babe'). Indeed, the babe, Brooks suggests, is 'perhaps the most powerful symbol in the tragedy'[78] and, in his vision, it grows to remarkable proportions: it 'signifies the future which Macbeth would [...] but cannot control'[79] and 'symbolizes [...] all those emotional and – to Lady Macbeth – irrational ties which make man more than a machine – which make him human. It signifies the pity which Macbeth, under Lady Macbeth's tutelage, would wean himself of[f?] as something "unmanly"'.[80] Macbeth tries to put on the cloak of manliness but the naked babe proves too strong for him.

On the basis of this analysis, Brooks offers an upward estimate, in comparison to Spurgeon's, of Macbeth's tragic stature:

■ [I]t is not merely his great imagination and his warrior courage in defeat which redeem him for tragedy and place him beside the other great tragic protagonists: rather, it is his attempt to conquer the future, an attempt involving him, like Oedipus, in a desperate struggle with fate itself. It is this which holds our imaginative sympathy, even after he has degenerated into a bloody tyrant and has become the slayer of Macduff's wife and children.[81] □

Brooks goes further in seeing Macbeth as a universal figure. 'Macbeth in his general concern for the future is typical – is Every Man. He becomes the typical tragic protagonist when he yields to pride and *hybris* [or 'hubris', 'the ancient Greek word for insolence or affront applied to the arrogance or pride of the protagonist in a tragedy' (Baldick, 1992, p.103)]'.[82]

Brooks' essay received some ripostes – for example, Oscar James Campbell (1897–1970) observed wryly that 'Macbeth, like all murderers in Elizabethan plays, is afraid, not of his inability to control the future, but of the knife in the hands of a human avenger'.[83] But Brooks showed decisively that New Criticism could tackle a Shakespeare tragedy and produce a fruitful reading that combined close attention to the text with a grasp of its overall significance and that rose above a supposedly 'mechanical' approach such as Spurgeon's. It was a significant contribution to the rise of New Criticism to become the critical North American orthodoxy of the 1950s, in Shakespeare criticism as elsewhere, and it complemented the Leavisian orthodoxy of 1950s Britain. But by the 1960s there was a sense that these orthodoxies, while still powerful and still able to generate interesting interpretations and debates, had lost their innovative and challenging edge; that, in an era of quickening social change, new perspectives were needed. In the next chapter, we shall examine the fresh approaches offered by Northrop Frye and Jan Kott in the 1960s, and by René Girard and Naomi Conn Liebler in the later twentieth century.

CHAPTER SEVEN

Archetype and Absurdity

In the 1950s, Leavisian criticism in the UK and New Criticism in
the USA gave a sense of 'business as usual' as far as the criticism of
Shakespeare, and of literature in general, was concerned. There was a
loose consensus that Shakespeare study, while it might draw on relevant scholarship, was primarily a matter of generating readings that
eschewed what was seen as excessive political and religious commitment (though the latter was more acceptable than the former) and that
confirmed Shakespeare's endorsement of a morality that turned out to
be remarkably like the kind of morality that a middle-class academic
professional in the mid-twentieth century might have. But there was
an underlying uncertainty. Both Leavisism and New Criticism had originally had a radical edge, in the sense that they challenged the industrial
roots of modern society, but with their assimilation into the academy
this edge became blunted; both had offered a new methodology but
this had turned into a routine, one that still required considerable
knowledge and skill but that, in terms of its results, offered more of the
same, variations on a theme rather than fresh compositions. Along with
this sense within academic literary criticism that new departures were
needed went the social and cultural changes starting to gather force in
the later 1950s – represented in literary terms, however roughly and
inadequately, by the 'Angry Young Men' in England and the Beat writers in America – and that would erupt as the 1960s went on. Changes
in academic criticism cannot of course be crudely correlated to social
and cultural changes, and the phenomenon of 'university lag', whereby
higher education can fall behind cutting-edge intellectual developments,
may delay change. But nonetheless there were signs even in the later
1950s that change was imminent. A key text here was Northrop Frye's
magisterial *Anatomy of Criticism* (1957) which, breaking away from the
words-on-the-page approach, and informed by Frye's staggering range
of reading, offered a comprehensive theory of genres and myths within
which to locate specific literary texts, including Shakespeare. But Frye
focused more closely on Shakespeare in his Alexander Lectures, delivered at the University of Toronto in 1966 and published the following

year as *Fools of Time: Studies in Shakespearean Tragedy*. We discuss Frye's
text first in this chapter.

Northrop Frye

In *Fools of Time*, Frye identifies 'three main kinds of tragic structure
in Shakespeare and his contemporaries': a 'tragedy of order', that is,
'a social tragedy, with its roots in history, concerned with the fall of
princes'; a 'tragedy of passion' that 'deals with the separations of lovers,
the conflict of duty and passion, or the conflict of social and personal
(sexual or family) instincts'; and a 'tragedy of isolation' in which 'the
hero is removed from his social context' and 'compelled to search for a
purely individual identity'. According to Frye, *Julius Caesar*, *Macbeth* and
Hamlet are 'tragedies of order'; *Romeo and Juliet*, *Antony and Cleopatra*,
Troilus and Cressida and *Coriolanus* are 'tragedies of passion'; and *King
Lear*, *Othello* and *Timon of Athens* are 'tragedies of isolation'. These are
not, however, rigid categories: 'most of the plays have aspects that link
them to all three groups'.[1]

The 'tragic action', according to Frye, is 'based on three main char-
acter-groups': an 'order-figure'; a 'rebel-figure or usurper' who kills the
'order figure'; and a 'nemesis-figure' or group who kill the 'rebel-figure'
and, in a secondary role, try to restore order. The 'order-figure' is, in
Julius Caesar, the titular hero; in *Macbeth*, Duncan; and in *Hamlet*, the
protagonist's father. The 'rebel-figure or usurper' is, in *Caesar*, Brutus and
his co-conspirators; in *Macbeth*, the eponymous protagonist; in *Hamlet*,
Claudius. The 'nemesis-figure' or group consists, in *Caesar*, of Antony
and Octavius; in *Macbeth*, of Malcolm and Macduff; and in *Hamlet*, the
Prince himself.[2]

Frye rejects the idea that Shakespeare's tragedies offer any significant
reflection of the actualities of his times. *Lear*, *Macbeth*, *Hamlet* and *Coriolanus* are, he asserts, set in a world that would have been 'primitive' to
Elizabethan as well as twentieth-century audiences, and 'because they
are primitive they are archetypal, reflecting the immutable facts of passion and power and loyalty that are always present in human life'. Here,
Frye affirms an idea of a universal and unchangeable set of human, social
and political facts that, in various guises, would be strongly challenged by
the more radical historicist criticism of Shakespeare that would emerge
in the 1980s. For Frye, the 'archaic settings of Shakespeare's tragedies'
are the clearest revelation of 'the self-destroying passions' by which
'[e]very man' (the gendered noun is appropriate to Frye's approach)
'lives, or would like to live'. In Shakespeare's 'tragic vision', 'death is the

end of all action' and 'the actions that lead most directly to death are the strongest ones'.[3]

An important distinction, for Frye, is between the tragic and ironic vision. He sees irony as based on 'the independence of the way things are from the way we want them to be'. In tragedy, 'a heroic effort against this independence is made and fails; we then come to terms with irony by reducing our wants'. While '[t]he ironic vision' in tragedy 'survives the heroic one', it is, Frye affirms, the latter that we remember, and 'the tragedy is for its sake'. Thus, Frye tentatively suggests, tragedy arouses the following feeling: 'the heroic and infinite have been; the human and finite are'.[4]

If Frye removes Shakespearean tragedy from its contemporary historical context, he does not remove it from a social one. Indeed, according to Frye, 'man', in Shakespearean tragedy, only truly becomes man within 'a social contract', 'when he ceases to be a "subject" in the philosophical sense and becomes a subject in the political one, essentially related to his society'.[5] While 'sacrificial imagery may occur anywhere in a Shakespeare tragedy', in a 'tragedy of order', it generally relates more closely than elsewhere to 'the analogy between the individual and the social body'.[6] Frye gives an example from Marcus's speech in *Titus Andronicus*:

■ O let me teach you how to knit again
This scattered corn into one mutual sheaf,
These broken limbs again into one body. (5.3.70–2) □

In some Shakespeare tragedies, however – especially *Romeo and Juliet, Troilus and Cressida* and *Antony and Cleopatra* – 'the social order is split and there is no symbol or centre of social unity'.[7] As a result, 'personal loyalty is likely to be deflected from society and to concentrate on sexual love or family loyalties'. These three plays are, in particular, 'tragedies of love or passion' and 'Shakespeare's version' of what Frye calls 'the tragedy of the son', in which the 'vitality' a young son represents is crushed 'in a world where two social powers grind on each other'. Frye calls this vitality 'Dionysian' – relating to the ancient Greek god Dionysus – and defines it as 'the energy of physical nature' which, because 'it is crushed' in Shakespeare, makes 'the hero resemble [...] Dionysus rather in his role as a suffering or dying god'. In the earlier versions of the life-and-death-in-nature myth, Dionysus dies due to his relationship with 'a female figure' representing 'the basis of that myth, or Mother Earth'.[8] Similarly, in Shakespeare, 'the women loved in the passion-tragedies' are all femmes fatales 'whom it is death to love': 'Cleopatra is the tantalizing mistress'; Cressida 'the treacherous siren'; and Juliet 'the bride in the midst of enemies'. All 'assume the ancient prerogative of choosing their own lover, and are abused or despised in consequence by the male-dominated societies they belong to'.[9]

Although Frye's reference to 'male-dominated societies' might seem to anticipate the critiques of patriarchy that feminist critics would later launch, his use of supposedly mythological constructions of women could seem itself a form of patriarchy in which stereotypes were disguised as archetypes. His account of *Antony and Cleopatra* is especially interesting in this respect, catching the fascination of the play and multiplying the mythic resonances of Cleopatra herself in a way that might seem to fix Cleopatra in pre-set roles. Frye affirms that *Antony and Cleopatra* is 'the definitive tragedy of passion' in which 'the ironic and heroic themes, the day world of history and the night world of passion, expand into natural forces of cosmological proportions'. Octavius Caesar, 'the very incarnation of history and the world's greatest order-figure', commands the 'Western and Roman world' that is 'pervaded by order, rule and measure'.[10] Cleopatra presides over the 'Eastern and Egyptian world'. 'Each world,' Frye contends, 'is a self-evident reality to itself and an illusion to its rival.' But if Octavius is 'the incarnation of history', Cleopatra is 'a counter-historical figure' who mainly 'substitutes [...] idleness and distraction' for 'heroic action'. Frye argues that there is ample 'textual justification for making her a straight temptress':

■ Cleopatra, the serpent of the Nile [1.5.30], is a Venus rising from it in Enobarbus' speech [2.2.230–4]; she wears the regalia of Isis (3.6.17–19); she is a *stella maris* [star of the sea], a goddess of the moon and sea. She has affinities with the kind of goddess figure that both Hebraic and classical religions kept trying to subdue by abuse: she is a whore and her children are all bastards; she is a snare to men and destroys their masculinity, making them degenerate slaves like Circe [in Homer's *Odyssey*]; she is an Omphale dressing her Hercules in women's clothes; she has many characteristics of her sister whore of Babylon.[11] □

But, Frye remarks, '*Antony and Cleopatra* is not a morality play'[12] and Cleopatra's Egypt can 'bring a superhuman vitality out of Antony that Rome cannot equal, not in spite of the fact that it destroys him, but because it destroys him'.[13]

Frye concludes *Fools of Time* with further general observations on 'the tragic structure in Shakespeare'. The deaths of Lear and Othello convey 'absurdity and anguish' but this is not the whole story because we have shared in the experience that leads up to those deaths, an experience too extensive and various to be reduced to its inevitable lethal end:

■ Tragedy finds its ultimate meaning neither in heroic death nor in ironic survival, nor in any doctrine deducible from either, but in its own re-enactment as experience [...] The hero of a tragedy ultimately includes the audience who form the *substance* of the hero [and] who participate in a ritual act of suffering in which the suffering is not real but the awareness of it is.[14] □

Fools of Time shows the advantages of drawing back from the words on the page – not, of course, ignoring them, but suggesting how they may fit into a bigger picture. Frye's book is also valuable for the way in which, as part of its larger perspective, it offers suggestions about the structure and substance of Shakespearean tragedy in a way that has not been done since Bradley. The major objections to Frye would be that he gets too far away from the text and history, manipulating abstract categories in an ahistorical zone, with scant regard for textual and historical specificity and with no self-reflexiveness about how his own position might be historically determined – for example, by gender stereotypes, and also by an emphasis on absurdity and anguish that, as perhaps seems clearer from a twenty-first-century vantage point, is due more to his mid-twentieth-century historical and cultural situation than to archetypal apprehensions. But in the mid-1960s, another critic emerged who was to declare unashamedly that Shakespeare was to be read as a writer for the mid-twentieth-century and to announce it in the title of his book: *Shakespeare Our Contemporary* (1967). This critic, whom we consider next, was Jan Kott.

Jan Kott

In the nineteenth century, the European critics who made a big impact on Shakespeare studies in England were two Germans, August Wilhelm von Schlegel and G. G. Gervinus, and George Brandes, a Dane (discussed in Chapters 2 and 3 of this Guide). In the mid-twentieth century, it was a Pole who made the big impact – that is, the native of a country which had suffered the Nazi invasion that had compelled Britain to enter the Second World War and which, in the postwar era, had come under Soviet dominance with a repressive communist government. The Preface to the English edition of *Shakespeare Our Contemporary*, by the renowned theatre director Peter Brook (b.1925), links Kott's book to this life experience: 'Kott is undoubtedly the only writer on Elizabethan matters who assumes without question that every one of his readers will at some point or other have been woken by the police in the middle of the night.'[15] Brook finds it 'disquieting' that 'the major part of the commentaries on Shakespeare's passions and his politics are hatched far from life by sheltered figures behind ivy-covered walls'.[16] If this stereotypes academic critics and caricatures the Oxbridge that Brook himself attended, it does express a wider mood of dissatisfaction with established Shakespeare criticism at the time, which could seem too safe and predictable, too remote from the real world. Brook, as an innovative theatre director, was able to make startling creative use of Kott in his productions of *Lear* and

A Midsummer Night's Dream. But Kott proved more difficult to assimilate into academic literary criticism at the time and his unquestioned sexist and racist assumptions can cause discomfort today. He remains, however, an invigorating critic who can still provoke thought about, and offer insights into, Shakespeare's tragedies.

In his account of *Hamlet*, for example, Kott offers a striking simile: '*Hamlet* is like a sponge. Unless produced in a stylized or antiquarian fashion, it immediately absorbs all the problems of our time.'[17] He offers a summation of the play that shifts the spotlight away from Hamlet as a character and from his relationship to his mother, father and stepfather, to shine in another area:

> ■ [Hamlet] is the story of three young boys and one girl. The boys are of the same age. They are called Hamlet, Laertes, Fortinbras. The girl is younger, and her name is Ophelia. They are all involved in a bloody political and family drama. As a result, three of them will die; the fourth will, more or less by chance, become the King of Denmark.[18] □

As Kott later points out, the fathers of all these young people – Hamlet, Fortinbras, Laertes and Ophelia – have been, or will be, killed.[19] All four are 'involved in a drama' in which '[n]one of them has chosen his part; it is imposed on them from outside'. For Kott, *Hamlet* is 'a drama of imposed situations'.[20]

Kott's discussion of *Othello* approves Coleridge and Hazlitt's descriptions of Iago as cited in Chapter 2 of this Guide – respectively, 'the motive-hunting of a motiveless malignity'[21] and 'an amateur of tragedy in real life'.[22] But Kott turns Hazlitt's amateur into a professional, calling Iago a 'diabolical', or 'rather, Machiavellian stage manager' and locating him philosophically both as a practitioner of the ideas of Machiavelli and as an anti-idealist: 'Iago is an empiricist, he does not believe in ideology and has no illusions.'[23] Through his machinations, he proves the folly and villainy of the world and 'goes to be tortured in a tragedy devised by himself'.[24] In contrast, Othello is an idealist caught in Iago's machine. Kott contends that if we strip *Othello* of its romantic, operatic and melodramatic encrustations, 'the tragedy of jealousy and the tragedy of betrayed confidence become a dispute between Othello and Iago [...] on the nature of the world' which poses questions such as: '[i]s this world good or bad?'; '[w]hat are the limits of suffering?'; 'what is the ultimate purpose of the few brief moments that pass between birth and death?' Iago wins the dispute in an intellectual but not moral sense: it seems that 'the world is as Iago sees it', but 'Iago is a villain'. In *Othello*, 'everybody loses in the end'.[25]

In Kott's perspective, *Othello* offers a further example of how in Shakespeare's plays, from *Hamlet* onwards, 'the moral order and the intellectual order are in conflict'.[26] The major Shakespearean tragedies show an 'earthquake' in which '[b]oth human orders have fallen; the feudal hierarchy of loyalty [and] the naturalism of the Renaissance', so that the 'world's history is just that of spiders and flies'.[27] These elements of the tragedies help to make Shakespeare our contemporary: '[l]ike our world, Shakespeare's world did not regain its balance after the earthquake' and 'remained incoherent'.[28]

In considering *Lear*, Kott examines the relationship between the tragic and the grotesque. 'Grotesque,' he declares, 'means tragedy rewritten in different terms.' The tragic and grotesque worlds share key features. In both, 'situations are imposed, compulsory and inescapable', and 'freedom of choice' and failure are ineluctable: 'the tragic hero and the grotesque actor must always lose their struggle against the absolute'. But while 'tragedy is an appraisal of human fate, a measure of the absolute', 'grotesque is a criticism of the absolute in the name of frail human experience' in which the 'absolute is transformed into a blind mechanism, a kind of automaton'. Whereas the tragic hero's downfall confirms and recognizes the absolute, the grotesque actor's downfall mocks and desecrates it. '[T]ragedy brings catharsis, while grotesque offers no consolation whatsoever.'[29]

Kott examines *Lear* in the perspective of the tragic/grotesque distinction, focusing especially on the scene in which Edgar, disguised as a mad beggar, supposedly leads his father, Gloucester, to the top of Dover Cliff. 'This entire scene,' Kott contends, 'is written for a very definite kind of theatre, namely pantomime.'[30] It uses 'all the means of anti-illusionist theatre in order to create a most realistic and concrete landscape'. The 'Shakespearean precipice at Dover exists and does not exist. It is the abyss, waiting all the time. The abyss, into which one can jump, is everywhere.'[31] Gloucester, 'falling over on flat, even boards, plays a scene from a great morality play'; he is 'Everyman' wandering through the world on a stage that becomes 'the medieval *Theatrum Mundi* [Theatre of the World]'. But neither medieval nor early modern guarantees are any longer fully available; in *Lear*, 'both the medieval and the renaissance orders of established values disintegrate'. *Lear* has 'neither Christian heaven, nor the heaven predicted and believed in by humanists'. In fact, the play 'makes a tragic mockery of all eschatologies [those parts of theology concerned with death, judgement and destiny]',[32] whether Christian or secular.

Lear shows the 'decay and fall of the world [...] on two levels, on two different kinds of stage, as it were': 'Macbeth's stage' and 'Job's stage'. 'Macbeth's stage is the scene of crime' in which social and familial bonds disintegrate and Goneril and Regan and Edmund and Cornwall become 'huge renaissance monsters, devouring one another like beasts of prey'. On Job's stage, the main one in the play, 'the ironic, clownish morality play on human fate will be performed'.[33] But with a difference. In the

Old Testament, Job can still, in the midst of his suffering, talk to God. In *Lear* the gods are often invoked but stay silent. Kott invokes the antagonism between the 'priest' and the 'clown' formulated in a 1959 essay by the Polish philosopher Leszek Kolakowski (1927–2009), and, more influentially, compares *Lear* to the play *Endgame* (first performed 1958; orig. *Fin de Partie* [1957]) by Samuel Beckett (1906–89) – a play which the American critic Marjorie Garber (b.1944), in her *Shakespeare and Modern Culture* (2008), calls 'a kind of astringent philosophical redaction of the essence' of *Lear*.[34] Drawing on both Kolakowski and Beckett, Kott sees the Book of Job as 'a theatre of the priests' but asserts that 'in both the Shakespearian [*sic*] and Beckettian *Endgames*', the Book of Job 'is performed by clowns'; in both 'it is the modern world that fell; the renaissance world and ours'.[35]

Here, then, Kott broadly locates *Lear* both in its time and in his own, implicitly arguing that he is bringing it up to date, not by imposing modernity upon it but by burning off its eighteenth- and nineteenth-century veneers to reveal what he takes to be its substance – a substance in which tragedy moves into the grotesque and the absurd in a way that does not dissolve its tragic aspects but makes them more angular and abrasive. He is aware, as his *Hamlet* chapter shows, that interpretations of Shakespeare's tragedies, on page or stage, are dependent to some extent on the times in which such interpretations are generated, but his chapters on *Othello*, and especially *Lear*, treat them not as sponges but as templates for a mechanism of cruelty and absurdity analogous to that of modern life. Thus in Kott, a harder-edged concept of Shakespearean tragedy, overlapping with the grotesque, emerges. Like Frye, but in a different way, Kott wants to get down to structural fundamentals. A third way of doing this was offered by the French anthropologist René Girard, in a series of essays published between 1972 and 1990 and collected and expanded in *A Theatre of Envy* (1991; 2000).

René Girard

In *A Theatre of Envy*, Girard starts by outlining his theory of 'mimetic desire', and it is important at the outset of this section to clear up a possible confusion in the use of the term 'mimesis' and the adjective deriving from it. 'Mimesis' is the ancient Greek word for 'imitation', used by Aristotle in the *Poetics*. In literary and artistic theory it refers to the imitation of reality in literature, drama and painting and is thus often linked to realistic fiction, poetry and drama and figurative painting that reproduces the appearances of external reality. But Girard uses the term to mean the way in which – in actual life and in fiction and drama – a human being wants something because someone else wants it; one's desire is the imitation, the mimesis, of another's, and mimetic desire is the 'fundamental source of human conflicts'.[36]

In Girard's perspective, humans can live in peace as long as 'Degree' is maintained – he takes the term (capitalized as it is in some editions) from Ulysses' long speech in *Troilus and Cressida* (1.3.76–138). Girard defines 'Degree' as meaning, generally, 'rank, distinction, discrimination, hierarchy, *difference*'.[37] It is 'a principle of separation' that is also, paradoxically, 'a principle of unity'.[38] The reason for this paradox, Girard says, is that '[a]s long as models and imitators live in separate worlds they cannot become rivals, because they cannot select the same objects' – mimetic rivalry is checked by what Girard calls 'external mediation'. But as the worlds of 'models and imitators overlap more and more', those models and imitators 'can and therefore do select the same objects' so that a society becomes 'undifferentiated' and mimetic rivalry is fostered by 'internal mediation'.[39] The result is conflict, and, ultimately, a 'crisis of Degree' that can only be resolved by 'the collective violence of scape-goating', in which someone is selected as a scapegoat and sacrificed – as happens with Julius Caesar, in real life and on Shakespeare's stage.[40] Girard makes bold claims for the mimetic approach to Shakespeare, affirming that it results in new readings of, among the tragedies, *Julius Caesar*, *Troilus and Cressida*, *Hamlet* and *Lear*; that it 'reveals the dramatic unity [...] and thematic continuity' of Shakespeare's work; and that it shows Shakespeare as 'an original thinker centuries ahead of his time'.[41]

Girard's approach is perhaps most illuminating when applied to *Julius Caesar*, which he sees as so 'radically mimetic' that 'almost every word uttered even by the most insignificant character can be simulta-neously true of all parties involved – subjects, object, and mediators alike'.[42] The Degree crisis is highlighted in the opening lines, when the two tribunes, Flavius and Murellus, castigate the artisans for being in the Forum on a working day with nothing to identify their professions, so that they become undifferentiated:

■ Hence! Home, you idle creatures, get you home:
  Is this a holiday? What, know you not,
  Being mechanical [working men, artisans], you ought not walk
  Upon a labouring day, without the sign
  Of your profession? (1.1.1–5) □

For Girard, *Julius Caesar* is 'the essential and indispensable work' about 'the scapegoat or victimage mechanism' that ends – for a time – the crisis of Degree.[43] The play shows three successive characters joining the conspiracy against Caesar – Brutus, Casca and Ligurius – and they embody in turn, like three descending steps, a progressive diminution of independence of mind, rationality and responsibility. This is due less to 'individual psychology' and more to 'the rapid march of mimetic desire'. As the conspiracy grows, gaining new members gets easier. 'The combined mimetic influence of those already attracted makes the chosen target more and more attractive mimetically.' But '[b]eing part of the crisis [of Degree], the genesis of the conspiracy is itself a dynamic process, a segment of an escalation in which the murder of Caesar comes next, then the murder of Cinna, and finally the ever intensified violence that leads to [the battle of] Philippi'.[44] Beyond that, however, lies the restoration of Degree and the Roman republic of order built on Caesar's death. The assassination of Caesar is therefore an example of what Girard calls 'foundational violence' – the act of sacrifice, the killing of a scapegoat, that is necessary to resolve the crisis of Degree and provide the basis of a new order that duly observes Degree.

Julius Caesar, Girard affirms, 'is unquestionably tragic [...] in the most traditional sense', but 'absolutely unique' because 'it goes straight to the heart of tragedy, the foundational murder'. Indeed, he declares, it 'is the first and only tragedy that focuses on this murder itself and nothing else'. Girard considers the objection that, because Caesar's murder takes place in the middle rather than at the end, the play lacks 'aesthetic unity' and is really two tragedies, one about Caesar and a second about the murderers; but he rebuts this by arguing that the play 'is centered neither on Caesar nor on his murderers' and 'is not a play about Roman history but about collective violence'. Its 'real subject is the violent crowd' and it reveals 'the violent essence of the theatre and of human culture itself'.[45] Girard expresses amazement at Shakespeare's ability to 'combine a full revelation of the foundational murder with a production of cathartic-sacrificial effects that this revelation should preclude but that prove, on the contrary, all the more effective for being deliberately engineered'. But the 'cathartic-sacrificial' reading 'corresponds to what [Girard] calls the *superficial play*', while 'the revelation of mimetic rivalry and structural scapegoating correspond to the *deeper play*'.[46]

Girard, then, provides a set of concepts – mimetic rivalry, the crisis of Degree, collective scapegoating and sacrifice to restore Degree – with which to grasp not only the bases of Shakespeare's tragedies and his other plays, but also, it seems, of all human and social orders. These are universalizing and transhistorical concepts – they apply everywhere and at any time. According to Girard, he is not imposing them on Shakespeare's texts but discovering them there; Shakespeare has insights that Girard merely conceptualizes and confirms. Clearly these concepts can be challenged in two ways in relation to Shakespeare: first, by asking in general terms, as with psychoanalysis, whether they are true; second, by asking how far they account for the phenomena of Shakespeare's tragedies. On a general level, it could be questioned whether such concepts are valid at all, let alone for all times and places. On a specific level, it could be argued that while they could indeed seem to account for some aspects of Shakespeare's plays – particularly perhaps *Caesar* – there is quite a lot they do not account for, and Girard's insistence on the omnipresence of the mimetic themes narrows and distorts the focus to a single set of issues. But provided this is allowed for, Girard's approach does offer insights into specific tragedies and a stimulating systematic view of them. In *Shakespeare's Festive Tragedy* (1995), Naomi Conn Liebler offers a no less stimulating and systematic perspective that draws to some extent on Girard, though less on *A Theatre of Envy* than on his *Violence and the Sacred* (1972).

Naomi Conn Liebler

Right at the start of *Shakespeare's Festive Tragedy*, Liebler declares that '"[f]estive tragedy" is not an oxymoron' (a figure of speech that uses two contradictory words, like 'bitter-sweet'). Instead, it 'expresses complexity rather than contradiction'.[47] She asserts that 'Shakespeare's tragedies perform social and communal concerns', akin to those explored in a book whose title hers deliberately echoes: *Shakespeare's Festive Comedy* (1959) by C(esare) L(ombardi) Barber. Examining the etymology of 'festive', she points out that it does not only mean 'merry' but also, in its Latin root – *festum*, 'feast' – it includes 'the sacramental, patterned, and entirely serious functions of ritual in communal activity'.[48] Used with these connotations, 'festive' is a word which 'recognizes that, like comedy, tragedy consecrates and celebrates something [which] varies *in*significantly from play to play' [Guide author's emphasis]. An undue critical focus on individual protagonists tends 'to occlude the fact that tragedy is at least equally interested in the *agon* [contest, struggle] of the community, and that protagonists along with all the other characters are representations of component positions'.[49] But, Liebler goes on to stress, the 'community' in a play, like the play's characters, is not 'real': 'They are representational models designed to express the complex relations of an exemplary society whose story is frozen for examination purposes at a particular moment in its fictionalized history.'[50] If the story is 'frozen' so that it can be examined, as in a cross-section, this does not mean the society it portrays is static; on the contrary, it is plunged into turbulence: '[i]n every Shakespearean tragedy the status quo is at risk from the first moments of the play'.[51] 'Shakespearean tragedy foregrounds an openly artificial but credible set of social constructions and anatomizes the consequences of destabilizing those constructions.'[52]

Liebler draws on a rich range of anthropological and philosophical perspectives and one of the most important of these is René Girard's idea, in *Violence and the Sacred*, of 'the hero as *pharmakos* [φάρμακος]', an ancient Greek term that originally meant a drug, then got applied to a sorcerer, poisoner or magician (from which the modern word 'pharmacist' derives), and also came to mean a human sacrifice used in some state rituals and selected because of signs that supposedly characterized the sacrificial victim as an outsider – for example, perceived ugliness. For Girard, Liebler explains, 'violence is that "excess" which threatens to break through the surface of community'. The *pharmakos* serves as a focus for what Girard calls 'the very real (though often hidden) hostilities that *all the members of the community feel for one another*', and 'sacrificial ritual imitates and re-enacts this "spontaneous collective violence"'. Liebler sums up Girard's argument thus: '[s]acrifical ritual, or "good" violence, channels otherwise random slaughter into an act of purification ratified by the structure and the membership of the community.'[53]

Thus the tragic hero becomes *pharmakos* when his body is objectified '*as* the body of the state', so that he 'literally *embodies* the socio-political taint, disease, or disruption that produces political anxiety and destabilizes the *polis* [the political and social order; orig. a city state in ancient Greece]'. The death of a tragic protagonist at the end of his play stands for a form of 'self-surgery by the community' – Liebler cites Sicinus's description in *Coriolanus* of the titular hero as 'a disease that must be cut away' (3.1.348). Such 'self-surgery' is linked to an attempt 'to restore some semblance of order and reclaim the culture's primary values', even though things cannot be as they were before.[54]

In this perspective, it makes no sense to blame the tragic hero, since he is in fact a kind of victim, given that he 'is selected and shaped to represent specific aspects of the communal situation' and to serve as a *pharmakos* and sacrifice. As Liebler puts it: '[t]ragedy does not represent the failure to do noble, difficult, necessary things; it represents the attempt to do them in a context that will not permit them to be done'.[55] To see its heroes as at fault, possessed, for example, of a 'fatal flaw' that leads to their downfall, 'is to erase the intense identification of hero and community that is central to the workings of tragedy'.[56] 'Festive' tragedy is 'the drama of communities in crisis and of the redress available to them, in which the protagonist is both priest and *pharmakos*, victim and villain, actor and acted upon, in the reciprocal relations of a community and its individual members'.[57]

Applying this approach to *Lear* and *Macbeth*, Liebler stresses that it is not only their protagonists but also their communities which are in crisis. Both plays 'present a society in a liminal moment, in transition from one type of structure to another'. The adjective 'liminal', from the Latin *limen*, 'threshold', means 'relating to a transitional or initial stage' or 'at a boundary or threshold'. Arnold van Gennep (1873–1957), the French ethnographer and folklorist, used it in his book *Les Rites de Passage* [*Rites of Passage*] (1909) to mean the transitional stage in a rite of passage from one social identity to another, and the British cultural anthropologist Victor Turner (1920–83) developed the idea in his work, for example *The Ritual Process: Structure and Anti-Structure* (1966).

Lear and *Macbeth* both dramatize such a liminal stage in a society as well as in its titular protagonist. *Lear* 'enacts the rupture of Britain', from the partition of the realm at the start to Albany's appeal to Edgar and Kent at the end – '[f]riends of my soul, you twain / Rule in this realm, and the gored state sustain' (5.3.340–1). Lear's 'disintegration throughout the play is a sustained personified emblem' of this rupture.[58] Similarly, at the start of *Macbeth*, Scotland is threatened from both within and without, by the treachery of Macdonwald and the original Thane of Cawdor, and by the invaders from Norway, and, at the end, it is turned, without debate, into a country governed on English lines when Malcolm says: '[m]y thanes and kinsmen, / Henceforth be earls, the first that ever Scotland / In such an honour named' (5.7.107–9).

Both *Lear* and *Macbeth* focus on how vulnerable identity is 'at the margins, the boundaries of bonds', and both plays question 'virtually every kind of human interrelatedness and definition of identity: feudal, familial, spousal, national'. This is most evident in the first act of *Lear*, which features 'a concrete objectified symbol of identity, boundaries, and margins, the map of Britain'[59] and shows the breaching of all the different boundaries that circumscribe the world of the play. In both plays (as also in *Hamlet*), '"real" homes, specifically castles, are sites of violations' – especially the blinding of Gloucester in *Lear* and the murder of Duncan in *Macbeth*. When Cornwall and Regan's servants, on Cornwall's orders, seize Gloucester in his own castle, the old Earl's first thought is 'the violation of his role as host':[60]

■ What means your graces?
Good my friends, consider you are my guests
[...]
I am your host:
With robbers' hands my hospitable favours
You should not ruffle thus. What will you do? (3.7.28–30, 40–2) □

Macbeth likewise invokes a code of hospitality as he contemplates Duncan's murder:

■ He's here in double trust:
First, as I am his kinsman and his subject,
Strong both against the deed: then as his host,
Who should against his murderer shut the door,
Not bear the knife myself. (1.7.12–16)

For Macbeth to speak of king-killing as a failure of hospitality, Liebler suggests, indicates the gravity that the code of hospitality still possessed in Shakespeare's time. According to Liebler, it survives from 'the Anglo-Saxon code of *comitatus*, the system in which the most prominent relationship was a lord's protection of his followers, and the most prominent locus for that relationship was the mead-hall, where all significant social operations were defined'.[61]

Pursuing her discussion of *Macbeth*, Liebler acknowledges that its titular 'hero/villain remains one of the most vexing definition-denying constructs in Shakespearean tragedy'. Macbeth's 'status as "butcher" [5.7.114]' is straightforward, but 'if he is not at the same time the tragic hero, then he is the only titular protagonist in Shakespearean tragedy (except perhaps for Julius Caesar) who is not'. To resolve this problem, Liebler calls on Jacques Derrida's interpretation of '*pharmakon*', in his essay 'Plato's Pharmacy' (1981), as ambivalent, both 'poison and cure'. Macbeth 'embodies all that is feudal Scotland at the start of the play'; he 'is Scotland's "monstrous double"', who 'replicates its contradictions, its feudal values, and the violence that sustains them'.[62]

In this context, Liebler offers an interesting reading of *Macbeth* 4.3 in which Malcolm falsely confesses his sins to Macduff and then admits he was lying. In Chapter 6 of this Guide, we saw L. C. Knights' interpretation of this as a point where Malcolm takes on a choric role; he has 'ceased to be a person' and his 'lines repeat and magnify' Macbeth's evils and implicitly 'contrast [them] with the opposite virtues'.[63] Liebler interprets the scene as follows:

■ In a complicated process of repeated inversions and identifications, Malcolm turns himself inside-out, 'opened', exposing vices in comparison with which Macbeth appears as 'a lamb' [4.3.59, 61], the emblem of innocence and sacrifice. The ritual subject identifies with his opponent and becomes what must be destroyed, and then redifferentiates himself as he emerges, newly forged, new born.[64] □

Liebler's perspective here converges with Knights' in that, for both, Malcolm at this point 'ceases to be a person'; but whereas Knights presents it as a sudden and unexplained shift from personhood to a choric role as moral demonstrator (and later back to personhood again), Liebler sets it in a wider context in which all the characters are functions, rather than persons, in a dramatic re-enactment of a communal ritual.

Where Knights sees 'order emerging out of disorder'[65] at the end of *Macbeth*, Liebler sees 'only an illusory order emerging out of paradox and contradiction'. Scotland's saviours are Macduff, not 'born of woman' [5.7.15] and childless because Macbeth has slain his wife and family, and Malcolm, 'yet unknown to woman' [4.3.140–1]. Their 'combination of unusual birth, childlessness and virginity suggest[s] no potential for procreative renewal'. It seems at the end that 'Scotland will not be restored; it will be reconstructed in the image of its southern neighbour'.[66]

Shakespeare's Festive Tragedy is an extremely rich book whose many veins have yet to be fully mined. For the first time since Bradley, it offers a comprehensive theory of Shakespearean tragedy, informed by a range of anthropological and philosophical sources – Girard, Turner, Derrida, among others. But, over a decade in the making, it perhaps appeared at slightly the wrong time. Although Liebler rejects what she calls 'the totalizing circularity' of Girard's claim of violence as 'the irreducible foundation of all human societies',[67] her own work has strong totalizing tendencies, offering a theory that applies not only to Shakespeare's tragedies, but also, it seems, to all actual societies in transition. Published in 1995, her book confronted an intellectual and critical environment that had grown inimical, under the influence of postmodernism, to totalizing theory – except for the totalizing theory that all totalizing theories were invalid and might well serve to foster totalitarianism. Moreover, much had happened in the 1980s, and although Liebler refers to some of this, it is not really integral to her theory and seems tacked on as a gesture towards then-dominant critical modes. In the next chapter, we will go back slightly in time, to the 1980s, and explore three new critical approaches to Shakespearean tragedy which emerged in that decade: New Historicism in the USA, which we shall represent by Stephen Greenblatt and Leonard Tennenhouse; and, in the UK, cultural materialism, represented by Jonathan Dollimore, and British poststructuralism,[68] represented by Catherine Belsey.

CHAPTER EIGHT

History and Subjectivity

In the 1980s, Anglo-American criticism of Shakespeare's tragedies, like other fields of literary criticism, began to change dramatically. A combination of social movements, particularly feminism, and of European, especially French, literary and cultural theories (deconstruction, poststructuralism, Lacanian psychoanalysis and power/knowledge perspectives derived from the French thinker Michel Foucault [1926–84]) broke down the empirical dykes roughly erected around Anglo-American criticism and a new set of critical concepts gushed in. These submerged, at least for a time, older ideas of resolution, homogeneity, unity and ultimately benign hierarchical order.

The decade was also notable for the development of three loosely defined but potent critical schools – New Historicism (as distinct from Marxist or positivist historicism) in the USA and cultural materialism (as distinct from historical materialism) and British poststructuralism in the UK. These approaches tended to relocate Shakespeare's plays in the broader context of the dramatic and discursive practices of his time rather than seeing them as the stand-alone product of a supreme genius (though New Historicism in particular also challenged the idea of 'context' or 'background' and the subordination of supposedly 'non-literary' texts to 'literary' ones). These approaches also argued that interpretations of Shakespeare were always political, serving or subverting ruling interests in the past and present. While there were overlaps between these two movements, there was also a key difference in that New Historicism tended to see subversion as produced by and ultimately serving the ends of power, while cultural materialism and British poststructuralism stressed that subversion was not wholly containable by power and could challenge and change the institutions of power. New Historicism was also particularly concerned with the construction of subjectivity at a time when, it was argued, the idea of the individual in the modern sense was only just starting to emerge, and this concern is echoed in Catherine Belsey's work, which retains the political edge blunted in New Historicism and the psychoanalytical and post-structuralist dimensions played down in cultural materialism.

This chapter starts by considering Stephen Greenblatt's essay 'Shakespeare and the Exorcists' from *Shakespearean Negotiations: The Circulation of Social Energy in Renaissance England* (1967).

Stephen Greenblatt

'Shakespeare and the Exorcists' starts from the link, known since the eighteenth century, between *King Lear* and the book *A Declaration of Egregious Popish Impostures* (1603) by the cleric and academic Samuel Harsnett (bap.1561–d.1631). Greenblatt contends that Shakespeare in *Lear* 'stages not only exorcism but Harsnett *on* exorcism'[1] and quotes Edgar's lines in his Poor Tom guise: 'Five fiends have been in poor Tom at once: of lust, as Obidicut, Hobbididence, prince of dumbness, Mahu of stealing, Modo of murder, Flibbertigibbet of mopping and mowing, who since possesses chambermaids and waiting-women' (Q, 132–7, RSC Shakespeare p. 2078). Greenblatt suggests there is an allusion in these lines to the chambermaids, Sara and Friswood Williams, and the waiting woman, Ann Smith, who featured in the exorcisms conducted by a group of English Catholic priests in Buckinghamshire between 1585 and 1586 and which Harsnett discusses in his book. This anachronism is, Greenblatt argues, like that of the Fool's remark, 'This prophecy Merlin shall make, for I live before his time' (3.4.94). In legendary British 'history', Lear's reign was centuries before Arthur's (when Merlin the magician was supposed to have lived), and the Fool jokingly prophesies a prophecy while drawing attention to the fictionality of his historical setting (since he knows about Merlin, he can hardly be completely confined in Lear-time; but Lear and Merlin are both legends). The Fool's remark highlights what Greenblatt calls *Lear*'s 'conspicuous doubleness, its simultaneous distance and contemporaneity'.[2]

Greenblatt argues that Harsnett's *Declaration* provides Shakespeare 'not only with an uncanny anachronism but also with the model for Edgar's histrionic disguise'. When an author consults 'a specialized source', such as 'a military or legal handbook', it is usually to find authentic material on which to base his work; but Shakespeare found in Harsnett, Greenblatt suggests, not genuine demons, but 'the inauthenticity of a theatrical role'. 'Shakespeare appropriates for Edgar a documented fraud'.[3]

Another source for *Lear* was the prose romance *Arcadia* (1590) by Sir Philip Sidney (1554–86). *Arcadia* gave the basis of the Gloucester subplot in *Lear*, but with the difference that in Sidney's work, the virtuous son escapes from his father and gains distinction as a soldier in another country. Edgar, by contrast, is not only outlawed by his father but also pushed to the edge of society as a near-naked madman. While this is an act, a role he casts off once he can return to the centre of society at the end of the play, its nature as an act – as the kind of fraud Harsnett presented in *Declaration* – makes it, Greenblatt contends, 'even more marginal and desperate' than real possession.[4]

Edgar's plight is sharpened by the strain of putting on an act. In the hovel with Lear, he says '[m]y tears begin to take his part so much / They mar my counterfeiting' (3.7.16–17). When he encounters his blind father and continues – as Greenblatt points out, quite why is uncertain – to maintain his 'Poor Tom' role, he almost breaks down: 'I cannot daub it ['put on a false face, pretend'] further' (4.2.60). The pseudo-suicide scene that follows can also be seen, according to Greenblatt, as drawing on fraudulent exorcist practices. Greenblatt quotes Harsnett's comparison of Catholic priests performing an exorcism to a play that 'gives us empty names for things' and 'tell[s] us of strange Monsters within, where there be none'. Likewise, the 'priests do report often in their patients [that is, those supposedly possessed by spirits] hearing the dreadful forms, similitudes, and shapes, that the devils use to depart in out [*sic*] of those possessed bodies', and 'this they tell with so grave a countenance, pathetical terms, and accommodate action, as to leave a very deep impression in the memory, and fancy of their actors'. In Harsnett's perspective, the priests create a theatrical illusion in which the supposedly possessed see the demonic spirits leaving their bodies and believe these spirits to be real. Edgar likewise aims to create a therapeutic illusion when he evokes the high cliff on which Gloucester stands, lets Gloucester 'leap' over, and then assumes the role of a bystander on the beach below telling the blind Earl of the monster he saw with him on the cliff top:

■ As I stood here below, methought his eyes
   Were two full moons: he had a thousand noses,
   Horns whelked and waved like the enragèd sea.
   It was some fiend: therefore, thou happy father,
   Think that the clearest gods, who make them honours
   Of men's impossibilities, have preserved thee. (4.5.82–7) □

To try to cure Gloucester of his suicidal impulses, Edgar stages an elaborate illusion complete with a devil, like a Catholic priest performing an exorcism – in Harsnett's view, an elaborate fraud that purports to cure people of demonic possession. But *Lear*, especially when acted, clearly shows Edgar is perpetrating an illusion, since Gloucester falls only on to the stage. In this, Edgar is doing to Gloucester what a play does to its audience, persuading them that an illusion is the truth. But the audience at a play knows it is an illusion and goes along with it for the sake of pleasure; Gloucester, like the supposedly possessed clients of an exorcist, is fooled, at least sufficiently to alter his attitudes profoundly. As Greenblatt puts it: 'the scene at Dover [which need not be at Dover at all] is a disenchanted analysis of both religious and theatrical illusions'.[5] But, unlike religious illusions such as exorcism, 'the theatre elicits from us complicity rather than belief'.[6]

Lear's staging, via Edgar, of an illusion akin to that of exorcism links up, for Greenblatt, with a more general sense of empty 'rituals and beliefs' in the play.[7] Greenblatt points out several examples of this emptiness. The pagan gods are invoked but none answer. Unlike *Hamlet, Lear* has no ghost; unlike *Macbeth*, no witches (Banquo's ghost, in that play, is already sceptically marked as a likely hallucination, since no one but Macbeth sees it); unlike *Antony and Cleopatra*, no music to mark what may be a god's exit. And there is no possession, except that feigned by Edgar; no devils, except the moon-eyed, multi-nosed, whelk-horned 'fiend' (4.5.85) Edgar creates in words. Lear's madness is not due to possession but related to '*hysterica passio*' (an inflammation of the senses rising up from the abdomen), being out and ill-clothed in bad weather, and extreme mental suffering; it is a gentleman rather than a divine who prescribes, not Catholic or Protestant spiritual remedies, but the natural cure of herb-induced sleep:

■ Our foster-nurse of nature is repose,
    The which he lacks: that to provoke in him
    Are many simples operative [effective medicinal herbs], whose power
    Will close the eye of anguish. (4.3.12–15) □

In Greenblatt's view, *Lear* reiterates Harsnett's *Declaration* and this indicates a larger implicit trade-off between church and theatre: '[the] official church dismantles and cedes to the players the powerful mechanisms of an unwanted and dangerous charisma; in return the players confirm the charge that those mechanisms are theatrical and hence illusory.'[8]

Greenblatt does not stop there, however; and it is his ability not to stop at an initial but illuminating conclusion, to pursue the argument into further twists and subtleties, that characterizes his most exciting critical work. For *Lear* does not only reiterate Harsnett; it also challenges him. For Greenblatt, this is one instance of a more general rule: 'the closer Shakespeare seems to a source, the more faithfully he reproduces it on stage, the more devastating and decisive his transformation of it'. As an example, Greenblatt takes Shakespeare's use of the term 'corky', which Greenblatt defines as 'sapless, dry, withered'.[9] This occurs in Harsnett's *Declaration* when he satirizes the penchant of Father Edmunds, the leader of the Buckinghamshire exorcists, for ignoring the rule that only old women were to be exorcised and tying young women in chairs to drive the devil out of them. Young rather than old women were necessary, Harsnett sardonically explains, because playing a possessed person demanded:

> ■ certain actions, motions, distortions, dislocations, writhings, tumblings, and turbulent passions [...] not to be performed but by suppleness of sinews [...] It would (I fear me) pose all the cunning Exorcists, that are this day to be found, to teach an old corky woman to writhe, tumble, curvet, and fetch her morris gambols.[10] □

Lear redeploys the term 'corky' in the brutal scene of Gloucester's blinding when Cornwall orders his servant to '[b]ind fast' Gloucester's 'corky arms' (3.7.27). Harsnett's satirical note is still there but now it issues from a man about to perform an act of torture. For Greenblatt, this 'one-word instance of repetition as transvaluation may suggest in the smallest compass what happens to Harsnett's work in the course' of *Lear*. The play reiterates Harsnett's arguments but partitions them out strangely. Cornwall, Goneril and especially the illegitimate Edmund are the sceptical voices but they assault and destroy the paternal figures. Persecution drives Edgar to feign possession as Poor Tom, and exorcism, in driving out his father's suicidal demon; but these dubious practices enable him to survive and help his father do the same. Are such practices therefore really as bad as Harsnett wants us to think them? And – this is a further bold move by Greenblatt – is there not an analogy between Edgar's plight, cast out, persecuted, hunted, forced to feign but continuing to perform covert, private exorcism and that of a Jesuit priest such as Father Edmunds whom Harsnett purports to expose and denounces? From an unofficial viewpoint, might not Edgar stand, more generally, as a figure for the proscribed position of the Jesuits in England?

Greenblatt is careful *not* to claim that the Edgar strand of *Lear* is 'an allegory in which Catholicism is revealed to be the persecuted legitimate elder brother forced to defend himself by means of theatrical illusions against the cold persecution of his sceptical bastard brother Protestantism'.[11] But the possibility of a more indefinite subversion of the official Anglican stance is there, and not only in historical retrospect. Greenblatt gives an example of the travelling players who performed *Lear*, *Pericles* and a 'St. Christopher Play' in the Yorkshire house of a recusant couple (that is, a couple who refused to attend Church of England services), Sir John and Lady Julyan Yorke. A Puritan neighbour, Sir Posthumus Hoby (1566–1640), denounced the players and their impresario, Sir Richard Cholmeley (c.1579–1631), for recusancy and the case became known to the Star Chamber (an English court of law that sat in secret, without charges or witnesses, and had become a powerful political weapon in Shakespeare's time). Greenblatt suggests – though he supplies no documentary evidence of this – that the denunciation may have been partly prompted by the perception that *Lear*, though ostensibly reinforcing Harsnett by presenting a fraudulent case of possession acted out by Edgar, was, perhaps more strongly, subverting Harsnett by evoking sympathy for a figure compelled to fraud by persecution and by a desire to save his father's life.

Moreover, there is also a sense in *Lear* that a world in which people no longer believe in possession creates, not clarity and freedom from fraud, but a greater uncertainty in accounting for evil. Lear asks: 'Is there any cause in nature that makes these hard hearts?' (3.7.31–2) and, as Greenblatt puts it, the play seems to suggest 'there is no cause *beyond* nature'. Possession is not responsible for such amoral and cruel utterances as Edmund's 'Thou, nature, art my goddess' (1.2.1), Regan's 'What need one?' (2.2.452) and Cornwall's 'Bind fast his corky arms' (3.7.28). 'Is it a relief', Greenblatt asks, to grasp that demonic possession did not produce the evil but that 'Lear himself' loosed it 'from the structure of the family and the state?'[12]

While actual possession cannot account for the evil in the play, Edgar's pretended possession, Greenblatt observes, is 'highly moral', like that of the supposedly devil-possessed people in Harsnett's book who praise the Catholic Church and its practices: 'Take heed o' th' foul fiend: obey thy parents, keep thy word's justice, swear not, commit not with man's sworn spouse ['i.e. do not commit adultery'], set not thy sweetheart on proud array' (3.4.70–1). The Norton edition of *Tragedies* (p. 627) comments: 'these are fragments from the Ten Commandments' (which reinforces Greenblatt's comment on the moral uprightness of Edgar's performance).[13] But these moral certainties emerge in the course of a pretence rather than through any extraworldly intervention. In this respect, they fit into a pattern in the play which shows the absence, or least non-interventionism, of any extraworldly forces, supernatural, pagan or divine. Edmund, though a villain, is likely, within the context of the play, to win audience assent when he mocks Gloucester's superstitious astrological discourse – 'These late eclipses in the sun and moon portend no good to us' (1.2.83) – as 'the excellent foppery of the world' (1.2.93). Lear often invokes the gods, but in vain:

■ O heavens,
   If you do love old men, if your sweet sway
   Allow obedience, if you yourselves are old,
   Make it your cause; send down, and take my part! (2.2.370–3) □

Greenblatt argues that in *Lear*, 'as Harsnett says of the Catholic Church, "neither God, Angel, nor Devil can be gotten to speak"'. But whereas Harsnett regards 'this silence' as 'a liberation from lies', it results, in

Lear, in the play's desolating end, as Lear, hunched over Cordelia's dead body, says:

> ■ Lend me a looking-glass:
> If that her breath will mist or stain the stone,
> Why, then she lives. (5.3.268–70) □

These lines, Greenblatt contends, raise the possibility that Cordelia will live and that Lear's suffering will be redeemed on earth, that *Lear* is not a tragedy but a '*tragedia di fin lieto*' [Italian for 'tragedy-with-comic-ending'] where the bad characters suffer the tragic punishment and the good miraculously survive[14] (this is akin to the idea of 'poetic(al) justice', which, as we saw in Chapter 1 of this Guide, Thomas Rymer formulated in the late seventeenth century). Lear himself identifies this redemptive possibility when he applies the feather-test to Cordelia for signs of life:

> ■ This feather stirs: she lives! If it be so,
> It is a chance which does redeem all sorrows
> That ever I have felt. (5.3.274–6) □

But the feather, in the fiction, stays still (on stage, of course, the actor's breath would stir it). *Lear* offers no image of redemption but does awaken the desire for it. Similarly it arouses the wish to believe in possession while demarcating it as pretence. In this, it resists the Harsnett kind of scepticism partly because the latter is, after all, the official state and church line in Shakespeare's time. Here lies the subversive element of *Lear* and the source of the play's continued appeal; it both endorses and questions any kind of social order in which central power displays itself by legally torturing and expelling what it categorizes as evil.

Another reason the play's resistance to Harsnettian scepticism still appeals depends on an assumption Greenblatt makes about human nature. If *Lear* continues to speak to us today, he contends, this is because it 'recuperates and intensifies our need' for 'magical ceremonies' such as exorcism, 'even though we do not believe in' such ceremonies, and 'performs them, carefully marked out for us as frauds, for our continued consumption'. It seems, then, that in Shakespeare's day as in our own we all have a need for exorcism and redemption that traditional religion, for many, cannot satisfy, but which the theatre can insofar as it is able to combine spectacle with scepticism – to produce what Greenblatt calls 'spectacular impostures'.[15] In *Hamlet in Purgatory* (2002), which we consider in Chapter 12 of this Guide, Greenblatt will pursue the idea of the theatre as the satisfaction of a human need that religion (or at least Protestantism in post-Reformation England) can no longer satisfy. But we turn now to a more directly political New Historicist reading of Shakespeare's tragedies, in *Power on Display* (1986) by Leonard Tennenhouse (b.1942).

Leonard Tennenhouse

We saw with L. C. Knights' essay 'How Many Children Had Lady Macbeth?' that its lesser-known subtitle, 'An Essay in the Theory and Practice of Shakespeare Criticism', was especially significant in its own right. This is also true of *Power on Display*'s subtitle: *The Politics of Shakespeare's Genres*. Here, two often separated fields of study, politics and genre, are brought together and genre is seen not in formalist terms but as serving political interests in Renaissance England. Tennenhouse makes a distinction between tragedies written in the 1590s, in the last years of Elizabeth's reign, and those written in the Jacobean era, the reign of James I. *Hamlet* is in some sense a transitional work which dramatizes two claims to power: a patrilineal one, which runs through Hamlet, and a matrilineal one, which runs through Gertrude and (as Claudius is her husband) ratifies Claudius's sovereignty. In this perspective, according to Tennenhouse, the 'dilemma of the play therefore turns upon the meaning and disposition of Gertrude's body', which 'becomes the place where the iconic bonding of blood and territory breaks down into competing bases for political authority'. Is 'blood' or the 'possession of territory' a more solid foundation of legitimate power?[16] It is the 'fate of Gertrude that makes *Hamlet* an Elizabethan play' because upon 'the condition of her body depends the health of the state'[17] – just as the health of the Elizabethan state could seem to depend upon the condition of its female monarch's body. Hamlet's play-within-a-play is intended to convict Claudius of fratricide and king-killing and restore the patrilineal, patriarchal order; but he is unable to do this and the patrilineal line dies with Hamlet. *Hamlet* as a whole remains within Elizabethan terms of reference. But after the accession of James I, patriarchal ideology is restored in *Othello*, *King Lear*, *Macbeth* and *Antony and Cleopatra*.

Tennenhouse considers these plays in the perspective of what he calls 'the Jacobean theatre of punishment'. Here he draws on the book *Surveiller et Punir* [*Discipline and Punish*] (1975) by the French thinker Michel Foucault, which posits that, in a culture that lacks a largely literate population (so that the function of written documents is limited), or a standing army or police force, displays of power in the form of spectacular punishments – such as public torture and execution – are important means of keeping the populace in order. Tennenhouse contends, however, that such displays are not as fully formed as Foucault implies but are always in process, an ongoing formulation of the ideology of state power constantly in competition with other displays that challenged that ideology. In Shakespeare's time, the theatre is one of the places in which state power is formulated and this formulation changes in the Jacobean era, as a male monarch replaces a female one and patriarchal values must be reaffirmed.

Tennenhouse identifies three key elements in Jacobean drama: 'kingship versus kinship; natural versus metaphysical bodies of power; the signs and symbols of state versus the exercise of state power'.[18] Indeed, he claims that 'all the oppositions which organize the great tragedies – including that of gender – cooperate to flesh out a problematic relationship between kinship and kingship'. In his discussion of *Othello*, Tennenhouse takes up Greenblatt's claim that Iago is not, as Hazlitt would have it, 'an amateur of tragedy',[19] or, as Kott put it, 'a Machiavellian stage manager',[20] but, as Tennenhouse paraphrases Greenblatt, 'a plotmaker/playwright of a comic narrative' – 'a romantic comedy' about Desdemona and Cassio. Iago also alters the way the Elizabethan stage represented sexual relations as he fools Rodrigo into thinking Desdemona is tired of her husband. As Tennenhouse puts it: 'Iago's plot transforms comic materials into those of a Jacobean tragedy.' His 'magic as dramatist is such that he transforms the chaste signs of desire into those of a monstrous betrayal right before Othello's eyes'. Desdemona, at first confident and articulate in winning the support of the Venetian senate in her successful struggle to choose her own husband, is reduced, not only by Iago but also by Shakespeare, to silence. Indeed, for Tennenhouse, Shakespeare and Iago are doubles: 'Shakespeare idealizes' and Iago 'defames' Desdemona but both share the same foundation for their 'gender distinctions' and both rob 'the female body' of 'its capacity to exercise patriarchal authority'. Othello's vengeance stages 'a theatre of punishment' in which it is Desdemona's incarnation of a challenge to patriarchal authority that is smothered.

This is only one example of the way Shakespeare reinforces patriarchal authority in his Jacobean drama, contributing to the ideological work necessary to sustain James I's power. In *Macbeth*, *Lear* and *Antony and Cleopatra*, Tennenhouse claims, 'Shakespeare takes the signs and symbols of legitimate authority and inverts them. He hands them over to illegitimate authority, but he does this in order to demonstrate that the iconography of the stage cannot possibly be used against the aristocratic body'. In *Macbeth*, for example, Lady Macbeth at first doubles herself as 'the punitive patriarch' and puts the promise to kill the king above the maternal bond. When she makes the guards drunk, she uses 'festival practices' to facilitate a regicide. Lady Macbeth and her husband then become 'counterfeit king[s]'. But all these elements are then reclaimed by patriarchal ideology. In her sleepwalking, Lady Macbeth doubles not as the patriarch but as the guilty party striving in vain to expel her own pollution. 'Out, damned spot! Out [...] . What, will these hands ne'er be clean?' (5.1.26, 31–2). Her attempt to engage in festive practices with Macbeth as monarch is thwarted by her husband's vision of Banquo at the banquet and it later seems that this has blighted all Scotland's festivities while Macbeth rules. As an unnamed Lord says to Lennox, the successful overthrow of Macbeth would mean that:

> ■ ... we may again
>   Give to our tables meat, sleep to our nights,
>   Free from our feasts and banquets bloody knives (3.6.34–6) □

On the morning after Duncan's murder, Macbeth writes the crime not on his own body but on Duncan's: 'His silver skin laced with his golden blood, / And his gashed stabs looked like a breach in nature' (2.3.116–17). Macbeth, the future king, has already effectively condemned himself as a violator of nature.

In the first scene of *Lear*, the king 'violate[s] the most important prohibition of his culture' and threatens 'to destroy the whole iconography of nationalism centered in the monarch's body'. The monarch's body should unite four powers, as Lear's does before he divides his kingdom: the power of the monarch's blood and bloodline which is sustained by primogeniture; the power of patronage; the power of fatherhood; and the power to command loyalty. By his division of the kingdom and his banishment of Kent and Cordelia, Lear disperses these powers and triggers 'a series of conflicts' that 'threaten' both 'the stability of the state' and 'the coherence of its signs and symbols'.[21] As Tennenhouse summarizes it: '[b]y privileging kinship over kingship, Lear produces an unruly state where women can rule men, where daughters can rule their fathers, and where bastards [that is, Edmund] can dispossess the aristocracy'.[22]

Patriarchal order is restored in several ways. The blind Gloucester renews his relationship with his son, the legitimate heir, and Edgar saves him from suicide. Gloucester renews his loyalty to Lear, unable to see the old monarch's natural body, stripped of its vesture of kingship. Goneril and Regan are no longer malcontents driven by their dissatisfaction with male patronage relationships but lustful women fiercely desiring Edmund – even though they had not previously seemed to exhibit such desire. Edgar's duel with Edmund is a foregone conclusion and simply serves to show 'the dissymmetrical power relations between bastard and legitimate son'.[23] Finally, Cordelia has to die because, if she had lived, she would either take the crown on Lear's death, or the play would have to challenge the idea of the king's bloodline by showing a male not of the king's direct bloodline acceding to the throne. Elizabeth I had demonstrated historically that a woman of royal blood could take the throne and that kinship and kingship could be thus linked; but *Lear* aims, in the reign of a male king, James I, to make its original audiences think of both kinship and kingship in male terms.

Antony and Cleopatra is like *Lear* in that, in both plays, 'kinship and kingship constitute a single strategy for distributing political power and thus for understanding the operations of such power in the world'. But the greater mythical quality of the former play is due to the way it highlights the complexities of the 'most important categories' of Jacobean culture – 'sexuality and politics'.[24] The play shows that Antony cannot leave history for sexuality because the two are interrelated. In Jacobean drama more generally, the aristocratic female is severed from the body politic and shown as a possible source of pollution. Shakespeare's Cleopatra is the ultimate example of this. In the way it portrays the lovers and their eventual deaths, the play re-establishes and reinforces the authority of Rome and the power of the male over the female who represents the grotesque, popular body. Cleopatra's death is an 'elaborate scene of punishment' that 'purges the world of all that is not Roman'. *Antony and Cleopatra* demonstrates that 'a whole way of figuring out power' is now 'obsolete'. In Tennenhouse's perspective, it might be seen as an 'elegy for the signs and symbols which legitimized Elizabethan power', the most important of which 'was that of the desiring and desired woman, her body valued for its ornamental surface, her feet rooted deep in a kingdom'.[25]

Tennenhouse's analysis of Shakespeare's tragedies as displays of power is itself a powerful one, trenchant and vibrant. Its history is broad-brush and relies strongly on an idea of two main periods – the Elizabethan and the Jacobean – and on iconographic and literary ingredients (rather than on, say, economic and social history based on factual documents). It is also rather reticent on a question which runs through this Guide: what makes a Shakespearean tragedy tragic rather than – as it tends to become in Tennenhouse's perspective – a dramatized piece of intense and intricate political propaganda that shows what goes wrong when ideas of kinship and kingship get split? There is a further issue which arises by comparison with Greenblatt: how much ambivalence is there in the political messages of the tragedies? Greenblatt argued, as we saw above, that *Lear* appears to reiterate the official Harsnett line which scoffed at possession and exorcism, while covertly subverting it and thus turning theatre into a means of satisfying human needs left unsatisfied after the disappearance of traditional Catholic practices. In this respect, the play gives off a double message. But for Tennenhouse, while there is a difference between Elizabethan and Jacobean messages, plays from each period reinforce the official line; there seems to be no room either for subversion or ambiguity. This means that the plays, on the highest level of abstraction, are all saying the same thing, all reinforcing the ideology of power even though the contours of that ideology may change historically. An alternative view, that takes tragedy as much more challenging, can be found in British cultural materialism as represented by perhaps its most influential exponent, Jonathan Dollimore, in his book *Radical Tragedy* (1984). We will explore this book next.

Jonathan Dollimore

The overall argument of *Radical Tragedy* is that 'a significant sequence of Jacobean tragedies, including the majority of Shakespeare's, were more radical than has hitherto been allowed'.[26] Indeed, Dollimore suggests that the 'sceptical, interrogative and subversive representations' of Jacobean drama may have helped to undermine the Crown, court, central administration, army and episcopacy and their legitimating ideologies and thus contributed to their collapse in the run-up to the English Civil War (1642–51). Jacobean drama's challenge to 'religious orthodoxy' produced other major subversions: 'a critique of ideology, the demystification of political and power relations and the decentring of "man"'[27] – the concept of an essential humanity that was the centre and source of things. Jacobean tragedy also implicitly contests the idea that art produces order, resolution and transcendence – an idea that ignores the social and political context and content of literature and finds 'supposedly timeless values which become the *universal* counterpart of man's *essential* nature – the underlying human essence'.[28]

Thus, *Lear*, for example, rejects the 'notion of man as tragic victim somehow alive and complete in death' as an 'essentialist mystification'; that is, the play does not endorse the view that there is an essence of human nature that finds vivid and full realization in a tragic protagonist's demise; rather, *Lear* exposes such a view as a way of trying to hide the unequal power relations that are the true source of tragedy. The play decentres the tragic subject and provides 'a more general exploration of human consciousness in relation to social being – one which discloses human values to be not antecedent to, but rather informed by, material conditions'.[29] The attempt as *Lear* ends to 'recuperate their society in just those terms which the play has subjected to sceptical interrogation' is balked by the deaths of Cordelia and Lear himself. As Dollimore puts it: '[t]he timing of these two deaths must surely be seen as cruelly, precisely subversive: instead of complying with the demands of formal closure – the convention which would confirm the attempt at recuperation – the play concludes with two events which sabotage the prospect of both closure and recuperation'.[30] It is interesting to compare this view with that of Leonard Tennenhouse which we discussed in the previous section: as we saw, Tennenhouse interprets Cordelia's death as contributing to recuperation and closure by removing the ideological conflict between kinship and kingship that would arise if Cordelia survived Lear and thus became next in line to the throne.

Both *Antony and Cleopatra* and *Coriolanus* offer 'a sceptical interrogation of martial ideology and in doing so foreground the complex social and political relations which hitherto it tended to occlude'.[31] Both male heroes embody an idea of aristocratic autonomy that is, in Jacobean society, fading but still potent; it is encapsulated in Coriolanus' idea that it is possible to 'stand / As if a man were author of himself / And knew no other kin' (5.3.36–8). Dollimore highlights the qualifying 'As if': for another idea is emerging to challenge the aristocratic one, in which Antony and Coriolanus are the products, instruments and effects of wider sociological and ideological forces: and 'as they transgress the power structure which constitutes them both their political and personal identities – inextricably bound together if not identical – disintegrate'.[32]

Dollimore acknowledges the 'captivating poetry' of *Antony and Cleopatra*, which can be 'rapturously expressive of desire', but contends that 'the language of desire, far from transcending the power relations which structure this society, is wholly informed by them'. Antony and Cleopatra 'experience themselves' in terms of 'possession, subjugation and conspicuous wealth'.[33] Dollimore gives several examples: Alexas, Cleopatra's attendant, delivers Antony's pledge to her queen to 'piece / Her opulent throne with kingdoms. / All the east, / Say thou, shall call her mistress' (1.5.53–5). In the ceremony in which Antony made good that pledge, he and Cleopatra, in Octavius Caesar's account, 'in chairs of gold / Were publicly enthroned' (3.6.4–5). Antony gives Cleopatra 'the stablishment ['confirmed possession'] of Egypt' and appoints her '[a]bsolute queen' of 'lower Syria, Cyprus, Lydia'. To Maecenas' question, 'This in the public eye?', Caesar replies: 'I'th'common show-place' (3.6.4–5, 9–13). Cleopatra despatches 'twenty several [separate] messengers' to Antony, a number that provokes Alexas to ask, 'Why do you send so thick ['such a throng']?' (1.5.70–1). When Maecenas asks Enobarbus, back from Egypt, whether it is true that '[e]ight wild boars roasted whole [were served] at a breakfast, and but twelve persons there', Enobarbus replies: '[t]his was but a fly by an eagle: we had much more monstrous matter ['strange, exotic foods'] of feast, which worthily deserved noting' (2.2.214–17).

There are also key references to the part power plays in the bonding of Antony and Cleopatra. Philo, a follower of Antony, speaks at the very start of the drama of Cleopatra's dominance over Antony, whose 'goodly eyes [...] now bend, now turn / The office and devotion of their view / Upon a tawny front' and whose 'captain's heart' has 'become the bellows and the fan / To cool a gipsy's lust' (1.1.2, 4–6, 9–10). Enobarbus reports that Cleopatra, on her first meeting with Antony on the river of

Cydnus, 'pursed ['pocketed'. RSC (p. 2181) also adds, in parenthesis: 'sexual connotations'] up his heart' (2.2.219). Cleopatra tells Antony 'I have no power upon you' but almost immediately asserts her monarchical status and defines him as a traitor: 'O, never was there queen / So mightily betrayed! Yet at the first / I saw the treasons planted' (1.3.28, 30–1).

Antony calls himself Cleopatra's 'soldier, servant, making peace or war / As thou affects' (1.3.81–2) and this, Dollimore suggests, is 'one of many exchanges which shows how their sexuality is rooted in a fantasy transfer of power from the public to the private sphere, from the battle-field to the bed'.[34] Dollimore goes on to argue that:

> ■ [Antony's] sexuality is informed by the very power relations which he, ambivalently, is prepared to sacrifice for sexual freedom; correspondingly, the heroic *virtus* which he wants to reaffirm in and through Cleopatra is in fact almost entirely a function of the power structure which he, again ambivalently, is prepared to sacrifice for her.[35] □

Like Antony, and perhaps even more so, Coriolanus embodies a contradictory martial ideal: he can seem to have an autonomous, self-sufficient identity but he is the product of powers that precede and construct him. In the course of the play, 'Coriolanus is forced to experience himself as decentred, identified [not by his inner essence but] by social forces which he cannot contain or [in the end] survive'. Prior to that, Coriolanus' '[e]ssential egotism, far from being merely a subjective delusion, operates in this play as the ideological underpinning of class antagonism'.[36] Moreover, Coriolanus' sense of an essential patrician identity depends on the plebeians, whose supposed difference from him confirms his own superiority while also exhibiting his fear of contamination by them, 'the mutable, rank-scented meinie ['common people, rabble' (pronounced 'many' or 'meeny')] (3.1.82).

Dollimore challenges the critical assumption that Jacobean dramatists shared the hatred of the mob Coriolanus expresses and contends that the play presents 'the plebeians [...] with both complexity and sympathy because [they are] understood in terms of the contradiction which the Third Citizen articulates'[37] when he says '[w]e have power in ourselves to do it [reject Coriolanus], but it is a power that we have no power to do' (2.3.3–4).

While *Coriolanus*, in Dollimore's view, is the most difficult of all Shakespeare's tragedies to recuperate for 'essential humanism', it is – or was, in the 1970s and 1980s – still done.[38] He quotes the affirmation of Sir Brian Vickers (b.1937), in his book *Shakespeare:* Coriolanus (1966), that he 'would rather have [Coriolanus'] integrity and innocence, however easily "put upon" than all the calculation and political skill in Rome or Corioli'.[39] Dollimore argues that the play does not present Coriolanus as innocent or having integrity, 'least of all in the autonomous ethical sense' that Vickers intimates. Furthermore, and more significantly, 'the very dichotomy of innocent, authentic individual versus corrupt society is false to the play; to accept that dichotomy is idealistically to recuperate the political and social realism of *Coriolanus*'; to import the idea of 'the ethically unified subject of a world elsewhere allows us to transcend the political and social realities foregrounded in and by the dislocated subject in this one'. Dollimore finds a 'more accurate assessment of Coriolanus' in Aufidius's words: 'So our virtues / Lie in th'interpretation of the time' (4.7.51–2) – that is, 'virtues', not merely 'reputation', are 'socially constructed' and historically relative rather than intrinsic.[40] In Aufidius' soliloquy, as throughout *Coriolanus* as a whole, Dollimore detects a 'fascinating tendency [...] to anchor traditional ideas of transience and mutability in an immediate perception of political and historical vicissitude'.[41] In other words, such 'traditional ideas' are given, in Shakespeare's time, a political and historical resonance that prevents them from simply ratifying a supposed human condition.

Dollimore's approach made it seem possible to read Jacobean tragedy as radical in its own time as well as ours and to account for its supposed artistic flaws in terms of the way these subverted, rather than confirmed, existing ideology. Dollimore, Tennenhouse and Greenblatt all see a close connection between Shakespeare's tragedies and power; but whereas Greenblatt sees covert subversion of Reformation orthodoxy and Tennenhouse perceives a dramatic replication of state propaganda, Dollimore sees a much more widespread radicalism that connects up, across the centuries, with British radical attitudes in the early 1980s. Dollimore does not claim, however, to be producing his interpretations for the present but to discern what is actually there, in the text. A related but rather different approach is offered by Catherine Belsey (b.1943) in *The Subject of Tragedy* (1985).

Catherine Belsey

The Subject of Tragedy has 'three main aims': first, 'to contribute to the construction of a history of the subject', the idea of the self, 'in the sixteenth and seventeenth centuries'; second, 'to demonstrate, by placing woman side by side with man, that at the moment when the modern subject was in the process of construction, the "common-gender noun"' – Man – 'largely failed to include women in the range of its meanings';[42] and third, 'to bring together history and fiction' (including drama).[43] The book also mounts an attack on liberal humanism with its central concept of '*man*, whose essence is *freedom*' and its idea that 'the subject is the free, unconstrained author of meaning and action, the origin of history' which freely chooses Western liberal democracy as the expression of human nature.

Hamlet is 'the classic case' of a statement of an inner reality which external appearance cannot capture, for example when he says:[44]

> ■ 'Tis not alone my inky cloak, good mother,
>   Nor customary suits of solemn black,
>   Nor windy suspiration of forced breath,
>   No, nor the fruitful river in the eye,
>   Nor the dejected 'haviour of the visage,
>   Together with all forms, moods, shows of grief,
>   That can denote me truly: these indeed seem
>   For they are actions that a man might play
>   But I have that within which passeth show;
>   These but the trappings and the suits of woe. (1.2.77–86) □

'That within' Hamlet, his supposed interiority, has been, as we have seen, the object of the quest of many critics – and that quest is, Belsey declares, 'endless', because no such interiority exists. As she points out, Hamlet is 'the most discontinuous of Shakespeare's heroes', who alternates between madness, rationality, vengefulness, inertia and determination in the first four acts of the play and is 'above all *not* an agent',[45] but, rather, a disunified subject 'traversed by the voices of a succession of morality fragments, wrath and reason, patience and resolution' – in none of which the 'real' Hamlet lies. It is only in Act 5, when Hamlet 'ceases to struggle towards identity and agency' and 'with and between reason and revenge', and provides no more soliloquies, that he can act.[46]

The sense of interiority is produced primarily by the device of the soliloquy, but it varies as to the extent that it purports to represent a full inwardness. Lady Macbeth's call to the spirits to unsex her shows, for Belsey, 'the contradictory nature of the subject in the early seventeenth century': [47]

> ■ Come, you spirits
>   That tend on mortal thoughts, unsex me here
>   And fill me from the crown to the toe top-full
>   Of direst cruelty. Make thick my blood,
>   Stop up th'access and passage to remorse,
>   That no compunctious visitings of nature
>   Shake my fell purpose nor keep peace between
>   Th'effect and it. Come to my woman's breasts
>   And take my milk for gall, you murd'ring ministers,
>   Wherever in your sightless substances

> You wait on nature's mischief. Come, thick night,
> And pall thee in the dunnest smoke of hell,
> That my keen knife see not the wound it makes,
> Nor heaven peep through the blanket of the dark,
> To cry 'Hold, hold!' – (1.5.38–52) □

Lady Macbeth, as the subject who is spoken about, hardly figures in the speech. The spirits are grammatical subjects of the actions and the moment the pronoun 'me' appears it splits into fragments: 'crown, toe, cruelty, blood, remorse, nature, breasts, milk'.[48] The speech ends with the heaven/hell opposition of a morality play or tale in which the human being is the playground of spiritual forces and her only freedom is to choose between them.

Lady Macbeth is one of those figures who 'speak with voices which are not their own' and are thus 'unfixed, inconstant', unable to sustain the pose of masculine virtue.[49] She ends by sleepwalking and revealing the truth about Macbeth's murder of Duncan and Lady Macduff. Likewise, Cleopatra demands to take part in the battle of Actium:

> ■ A charge we bear i'th'war,
> And, as the president of my kingdom will
> Appear there for a man. Speak not against it.
> I will not stay behind. (3.7.21–4) □

But Cleopatra flies from the battle. Nonetheless, she can seem a heroic figure. She at last rejects 'feminine' unfixedness and 'becomes agent of her own destiny, the absolute subject of suicide':[50]

> ■ My resolution's placed, and I have nothing
> Of woman in me: now from head to foot
> I am marble-constant: now the fleeting moon
> No planet is of mine. (5.2.282–5) □

As Belsey points out, the 'final visual image of Cleopatra' combines stateliness with the sense of a 'lass unparalleled' (5.2.356), with 'the asp at her breast, perhaps evoking the medieval emblem of lechery, a young woman whose breast and genitals are devoured by serpents'. It is an image of a woman who is simultaneously 'whore and mother', who says '[t]he stroke of death is as a lover's pinch' (5.2.331) and '[d]ost not thou see my baby at my breast' (5.2.348), but who also 'refuses the feminine'. The 'figure of Cleopatra is thus plural, contradictory, an emblem which can be read as justifying either patriarchy on the one hand or an emergent feminism on the other, or perhaps as an icon of the contest between the two'.[51]

Belsey thus opens up two crucial, interrelated issues in regard to Shakespeare's tragedies, and other tragedies of the period. One is the issue of the construction of subjectivity and the way in which the subject, the idea of a unified individual self, emerges in Shakespearean tragedy, especially through the soliloquy, but remains unstable, with elements of earlier modes, as in Lady Macbeth's division into body parts, supposedly active demons and morality-play elements (Heaven and Hell). The other is the way in which the emerging subject is male, working to displace and control the female subject, but not – as the representation of Cleopatra shows – with complete success. For Belsey, these two issues have implications for twentieth-century political change and for feminism.

With Belsey, Dollimore, Tennenhouse and Greenblatt, we can see that there were large changes in the 1980s in the ways in which Shakespearean tragedies were understood and interpreted. Greenblatt's New Historicism suggested how other texts, such as Harsnett's *Declaration*, might be deployed not as inert sources but as material that could be both reiterated and subverted in drama. Tennenhouse proposed that Shakespeare's tragedies be seen as serving the ends of a monarchical power that still relied crucially on public display to prove its potency but made a major distinction between the way that this was done in the Elizabethan era, with a woman as monarch, and the way it was done in the Jacobean era, when a man returned to the throne. In contrast to Tennenhouse, Dollimore found Jacobean tragedy to be subversive, challenging religion, ideology and power and decentring 'man' as an autonomous individual. Belsey, however, tends to find 'man' emerging through Elizabethan and Jacobean tragedy though still in an unstable form and subverted by representations of women which may challenge or confirm patriarchy. It is in Belsey's work that the strongest feminist emphasis is found and we shall pursue this further in the next chapter on gender and sexuality, exploring criticism by Janet Adelman, Philippa Berry, Coppélia Kahn, Madhavi Menon and Jason Edwards.

CHAPTER NINE

Gender and Sexuality

The last section of the previous chapter showed how a renewed concern with history and subjectivity in the 1980s combined, in Catherine Belsey's work, with a non-essentialist feminism that focused on the construction of female and male subjects through the interaction of social discourse and desire, and explored the representations and subversions of these subjects in Shakespearean tragedy, and Jacobean tragedy more generally. Drawing on an often eclectic mix that could include Freudian and Lacanian psychoanalysis, feminism, poststructuralism, deconstruction and postmodernism – and, still at the centre of critical practice, 'close reading' – a range of studies emerged towards the end of the twentieth century that examined issues of gender and sexuality in Shakespearean tragedy from a variety of angles. By this time, critics were freer to pursue projects without the need (evident to varying degrees in all four of the critics considered in the last chapter) to make an extensive case against older models of criticism ('liberal humanist' or 'old historicist', for instance) which were not necessarily wholly invalid but no longer attracted much critical energy. This more open situation also meant that it was possible to mix and merge a range of theoretical perspectives and interpretative approaches, with the result that the movements of the 1980s that had aimed at sharp self-definitions in order to advance their particular causes became, in the 1990s, blurred, broken up or blended, often in productive ways. Thus, while each of the critical texts we discuss in this chapter addressed issues of sexuality and gender in Shakespeare, none can be simply assigned to a particular category (e.g., feminism, deconstruction, psychoanalysis). We start with *Suffocating Mothers: Fantasies of Maternal Origin in Shakespeare's Plays* (1992) by Janet Adelman (1941–2010).

Janet Adelman

Suffocating Mothers draws on a mixture of feminism, psychoanalysis and close reading to explore 'masculinity and the maternal body in

Shakespeare'[1] and to argue that the return of 'the figure of the mother [...] to Shakespeare's dramatic world' in *Hamlet* 'is the point of origin of the great tragic period'.[2] In *Hamlet*, the fathers, 'despite their manifest differences', 'keep threatening to collapse into one another, annihilating in their collapse the son's easy assumption of his father's identity'. Adelman identifies Hamlet's mother as the 'initiating cause of this collapse': 'her failure to serve her son as the repository of his father's ideal image is the symptom of her deeper failure to distinguish properly between his father and his father's brother'.[3]

Adelman points out that, although Gertrude is central to *Hamlet*, we know little about her, and suggests this partly accounts for the apparent absence of what T. S. Eliot called an 'objective correlative' in the play (as discussed in Chapter 4 of this Guide). Gertrude 'becomes for Hamlet – and for *Hamlet*' – the basis of quite disproportionate 'fantasies of maternal malevolence [and] spoiling, that are compelling [...] exactly as they seem therefore to reiterate infantile fears and desires rather than an adult apprehension of the mother as a separate person'.[4]

In this perspective, Adelman offers an analysis of the opening lines of Hamlet's first soliloquy that has implications not only for *Hamlet* but also for Shakespeare's later tragedies, and indeed for tragedy in general:

■ O that this too too solid [sullied] flesh would melt,
   Thaw and resolve itself into a dew!
   Or that the Everlasting had not fixed
   His canon gainst self-slaughter! O God, O God!
   How weary, flat, stale and unprofitable
   Seem to me all the uses of this world!
   Fie on't! O, fie, fie! 'Tis an unweeded garden
   That grows to seed: things rank and gross in nature
   Possess it merely. That it should come to this!
   But two months dead [...] (1.2.129–38) □

Adelman argues that this soliloquy is effectively Hamlet's 'attempt to locate a point of origin for the staleness of the world and his own pull toward death' and that 'he discovers this point of origin in his mother's body'. According to Hamlet, as Adelman paraphrases it, 'the world has been transformed into an unweeded garden, possessed by things rank and gross, because his mother has remarried'. Hamlet offers, in effect, a 'highly compacted and psychologized version' of the Fall of Man in the Old Testament. For Adelman, 'the opening lines of the soliloquy point [...] toward a radical confrontation with the sexualized maternal body as the initial premise of tragedy, the fall that brings death into the world'. She continues: the 'structure of *Hamlet* – and [...] of the plays that follow from *Hamlet* – is marked by the struggle to escape from this condition, to free the masculine identity of both father and son from its origin in the contaminated maternal body'.[5] Adelman sums up her overall argument in this way:

■ The first mother to reappear in Shakespeare's plays is adulterous [...] because maternal origin is in itself felt as equivalent to adulterating betrayal of the male, both father and son; *Hamlet* initiates the period of Shakespeare's greatest tragedies because it in effect rewrites the story of Cain and Abel as the story of Adam and Eve, relocating masculine identity in the presence of the adulterating female.[6] □

In *Othello*, however, Desdemona takes the maternal role. At the start of the play, Othello 'leaves his martial identity behind to encounter maternal pity in the form of Desdemona'[7] and, in a sense, to return to childhood – 'She loved me for the dangers I had passed, / And I loved her that she did pity them' (1.3.181–2). In this perspective, Adelman offers an ingenious reading of the significance of that handkerchief which, as we saw in Chapter 1 of this Guide, Thomas Rymer mocked in the late seventeenth century as a case of much ado about nothing. 'The handkerchief,' Adelman argues, 'maintains its hold over Othello's imagination partly insofar as it records the moment at which this idealized maternal figure [Desdemona] is lost';[8] this moment is when he takes her virginity on the consummation of their marriage. The handkerchief can be seen as a 'miniature representation of the wedding sheets, "spotted with strawberries" [3.3.479] as those "lust-stained" sheets are "spotted" with "lust's blood" [5.1.38], it is a talisman that guarantees both virginity and its loss in the act of consummation'.[9] Moreover, 'the loss of the handkerchief itself only reconfirms what is lost in that act' of consummation. 'Othello's mother enters the play only by allusion to the moment of her death', when she gives him the handkerchief – 'she, dying, gave it me' (3.4.64) – and, likewise, 'the handkerchief becomes imaginatively present to Othello only in its absence, and only after he believes Desdemona [is] lost to him'.[10]

Adelman contends that as Othello relates 'the history of the handkerchief', it becomes evident that 'its magical power to stabilize male desire turns increasingly on the power of long-dead women':[11]

■ That handkerchief
Did an Egyptian to my mother give [...]
[...] There's magic in the web of it:
A sibyl, that had numbered in the world
The sun to course two hundred compasses,
In her prophetic fury sewed the work:
The worms were hallowed that did breed the silk,

> And it was dyed in mummy ['medicinal substance obtained from mummified bodies'] which the skilful
> Conserved of maidens' hearts. [3.4.56–7, 71–7] □

This history, which has an emotional if not literal truth for Othello, sets the weaving of the handkerchief in 'an unbroken line of female descent'[12] that leads to Desdemona's destruction, a lethal event that Adelman relates to the story of the handkerchief in this way:

> ■ In Desdemona's death, the transmission of the handkerchief becomes perfectly circular: the talisman that comes from the dying mother is returned to her through the dead body of the wife. And as the mother is preserved in the dead maidens, so Desdemona's death serves not only to punish but to preserve her, returning her to her status as maiden/mother and making her Othello's alone, in the terrible love-death that consummates the play.[13] □

Desdemona, Adelman argues, is unique in Shakespeare's tragedies in being 'both frankly sexual and utterly virtuous'. Shakespeare's later tragedies, however, will violently split apart and demonize 'the qualities momentarily brought together in Desdemona'. 'Female power' in itself 'will be dangerous'. '[S]exuality will become the sign of villainy, maternity the sign of overwhelming power' in Goneril and Regan (*Lear*), Lady Macbeth (*Macbeth*) and Volumnia (*Coriolanus*).[14] Cleopatra alone will be partly free of such splittings.

Moving on to *Lear*, Adelman acknowledges that it may seem strange to include this play in a book about male fantasies of maternal power, since it notably lacks mothers. But in a psychoanalytic perspective, the apparent absence of something may indicate its repressed presence. For Adelman, a central text of the play is the Fool's words to the King: 'thou mad'st thy daughters thy mothers [...] thou gav'st them the rod and put'st down thine own breeches' (1.4.125–6). This image, Adelman suggests, has 'painfully literal suggestions of both generational and gender reversal, of infantile exposure and maternal punishment' (104). Adelman argues that '[m]uch of [*Lear*'s] power comes [...] from its confrontation with the landscape of maternal deprivation or worse, from the vulnerability and rage that is the consequence of this confrontation and the intensity and fragility of the hope for a saving maternal presence that can undo pain'. A key Freudian concept on which Adelman calls is 'the return of the repressed' – the idea that what is repressed will return savagely. In the case of *Lear*, it is the mother who is first of all repressed to permit a fantasy in which males are the source of both men (Gloucester's sons) and women (Lear's daughters); but this 'ends by releasing fantasies far more frightening than any merely literal mother could be, fantasies that give emotional coloration to the entire play because they are not localized in (and hence limited to) any single character'.[15]

For example, one of the few references to mothers occurs near the start of the play, in an exchange between Kent and Gloucester, with Edmund present:

■ KENT   Is not this [Edmund] your son, my lord?
  GLOUCESTER   His breeding, sir, hath been at my charge. I have so often
                blushed to acknowledge him that now I am brazed to't.
  KENT   I cannot conceive [understand] you.
  GLOUCESTER   Sir, this young fellow's mother could; whereupon she grew
                round-wombed and had indeed, sir, a son for her cradle
                ere she had a husband for her bed. Do you smell a fault?
  KENT   I cannot wish the fault undone, the issue of it being so
                proper. (1.1.5–12) □

Whereas Gloucester is circumlocutory and evasive about his own part in Edmund's conception, there is no doubt about the role of his anonymous mother, who 'grew round-wombed'. But Gloucester then focuses his attention on his legitimate offspring – 'I have a son, sir, by order of law … ' (1.1.13) – thus marking the difference between the mother's illegitimate child and the father's legitimate one, whose mother is unmentioned. And it is Edmund's mother whom Edgar, near the end of the play, blames for his father's blinding:

■ My name is Edgar, and thy father's son.
  The gods are just, and of our pleasant vices
  Make instruments to plague us:
  The dark and vicious place where thee [that is, Edmund] he got
  Cost him his eyes. (5.3.181–5) □

As Adelman points out, Edgar here eliminates Cornwall, the actual blinder of Gloucester, and refers only in a relative clause to Edmund ('thee'), who left his father's castle knowing the old man was about to be brutalized (3.7.5–7). Edgar effectively 'names the female sexual "place" as the blinding agent', thus by a metonymy – a verbal device in which a part stands for a whole – 'making the darkness of that place equivalent to the darkness into which Gloucester is plunged'.[16] The repressed mother returns as the fantasy agent of Gloucester's blinding.

The same process of repression and return occurs in the Lear plot. Lear sometimes tries to suggest that Goneril and Regan are illegitimate: he calls Goneril a '[d]egenerate bastard' (1.4.199) and says that if Regan were not glad to see him (which of course she is not), 'I would divorce me from thy mother's tomb / Sepulch'ring an adult'ress' (303–4). Cordelia,

Adelman suggests, is, like Edgar, seen as 'purely her father's child' and, once more, 'the female sexual place is necessarily the place of corruption, the "sulphurous pit" (4.5.134) that is Lear's equivalent to Edgar's "dark and vicious place"' (5.3.184).[17] But Lear cannot deny that he is the father of all three of his daughters; he therefore tries to diagnose Goneril as an infection in his body:

> ■ But yet thou art my flesh, my blood, my daughter –
> Or rather a disease that's in my flesh,
> Which I must needs call mine: thou art a boil,
> A plague-sore, or embossèd carbuncle,
> In my corrupted blood. (2.2.405–9) □

As this quotation shows, Lear's acknowledgement of Goneril as 'his flesh and blood entails making his own body the site of her monstrous femaleness'.[18] The feared female flesh invades the male self. But its most fearful representation is not in Lear's daughters but in the storm which, if it is 'classically the domain of the male thunderer', is also 'the domain of disruptive female power'.[19] And although Cordelia is the 'site of [Lear's] deepest longings' she is also 'the suffocating mother within'.[20] Adelman describes the process thus:

> ■ in its longing for originary wholeness, the unstable masculinity that would escape its own finitude through a fantasy of merger with her recoils at finding the signs of her presence within, including the signs of his need for her, and its recoil transfers the dream of union into the nightmare of suffocation.[21] □

Adelman thus offers another reason why Cordelia has to die. In this psychoanalytic perspective, it is not, as Tennenhouse suggested (see the previous chapter of this Guide), that her survival would threaten the Jacobean restoration of patriarchy by potentially putting a woman on the throne; rather, her survival would threaten a psychological engulfment of the male by a figure assuming the functions of the mother whose very goodness is suffocating. The deaths of women – and 'feminized figures of speech'[22] – also figure centrally in Philippa Berry's *Shakespeare's Feminine Endings* (1999), which we will consider next.

Philippa Berry

Philippa Berry's *Shakespeare's Feminine Endings* argues that 'the dead or dying female body' in Shakespearean tragedy is linked, through metaphor and metonymy, both with 'popular festivity' (this gives another meaning to Naomi Conn Liebler's idea of 'Shakespeare's festive tragedy') and with an implied wonder-working principle concealed in nature. These links, Berry contends, partly offset the tragic idea of death as the end. She suggests that the tragedies, by 'redefining dying as a state that is open rather than closed [...] both problematize and amplify religious knowledge of and around death, disrupting the orderliness of such established significations in a complex layering of figurative detail that is often emblematically embodied, near the end of the play, by a dead or dying woman'.[23] According to Berry, the 'dying female body [...] figures a literal death in sexual terms' and thus becomes 'an oxymoronic image of life-in-death, whose simultaneous "deflowering" and "devouring" by death [...] juxtaposes the prospect of death as an individualized end to a finite existence with the possibility of a virtual infinity or endlessness of erotic "deaths"'.[24]

Gertrude's account of Ophelia's death provides a notable example of this:

■ There is a willow grows aslant a brook,
   That shows his hoar leaves in the glassy stream.
   Therewith fantastic garlands did she make
   Of crow-flowers, nettles, daisies and long purples,
   That liberal shepherds give a grosser name,
   But our cold maids do dead men's fingers call them:
   There on the pendent boughs her coronet weeds
   Clamb'ring to hang, an envious sliver broke,
   When down the weedy trophies and herself
   Fell in the weeping brook. Her clothes spread wide,
   And mermaid-like awhile they bore her up,
   Which time she chanted snatches of old tunes,
   As one incapable of her own distress,
   Or like a creature native and indued
   Unto that element: but long it could not be
   Till that her garments, heavy with their drink,
   Pulled the poor wretch from her melodious lay
   To muddy death. (5.1.149–66) □

Here Ophelia becomes, through the images that evoke her, 'a demented flower-goddess, a May queen who, even in tragedy, displays the attributes of popular festivity', and her 'muddy death' becomes 'a strangely pleasurable, but also implicitly fruitful, surrender to the dirtiness and ambiguity of bodily desire in her watery river-bed'.[25]

Turning to *Othello*, Berry regards its protagonist as an example of Western 'ocularcentrism' in his overvaluation of the ability of the visual faculty to perceive truth – hence his readiness to accept as an 'ocular proof' (3.3.398) of Desdemona's infidelity that handkerchief which

Thomas Rymer mocked (see Chapter 1 of this Guide) and Janet Adelman (see previous section) took as a talisman of maternal power. The 'ocular proof' that Iago gives Othello uses, as a metonymy for Desdemona, 'a flag or sign of love' (1.1.165). (This last phrase is in fact used by Iago to refer, not to the handkerchief, but to the need to mislead Othello into thinking Iago loves him in order to further his, Iago's, stratagems; Berry, however, applies it to the handkerchief to summarize the metonymic function of the latter.) The handkerchief – the term is used in the text (as distinct from the stage directions) 26 times – is also referred to on three occasions as a 'napkin',[26] and Berry pursues the connotations of both these terms. As she points out, 'handkerchief' links etymologically, through the term 'couvre-chef', meaning 'a cover for the head', to the French verb 'couvrir', meaning 'to cover', and thus 'has a buried association both with the oriental veil' and also with 'covered' in the sense in which Iago uses it when he tells Brabantio: 'you'll have your daughter covered with a Barbary horse' (1.1.118–19) – 'covered' here being 'a term for copulation between a stallion and a mare'. The alternative and much less frequent term 'napkin' links with 'the material matrix or "pattern" to which Othello compares Desdemona before he kills her' – 'Thou cunning'st pattern of excelling nature' (5.2.11). It is also linked 'with the contrasting activities of both discovery and concealment' and 'has an etymological affinity with "map", from the Latin for napkin, *mappa*'.[27] Moreover, in the early modern era, the verb 'to napkin' could mean 'to wrap up' – Berry does not give an example but the earliest instance *OED* cites is from 1621, from the *Sermons* of the theologian and clergyman Robert Sanderson (1587–1663): 'Let every man beware of napkining up the talent, which was delivered him to trade withal'. As Berry sums up the matter:

■ Rather than Desdemona herself, it is this textural figure for a revelation that is also a concealment which constitutes the centrepiece of the dumb show that Othello finally observes in [4.1]. From his hiding place, Othello can hear nothing, which suits Iago perfectly; what he wants is to offer him a purely visual perspective on his own exchange with Cassio, which will actually be about Bianca rather than Desdemona.[28] □

It is Othello's willingness to trust this 'ocular proof' without calling on his other senses that leads to 'his ocularcentric tragedy'.[29]

Moving on to *Macbeth*, Berry asserts that it is Shakespeare's most suggestive tragedy in its exploration of 'pre-modern conceptions of temporal recurrence'[30] – that is, conceptions which stress cyclical rather than linear time. Berry deploys the idea of what she calls 'double time', using this phrase to mean the way in which the ostensible period in which a play is set finds parallels and repetitions in events that are contemporary with the time in which that play was written and first performed. *Macbeth* is a particularly prominent example of this, since it includes echoes of both the accession of James I and the life and execution of his mother, Mary Queen of Scots. There are also wider temporal dimensions to the play such as 'implicit allusions to classical myth, Biblical typology [the idea that the Old Testament offers 'types' – stories, images and characters – that prefigure the life of Christ in the New Testament] and Celtic antiquity along with its contradictory prophetic focus upon a future which is now the present'.[31]

The sense of recurrence and of a doubling of events within the time of the play is most evident in the parallels between its first and last acts. In the first act, the 'bloody' captain stresses how Macbeth, '[d]isdaining Fortune', 'unseamed' the rebel Macdonald 'from the nave [navel] to the chops' and 'fixed his head upon our battlements' (1.2.1, 19, 24, 25). (Berry points to the homophonic pun on 'nave' as 'knave', meaning 'rebel'.[32]) But the captain goes on to offer a meteorological simile:

■ As whence the sun 'gins his reflection [shining/return],
   Shipwrecking storms and direful thunders,
   So from that spring whence comfort seemed to come,
   Discomfort swells. Mark ['note, pay attention'], King of Scotland, mark:
   No sooner justice had, with valour armed,
   Compelled these skipping kerns [lightly armed foot soldiers] to trust their heels,
   But the Norwegian lord, surveying vantage,
   With furbished arms and new supplies of men,
   Began a fresh assault. (1.2.27–35) □

Berry glosses the first two lines to mean 'the wild weather that accompanies the sun's springtime "reflection" on its tropical turning back to the place of the vernal equinox';[33] there is an idea here of time going backwards, returning to the place where it began. This also comes across in the account of the repulse of the fresh attack of Norway and of the treacherous Thane of Cawdor whose defeat and execution will release the title for Duncan to bestow it on Macbeth:

■ Norway himself, with terrible numbers,
   Assisted by that most disloyal traitor,
   The Thane of Cawdor, began a dismal conflict
   Till that Bellona's bridegroom, lapped in proof,
   Confronted him with self-comparisons,
   Point against point, rebellious arm gainst arm,
   Curbing his lavish spirit: and to conclude,
   The victory fell on us – (1.3.56–63) □

Norway, newly reinforced and armed, and assisted by the Thane of Cawdor, moves forward again only to be driven back. These lines also highlight the likeness between the opponents – '[p]oint against point, rebellious arm gainst arm' – and anticipate the way in which Macbeth himself will soon acquire the title of 'that most disloyal traitor, / The Thane of Cawdor' and later himself become a 'most disloyal traitor'. In this battle, Macbeth and Banquo are likened to Christ, fighting as if 'they meant [...] to memorize [make memorable] another Golgotha ['"place of skulls" where Christ was crucified'] (1.2.41, 42).

These first-act events find parallels near the end of *Macbeth* in the mortal combat between Macbeth and Macduff. In the first act, Macbeth slew Macdonald to safeguard Duncan's power; now Macduff slays Macbeth to clear the path of Duncan's son, Malcolm, to the throne. Like Macdonald, the '(k)nave' and 'slave' whose head, in the first act, is finally 'fixed upon our battlements', Macbeth's fate is fixed even before the final fight and his head will be 'fixed' on a pole or lance afterwards – 'Behold where stands / Th'usurper's cursed head' (5.7.98–9). Berry highlights Macbeth's use of ursine imagery as he braces himself for combat: '[t]hey have tied me to a stake: I cannot fly, / But bear-like I must fight the course' (5.7.1–2). In the simile of the 'bear', Berry hears intimations of the Christian vision of the last confrontation between Christ and the Antichrist or Great Beast, after which time will stop. Whereas in the first act Macbeth, along with Banquo, could seem Christlike, aiming to repeat in his own body the wounds and suffering of the Crucifixion, he now takes the role of the bear or beast while Macduff partly assumes the role of Christ, although unlike Christ he was not 'of woman born' (5.7.50) in the straightforward sense. For Berry, the ursine image also calls to mind the idea of a reversion, a backsliding in time, 'to a prehuman or animal state' like that of the *nigredo* in alchemy – the putrefaction or decomposition that reduces materials to black matter in the alchemical process. Another element in that process is *silva*, the Latin for 'wood', and this links up with the apparently moving wood near the end of *Macbeth* which reinforces the idea of 'a return of, or to, the state of primal matter'. Finally, Macduff's verbal salute to Malcolm, as he reappears with Macbeth's head – 'Hail, king, for so thou art' (5.7.98) – and its echo and more exact specification by 'All' – 'Hail, King of Scotland!' (5.7.104) – recalls the witches' hails in the first act to Macbeth and Banquo (1.3.50–3, 64–6, 70–1).

As these examples suggest, *Shakespeare's Feminine Endings* offers very ingenious interpretations of specific Shakespeare tragedies. Berry's approach involves close – very close – reading but not of a kind that aims to restrict itself to 'the words on the page' – or rather of a kind that assumes that grasping the meaning of 'the words on the page' always involves the nuanced and informed exploration of the wider networks of discourse in which those words take on meaning. In Berry's case, these wider networks are mainly those which once fell under the rubric of the 'history of ideas' – for example, early modern ideas about time as cyclical rather than linear; about alchemy and the transformation of matter; about a vital, renovating principle in nature that is revealed in the process of decay. Although Berry engages to some extent with history, for instance in her discussion of the relationship of *Macbeth* to the reign of a Jacobean king whose mother had been executed by his female predecessor, she is not as evidently concerned with political ideology as Leonard Tennenhouse. And she is certainly not a presentist in the manner suggested by the title of Jan Kott's book (discussed in Chapter 7 of this Guide): in Berry's perspective, if Shakespeare is our contemporary, he is only revealed as such if we first attend carefully to the ways in which his work and the discourses of his time differ from ours (though Kott does in fact sometimes invoke the meaning words had in Shakespeare's time, as in his observation that 'nunnery', in *Hamlet* (3.1.125), could also mean 'brothel'). Like Janet Adelman, however, Berry does valorize – ascribe value and validity to – the feminine, elevating its worth in understanding Shakespeare's plays; but the threatening mothers of Adelman's Shakespearean tragedy-scape give way to figures that are, at least potentially, more benign.

This is the most striking aspect of Berry's argument: her book might also be called 'Notes towards the Dissolution of Tragedy'. For, in her perspective, Shakespeare's 'feminine endings' – the diction and imagery in which the deaths of his chief female figures are evoked – macerate the hard rocks of tragedy, opening up the possibility of ongoing life beyond the individual, not in a spiritual but in a supposedly 'base' material sense; and this possibility is figured through women rather than men. Moreover, Shakespeare's tragedies, in Berry's perspective, implicitly contain a critique of cherished notions of Western civilization: for example, ocularcentrism, the idea that vision offers privileged cognitive access to truth; linearity, the idea that time is a matter of forward progress rather than cyclical reversion; masculinity, defined in terms of the exclusion of the feminine; the spiritual, seen as opposite and superior to the material. If Berry challenges the very notion of tragedy as applied to Shakespeare, she also elevates his tragedies to supreme status as diagnoses of the philosophical errors of Western culture that produce tragedy, not only on the stage, but also in real life. It is to the diagnoses of masculinity in the Roman plays, as analysed by Coppélia Kahn, which we now turn.

Coppélia Kahn

The 'central claim' of Coppélia Kahn's *Roman Shakespeare: Warriors, Wounds and Women* (1997) is 'that Shakespeare's Roman works [in which

Kahn includes the poem *The Rape of Lucrece* (1594)] articulate a critique of the ideology of gender on which the Renaissance understanding of Rome was based'.[34] The book develops the interest in 'identifying a gender-specific dimension – an identification with the masculine subject – in Shakespeare' that Kahn had pursued in an earlier study, *Man's Estate: Masculine Identity in Shakespeare* (1981),[35] but this time she puts less emphasis on psychoanalysis and more on 'an ideology discursively maintained through the appropriation of the Latin heritage for the early modern English stage'. Kahn seeks 'to identify and interpret the centrality of a specifically Roman masculinity to Rome as represented' in Shakespeare's Roman writings[36] and in this perspective analyses, among the tragedies, *Titus Andronicus*, *Julius Caesar*, *Antony and Cleopatra* and *Coriolanus*.

The subtitle of Kahn's book, *Warriors, Wounds, and Women*, indicates three main elements of the representation of Roman virtue in Shakespeare's work. 'Warriors' suggests 'the central motif of the Greco-Roman heroic tradition – the agon', or contest, in which the hero gains his reputation by confronting 'his likeness or equal in contests of courage and strength'. Kahn observes that '[f]rom Achilles and Hector to Antony and Octavius, pairs of evenly matched heroes act out a mixture of admiration, imitation and domination'– a mixture which is known, in the early modern period, as 'emulation'. *OED* defines the verb 'to emulate' as meaning '[t]o strive to equal or rival (a person, his achievements or qualities); to copy or imitate with the object of equalling or excelling'. But, Kahn points out, the effort 'to equal or rival' can become 'the desire to defeat or destroy [the emulated person] and take his place', creating a split within the idea of *virtus*. As Kahn puts it: '[e]mulation figures and enacts the differences *within* the masculine; thus it fractures a seemingly unified *virtus*'.[37]

The second element of Shakespeare's representation of manly virtue is 'wounds'. Kahn contends that the wound is 'a fetish of masculinity' that is crucial in signifying masculine virtue and constructing the Roman hero. But it is a contradictory signifier: as Kahn points out, the Latin noun for 'wound' is *vulnus*, from which the noun 'vulnerability' comes, and 'wounds mark a kind of vulnerability easily associated with women'. The extent to which wounds feature in Shakespeare's Roman texts varies, but, Kahn asserts, 'they are a central, recurring image that invariably signifies instabilities underlying the apparent firmness of Roman virtue'.[38]

'Woman' is the third element in Shakespeare's representation of manly virtue. Women are seen as opposite and inferior to men but masculine identity depends on them for its own superior self-definition. Qualities that do not conform to manly virtue are projected on to women and women are used as an excuse for the appearance of such qualities in men; but the projection is not always successful and the 'feminine' aspects can remain inside the masculine, causing self-division. Women as mothers are crucial to the continuance of Rome and may themselves take on the task of turning their sons into men but nonetheless produce a division in the male subject between supposedly masculine and supposedly feminine feelings, as does Coriolanus' mother, Volumnia.

Focusing on *Julius Caesar*, Kahn points out that Shakespeare adds an example of emulation to his source in Plutarch. This is when Cassius recalls his swimming contest with Caesar:

■ For once, upon a raw and gusty day,
The troubled Tiber chafing with her shores,
Caesar said to me, 'Dar'st thou, Cassius, now
Leap in with me to this angry flood
And swim to yonder point?' Upon the word,
Accoutrèd as I was, I plungèd in
And bade him follow: so indeed he did.
The torrent roared, and we did buffet it ['beat it back']
With lusty sinews, throwing it aside,
And stemming it with hearts of controversy.
But ere we could arrive the point proposed,
Caesar cried, 'Help me, Cassius, or I sink!'
I – as Aeneas, our great ancestor,
Did from the flames of Troy upon his shoulder
The old Anchises bear – so from the waves of Tiber
Did I the tired Caesar: (1.2.106–21) □

This swimming contest – which Caesar does not merely lose but in which he has abjectly to call on his opponent for help to save him from drowning – is an example, in microcosm, of the more general competitiveness of life in the ancient Roman republic, as mediated through Elizabethan culture. Such competitiveness generates a contradiction in Roman ideology and in the project of the conspirators against Caesar: their 'assumption that all Romans are brothers, united by their shared belief in the republic, is flatly contradicted by an equally Roman spirit of emulation'. While the envy of Cassius may seem to contrast with the altruism of Brutus, the latter, Kahn suggests, shares 'the drive to excel over his fellow republicans'; 'he competes in precisely republican terms which, paradoxically, make civic altruism the touchstone of distinction among men'.[39]

Wounds and women feature in the scene with Brutus and Portia (one of only two female characters in the play, the other being Calpurnia, Caesar's wife). Here Brutus's inner doubts are given voice through the feminine, through Portia, who also bears the masculine insignia of a self-inflicted wound in the thigh:

■ I grant I am a woman: but withal
  A woman well-reputed, Cato's daughter.
  Think you I am no stronger than my sex
  Being so fathered and so husbanded?
  Tell me your counsels, I will not disclose 'em.
  I have made strong proof of my constancy,
  Giving myself a voluntary wound
  Here in the thigh: can I bear that with patience
  And not my husband's secrets? (2.1.306–14) □

As Kahn points out, Portia acknowledges here that she is a female but asserts that she has a good reputation and that she draws strength from two men: her father, a sternly moral man who committed suicide rather than bow to Caesar, and her husband, Brutus. But, Kahn contends, it is 'above all by wounding herself that she imitates a man's constancy'.[40] This self-wounding, however, undermines the wound as a symbol of maleness. If a woman can produce, by her own act, this key mark of masculinity, it can no longer be the exclusive sign of a man and becomes a performance, behaviour that is learned rather than innate to a masculine 'essence'. Kahn sees this as an example of the return of the repressed, the psychoanalytic concept we discussed in considering Janet Adelman's readings of Shakespearean tragedy. The feminine is repressed to constitute maleness but returns to trouble maleness from within when it utters repressed 'feminine' feeling and takes on supposedly masculine characteristics, thus destabilizing their identity as the supposedly exclusive property of the male.

In the following scene, the woman – Caesar's wife, Calpurnia – again expresses the fears the man – Caesar himself – has repressed. She invokes a range of portents and tries to persuade him to stay at home. Caesar claims this would be cowardly but eventually agrees to do so 'for thy humour ['whim, fancy']' (2.2.59) and tells Decius of his wife's dream:

■ Calpurnia here, my wife, stays me at home:
  She dreamt tonight she saw my statue,
  Which, like a fountain with an hundred spouts,
  Did run pure blood, and many lusty Romans
  Came smiling and did bathe their hands in it.
  And these does she apply for warnings and portents
  And evils imminent, and on her knee
  Hath begged that I will stay at home today. (2.2.79–86) □

Decius responds with a positive interpretation of Calpurnia's dream that also, as Kahn points out, emasculates Caesar by its 'odd but suggestively Roman vision of a nursing mother':[41]

■ This dream is all amiss interpreted.
　It was a vision, fair and fortunate:
　Your statue spouting blood in many pipes
　In which so many smiling Romans bathed,
　Signifies that from you great Rome shall suck
　Reviving blood [...] (2.2.87–92) □

Caesar is thus feminized, and his assassination amplifies this process of feminization. Antony compares Caesar's knife wounds to 'dumb mouths' which 'do ope their ruby lips / To beg the voice and utterance of my tongue' (3.1.279–80). Kahn suggests that the wounds are like women in their voicelessness, requiring a male tongue in order to speak. Disingenuously disclaiming oratorical skill as he addresses the plebeians, Antony says that if he had Brutus's eloquence, he would 'put a tongue / In every wound of Caesar that should move / The stones of Rome to rise and mutiny' (3.2.24–6) – but of course that is precisely what Antony is doing. As Kahn summarizes it: 'Antony's rhetoric, his "tongue", is [...] the phallic instrument that transforms Caesar's inert, passively bleeding body into a vehicle of political power'. Antony appeals to 'feminine' emotions in his audience when he shows Caesar's bloodstained and punctured mantle (cloak) – 'If you have tears, prepare to shed them now' (3.2.166). He also, Kahn argues, presents vengeance in a feminized way. 'Its matrix is pity and fear, the release of tender and passionate feelings' which are then easily transmuted into '[d]omestic fury and fierce civil strife' (3.1.282). Prior to his address to the crowd, Antony forecasts that:

■ Blood and destruction shall be so in use,
　And dreadful objects so familiar,
　That mothers shall but smile when they behold
　Their infants quartered with the hand of war,
　All pity choked with custom of fell deeds [...] (3.1.284–8) □

Antony's forecast is fulfilled. As Kahn puts it, '[u]nrestrained emotions deaf to the general good and insensible to reason overtake the Roman republic and its new leaders'. The feminization and humiliation of Caesar, 'once the embodiment of *virtus* as conqueror of Europe and Asia [and] victor over Pompey', releases 'the most fearsome and destructive images of the feminine [to] possess Rome'.[42] For Kahn, this is another example of the return of the repressed.

Kahn argues that 'Brutus is a tragic hero' because 'in him the contradictions embedded in his culture are set at war'. These, as we have seen, are twofold. First, 'as a Roman [male], he acts both for the general good and out of emulation, in that he wants to stand above other men – in his devotion to the general good'.[43] Second, Portia's voicing of his own doubts about killing Caesar enables him to dismiss these doubts as feminine and reinforces his idea that the assassination will exemplify manly virtue.

Roman Shakespeare provides an insightful account of how Shakespeare's Roman works both use and question the ideas of Roman masculinity that the early modern period had appropriated and constructed. It demonstrates how *Julius Caesar*, a play with only two female characters, each of whom speaks in only two scenes, can nonetheless be pervaded by ideas of femininity which provide the supposedly inferior 'other' against which a 'superior' masculinity constructs itself but which can also invade that masculinity to subvert and destabilize it. Kahn's book also traces this construction and destabilization of masculinity through Shakespeare's other Roman work. It locates the source of tragedy in these plays, as with Brutus, in the denial of the feminine. But another kind of construction and destabilization to explore in Shakespeare's plays is that of fixed heterosexual orientation and, beyond that, of all fixed positions and boundaries. This is the topic of the next book we shall consider, by Madhavi Menon, which has a punningly defiant title: *Shakesqueer*.

Madhavi Menon, Jason Edwards

Madhavi Menon's multivoiced volume *Shakesqueer: A Queer Companion to the Complete Works of Shakespeare* (2011) aims, as its compound main title suggests, to bring together Shakespeare, queer theory and early modern studies. Queer theory is an eclectic movement that draws on feminism, gender studies, psychoanalysis, poststructuralism and deconstruction to question fixed meanings and presumed finalities. It does not focus only on same-sex relationships, or the intimations of such relationships, in fictional characters and texts or actual authors or cultures, although these may sometimes be the places where the unsettling of fixities becomes most evident. Given its aversion to containment, its remit can be anything and everything. Nonetheless, it has been inclined to focus on the post-1800 period, where the correlation between identity and sexual preference, and the idea of the homosexual emerge – before that, in the early modern period, there was sodomy but no homosexuals.

There is, however, one clear link between queer theory and Shakespeare: the answer to the question 'What is queer theory?' could be the same as the answer to the question: 'What is Shakespeare?', which is, in Menon's words: 'All things that militate against the obvious, the settled, and the understood – in other words, nothing that may be fully or finally grasped.'[44] The critical history we have traced so far in this Guide provides ample evidence that Shakespeare's meanings militate against 'the obvious, the settled, and the understood' and offer 'nothing that may be fully or finally grasped' – despite repeated critical attempts to arrest their significance. Shakespeare's works appeared before the modern concept of the 'homosexual', and it is anachronistic to define his characters and situations, or Shakespeare himself, as gay; but, by the same token, these can hardly be defined as straight either. In fact, they give the same answer to another question Menon poses: 'What does a homosexual look like?' Queer theory's answer, according to Menon, is 'I do not know'. If this question is put to Shakespeare's works, these also reply: 'I do not know'. In this refusal of definitions and boundaries, this acknowledgement of uncertainty, Shakespeare's works and queer theory operate in the same way.

There is a considerable amount of boundary breaking in Menon's book. One element of this is that, aiming to bring Shakespeare and queer studies together, she includes contributions from those who belong to both fields, such as Jonathan Goldberg and Alan Sinfield, and those queer theorists who most usually concern themselves with post-1800 literature and art. An example of the latter is Jason Edwards, who describes himself as 'a professional queer-theory art historian'[45] (at the University of York in the UK) and who specializes in the Victorian period and had avoided Shakespeare's work since the age of 19. He tackles *Coriolanus*, 'knowing little about it except the old joke [...] about the New Historicists being the scholars who put the anus back into *Coriolanus* and the knickers back into *Titus Andronicus*'.[46] As the second part of his title suggests – 'Queer Meditations on *Coriolanus* in the Time of War' – Edwards is, in some respects, an unashamed presentist, relating the play to his aversion to the UK/US military actions in Iraq and Afghanistan; but he is also concerned to draw out the queer meanings of the play. *Coriolanus* is, he contends, 'explicit about the male homosocial desire that binds military corpuses together and its tragic costs'[47] and he gives several examples. This is Martius (Coriolanus) to Cominius:[48]

■ O, let me clip [embrace] ye
   In arms as sound as when I wooed in heart,
   As merry as when our nuptial day was done,
   And tapers burned to bedward. (1.6.35–8) □

Aufidius speaks of Coriolanus as his enemy in phrases with homoerotic connotations:

■ If e'er again I meet him beard to beard
  He's mine, or I am his: mine emulation
  Hath not that honour in't had: for where
  I thought to crush him in an equal force,
  True sword to sword, I'll potch [poke, thrust] at him (1.10.11–15) □

Later, when Coriolanus comes to Aufidius' house in Antium to offer his services to his former enemy, Aufidius says to his old opponent:[49]

■ [...] Let me twine
  Mine arms about that body, where against
  My grained ash an hundred times hath broke
  And scared the moon with splinters: here I clip
  The anvil of my sword [the 'anvil' is Coriolanus, 'who has been struck
  by Aufidius' "sword" as an anvil is hit with a hammer'], and do contest
  As hotly and as nobly with thy love
  As ever in ambitious strength I did
  Contend against thy valour. Know thou first,
  I loved the maid I married: never man
  Sighed truer breath. But that I see thee here,
  Thou noble thing, more dances my rapt heart
  Than when I first my wedded mistress saw
  Bestride my threshold. (4.5.103–15) □

Despite Aufidius' assertion of heterosexual desire and attachment – 'I loved the maid I married' – it is now the sight of Coriolanus that makes his 'rapt heart' dance more.

The kind of reading Edwards offers here is a first-level queer analysis, which teases out homoerotic suggestions in ostensibly heterosexual characters and situations, 'queering' a supposedly straight text. But, Edwards continues, *Coriolanus* is 'perhaps also queer [...] in a second, less familiar and more recent way in that it displaces from center stage the notion of *sexual* identity'. It does this, first, by 'imagining desire as only one gravitational pull within a much richer, queerer, ever altering early modern constellation'[50] of attractions, pleasures and promptings; and, second, by challenging 'models of intersubjectivity imagined to be ideally and primarily predicated on the genital desire of one person for another'. Indeed, 'it almost entirely fails to mention the genitals or ass', despite its copious references to the body and to body parts.[51] Contact between bodies or what issues from them (for instance, smells) is mainly 'imagined as assault or defense'.[52]

This hostile bodily contact helps to make *Coriolanus* a tragedy; but the play contains intimations of other possibilities:

■ Its hero gets a fatal and martial, not a happy, marital ending, whether with Virgilia or Aufidius. But because all of our bodies are inextricably in 'the weal [commonwealth]' [2.3.162], and because one cannot, as the play insists, be entirely the author of one's self and know 'no other kin' (5.3.36–8), we might want to use *Coriolanus* as an opportunity to explore its unspoken, imagined, comic opposite – an alternative, possible, queerly utopian model of sociability to the phobic, militaristic, homosexually panicked one still experienced by many of Shakespeare's audience.[53] □

Here, then, we find a contemporary relevance asserted for *Coriolanus* – it is, in Edwards' view, a critique of a negative 'model of sociability' that still exists in the twenty-first-century and becomes evident in conflicts such as those in Iraq and Afghanistan – and a desire which extends, in the twentieth century, from A. C. Bradley to Philippa Berry, to go beyond tragedy, or, rather, to use the authority of tragedy to reveal how tragedy goes beyond itself, adumbrating other, positive possibilities beyond its bleak conclusions.

The movement of queer theory away from a focus on sexual identity may seem, of course, to rob such theory of its distinctive identity – even if, given the premises of queer theory, such an identity is illusory and undesirable. Certainly such a movement opens the way to examining other elements of that 'early modern constellation' that Edwards evokes, both in their difference from and resonance with us, a dual perspective which we might call 'Shakespeare Not/Our Contemporary'. In the next chapter, we explore two of these other elements – ethnicity and ecology – in that dual perspective, discussing work by Barbara Everett, Ania Loomba, Gabriel Egan and Simon C. Estok.

CHAPTER TEN

Ethnicity and Ecology

This chapter considers critical explorations of Shakespearean tragedy in relation to two modern approaches that take a global purview – ethnicity and ecology. Both approaches involve a mixture of close textual analysis, historical investigation and 'presentism', as they seek to analyse Shakespeare's plays in ethnic and ecological perspectives, to tease out Elizabethan and Jacobean attitudes to race and nature, and to relate them to the twenty-first century. We begin with Margo Hendricks's introduction to *Shakespeare and Race* (2000) and then focus on Barbara Everett's essay, '"Spanish" Othello: the Making of Shakespeare's Moor' (1982), from the same volume.

Barbara Everett

Shakespeare and Race (edited by Catherine M. S. Alexander and Stanley Wells) consists of 13 essays, 11 originally published in *Shakespeare Survey* between 1958 and 1999 and two (by Margo Hendricks and Celia R. Dailreader) written specially for the volume. The book aims to show that there was scholarly and critical work addressing the issue of Shakespeare and race prior to the emergence of postcolonial theory. In the first chapter, which effectively serves as an introduction to the whole book, Margo Hendricks describes her interest in race in Shakespeare as not limited to 'the obvious markers' – *Othello, The Merchant of Venice, Titus Andronicus* and *Antony and Cleopatra* – but extending to 'the epistemology of race'[1] in Shakespeare's time: what kind of 'knowledges' of race did the early modern period produce? Hendricks contends that 'early modern English usage of the word "race" reveals a multiplicity of loci, of axes of determinism, [of] metaphorical systems to aid and abet its deployment across a variety of boundaries in the making'. In 'all these variations', however, 'race is envisioned as [...] fundamental [...] immutable, knowable and recognizable', yet only becoming 'visible' when 'its boundaries are violated'. It is thus, 'paradoxically, mysterious, illusory and mutable'[2] – a paradox dramatized in Shakespeare's plays.

A fascinating example in this volume of a relatively early exploration of race in relation to the tragedy that most obviously engages with it is '"Spanish" Othello: the Making of Shakespeare's Moor' (1982) by Barbara Everett. 'Iago,' Everett observes, 'is, in Spanish, the same name' as that of King James I, a fact that could hardly have escaped Shakespeare's notice, given his elaborate tribute to his royal master in the vision of the line of kings leading from Banquo to James in *Macbeth*. Shakespeare's audience would have noticed it too, because 'at that time, "Iago" was of all names the most recognizable both as Spanish and as James'.[3] As Everett explains, St James was Spain's patron saint, with many shrines across the peninsula, most notably Santiago de Compostela, a place of pilgrimage second only to Rome in size. His adoption as Spain's patron saint was due to his supposed manifestation at several events, the most notable being the fictional battle of Clavijo between Spanish Christians and Muslims, where James's appearance was held to have enabled the Christians to win against heavy odds. After this saintly intervention, St James was called in Spain 'Santiago Matamoros', meaning 'St James the Moor-killer'. It is this link between Saint Iago and the Moor, Everett suggests, that accounts for Shakespeare's use of the name Iago in *Othello*, even at the risk of offending King James I. According to Everett, 'the reiteration, in the play's first scene, of "Rodrigo [another Spanish name, and the first character to be named after the opening stage directions] … Iago … the Moor" gave to the work and its hero a Spanish resonance that nothing else could effect so briefly and successfully'. Each of Othello's utterances of 'Iago' would have resonated with audiences in Shakespeare's time who would have known 'that Santiago's great role in Spain was as enemy to the invading Moor, who was figurehead there of the Muslim kingdom'.[4]

While acknowledging that not too much should be made of the significance of names, Everett nonetheless points to reasons why Spanish names, and the term 'Moor', might have had special resonance for the English in the early seventeenth century. Despite the Armada defeat, Spain was still the most powerful nation in Europe at this time and, as such, figured strongly in English consciousness. Moreover, from 1602 to 1604, a French spy in London, Saint-Etienne, tried to secure support for the rebellious Moors in Valencia from the British government; but James I's pro-Spanish policy made Britain hang back. For years before this, Protestant England, perhaps because of its defeat of the Armada, had become a place of asylum for Moors fleeing Spain and this had resulted in two royal edicts (1599, 1601) requiring that these refugees be transported from England, because '[the] Queen's Majesty is discontented at the great number of negars and blackamoors which are crept into the realm since the troubles between her Highness and the King of Spain, and are fostered here to the annoyance of their own people, which want the relief consumed by these people ...'[5] Everett observes that it was usual in England, on into the seventeenth century, to call Moors 'negars and blackamoors' but that 'the ancestors of these Spanish Moors, the Moors who invaded and conquered the peninsula in the eighth century, were principally of the Berber strain' and their 'culture' was 'Islamic'. [6] These Moors would not have stood out visually from other Spaniards in London. But in Spain itself, their position had become increasingly difficult. The nationalist and imperialist thrust of fifteenth- and sixteenth-century Spain had led to the expulsion of all Jews who refused to undergo Christian baptism and, after that, to a campaign against the Moors. When the Moors made it clear they would hang on to their cultural identity, intense ethnic and religious conflict followed, culminating in 1609, five years after *Othello* was first performed in November 1604, in the expulsion from Spain of all Moors, baptized as Christians or unbaptized.

Everett argues that 'the tragedy of the real-life Spanish Moor was that he was, whatever his colour, in all important senses indistinguishable from his fellow Spaniards'. Over 500 years of history in the Spanish peninsula 'had produced a "Spain", in the age of nationalism, that was one intense identity-crisis, of which the Moor was essentially no more than the point of breakdown'. When, at the start of *Othello*, two characters with Spanish names, Iago and Rodrigo, talk 'with hatred, envy and derision of "the Moor"', whom they regard as 'a civilized barbarian of fierce and repressed lusts', they evoke, by analogy, a political situation known to Shakespeare and his audience.[7] But for Everett, their creator does not share their attitudes; rather, she suggests that for Shakespeare:

■ The Moor is a member of a more interesting and more permanent people: the race of the displaced and dispossessed, of Time's always-vulnerable wanderers: he is one of the strangers who do not belong where they once ruled and now have no claim to the ancient 'royal siege'. [1.2.24][8] □

If these remarks may seem to make Othello a universal character in a way that elides his historical and ethnic specificity, Everett counters this by pursuing her idea of a 'Spanish Othello' in relation to sixteenth- and seventeenth-century cultural history. In doing so, she also partly accounts for the comic aspect of Shakespeare's play, the way its protagonist can seem a buffoon. She identifies a 'romantic–picaresque polarity and contrast' in sixteenth-century Spanish history and culture, which found rich artistic expression in the Spanish novel *Don Quixote* (Part 1, 1605; Part II, 1615) by Miguel de Cervantes (1547–1616), with its pairing of its idealistic titular hero and the down-to-earth Sancho Panza. This romantic–picaresque polarity, Everett asserts, must have informed the English idea of Spanish culture and entered into *Othello*. *Don Quixote*, along with picaresque novels such as the anonymous *The Life of Lazarillo de Tormes and His Fortunes and Adversities* (1554), and the first Don Juan play *El Burlador de Sevilla* [*The Trickster of Seville*] (1630), possibly by Tirso de Molina (pseud. of Gabriel Téllez (?1580–1648)) also initiated, in European literature 'the vitally significant theme of the master and the man', and Shakespeare puts this theme into *Othello* by making Iago the Moor's servant rather than, as in his source, his friend. Everett contends that the 'horror of Shakespeare's "temptation scene" [3.3] is its corruption and inversion of the master–servant relationship', which exemplifies how *Othello* is 'impregnated with the subject of power and social hierarchies'.[9]

The idea of Othello as a Spanish Moor links up with what Everett calls 'a strange compound of the high-idealistic and the derisively picaresque' that pervades the play. Its protagonist's 'imagination is enormously, preposterously vulnerable to the sense of social shame', while Iago, as the voice of rough common sense, is not utterly unsympathetic. Othello's preposterousness and Iago's brutally realistic 'voice from underground' give the play its capacity for what Everett calls 'frightful comedy': it is 'at once the most romantic of Shakespeare's tragedies and the one most filled by an ugly obdurate [...] humour', like that of the Elizabethan satirist and pamphleteer Thomas Nashe (1567–1601).[10]

Everett also identifies, however, another reason for the comic element of *Othello*. Its two major dramatic settings, the street and the dockside, are traditionally found in ancient Greek New Comedy, whose most prominent practitioner was Menander (341–290 BC) and which mildly mocked the mores of middle-ranking citizens in Athenian society, and in its successor, ancient Roman comedy. In the early modern period, learned or erudite Italian comedy (*commedia erudita*), written and privately performed for elite audiences and focusing on contemporary upper-class issues, inherited from ancient Greek and Roman comedy the figure of 'the braggart soldier' and, Everett argues, often fused this with a new figure generated within learned Italian comedy itself, that of the deceived husband, the cuckold (*cornuto*). Moreover, learned Italian comedy turned the braggart soldier into the *Spanish* soldier, as a way of hitting back, through drama, at the ruthless Spanish mercenaries who threatened the Italian territories in the sixteenth century. The *commedia erudita* passed these features on to popular professional comedy (*commedia dell'arte*), in which travelling troupes of masked actors played stock characters, and the traces of such elements persist in *Othello*. Clearly Othello is neither an actual cuckold nor a braggart soldier; but nonetheless Shakespeare's play 'contains devices that seem a distant disturbing ironical echo of braggart conventions' evident in Italian learned comedies.[11]

Everett's excellent essay certainly supports Margo Hendricks' claim that scholars and critics were working in the field of 'Shakespeare and

Race' before postcolonial criticism came fully on to the scene. With a mixture of historical scholarship, discourse analysis and genre study, Everett creates a new and illuminating perspective on *Othello* and a plausible explanation for its comic elements. Her essay is not dominated by 'close reading' of the primary text but moves outside 'the words on the page' to bring in other discursive and ideological features that alter our understandings of those words. More explicit engagement with issues of ethnicity in a postcolonial mode can be found in the work of Ania Loomba, who fittingly contributes the closing essay to *Shakespeare and Race* and develops her ideas more extensively in the next book we consider, *Shakespeare, Race, and Colonialism*.

Ania Loomba

Ania Loomba's *Shakespeare, Race, and Colonialism* (2002) pursues the usages of the term 'race' in Shakespeare and his culture, the way beliefs about skin colour and identity combined to produce altering ideas about the differences between races. Loomba discusses, among Shakespeare's tragedies, *Titus Andronicus*, with its dramatization of the intersection of notions about blackness and about deviant womanhood in the early modern period; *Othello*, which weaves into these notions an important religious element; and *Antony and Cleopatra*, with its deployment of the layers of discourses from different periods that constitute racial ideologies. In this section we shall focus on *Titus Andronicus* and see how Loomba's approach draws out fascinating aspects of a play which still sits uncertainly in Shakespeare's tragic canon.

Loomba contends that the figure of Aaron in *Titus* evokes 'older stereotypes about barbarism, black sexuality, and evil' which 'mediate newer anxieties about nation, religion, race, and femininity'.[12] While most of the characters partake in the play's slaughter and brutality, Aaron is the living scapegoat at the end, denounced as 'an irreligious Moor. / Chief architect and plotter of these woes' and 'breeder of these dire events' (5.3.121–2, 178), and condemned by Lucius to a slow and painful death:

> ■ Set him breast-deep in earth and famish him:
> There let him stand and rave and cry for food.
> If anyone relieves or pities him
> For the offence he dies. This is our doom [sentence]: (5.3.179–82) □

As Loomba points out, however, Aaron is not the 'chief architect and plotter' in the way that Iago is in *Othello*, though the two are often compared. Nonetheless, it may be possible to see a partial similarity in motivation. Loomba takes issue with Coleridge's famous attribution of 'motiveless malignity' to Iago,[13] which we considered in Chapter 2 of this Guide, contending that Iago can be seen as driven by 'racial and class envy of Othello'.[14] Aaron might also be motivated by the desire to improve his social position as slave, following the example of his lover, Tamora, the Queen of the Goths, which he outlines:

> ■ Then, Aaron, arm thy heart and fit thy thoughts
> To mount aloft with thy imperial mistress,
> And mount her pitch whom thou in triumph long
> Hast prisoner held, fettered in amorous chains
> [...]
> I will be bright, and shine in pearl and gold
> To wait upon this new-made emperess.
> To wait, said I? – To wanton with this queen,
> This goddess, this Semiramis ['Assyrian queen famed for beauty, cruelty and lust'], this nymph,
> The siren that will charm Rome's Saturnine
> And see his shipwreck [...] (2.1.12–15, 19–24) □

Aaron wants to 'mount aloft' with Tamora who is his mistress in both senses, his owner and lover. Perhaps, Loomba suggests, his organizing of her vengeance on the Romans is a way of making himself indispensable to her and, if Rome is defeated, of gaining real power. When Tamora suggests they make love, Aaron replies: 'Madam, though Venus govern your desires, / Saturn is dominator over mine [the 'influence [of the planet Saturn] was supposed to make men sullen and melancholy']' and asserts to her that '[v]engeance is in my heart, death in my hand' (2.3.30–1, 38). Loomba points out that Aaron only avoids conforming to 'the stereotype of the lusty Moor' in this scene by fulfilling another stereotype, that of the malignant, if not motiveless, black.[15]

Moreover, as Loomba points out, Aaron stresses this stereotype himself, making his blackness the sign and even the source of his evil. In the speech to Tamora quoted in the previous paragraph, he speaks of his 'fleece of woolly hair that now uncurls / Even as an adder [a poisonous snake] when she doth unroll / To do some fatal execution' (2.3.34–6). After he cuts off Titus' hand (at Titus' request), he declares: 'Let fools do good and fair men call for grace. / Aaron will have his soul black like his face' (3.1.205–6). In the first scene of Act 5, he assumes and magnifies the accusations of evil made against him in the course of the play:

> ■ Even now I curse the day – and yet I think
> Few come within the compass of my curse –

Wherein I did not some notorious ill,
As kill a man or else devise his death,
Ravish a maid or plot the way to do it,
Accuse some innocent and forswear myself,
Set deadly enmity between two friends,
Make poor men's cattle break their necks,
Set fire on barns and haystacks in the night
And bid the owners quench them with their tears.
Oft have I digged up dead men from their graves
And set them upright at their dear friends' door,
Even when their sorrows almost was forgot,
And on their skins, as on the bark of trees,
Have with my knife carved in Roman letters,
'Let not your sorrow die, though I am dead.'
Tut, I have done a thousand dreadful things
As willingly as one would kill a fly,
And nothing grieves me heartily indeed
But that I cannot do ten thousand more. (5.1.126–45) □

Loomba raises the question of whether 'Aaron's exultation in his own wickedness indicate[s] his defiant attempt to control a hostile environment and to manipulate a society in whose eye he can do no good anyway'. She points to twentieth-century black political movements that have deliberately and defiantly adopted as badges of pride the insults directed against them and have sometimes advocated retaliatory violence against their oppressors. But Loomba finds that Aaron's 'delight in crime is presented as haphazard, connected not to his race or class consciousness, but to his race and class themselves', thus reinforcing the stereotype of the 'motiveless malignity of blacks'.[16]

Loomba argues, however, that Aaron is not merely 'a stock figure of black villainy'.[17] She contends that, '[f]or all his wickedness, Aaron only intervenes in and redirects a dynamic of rivalry and revenge between the Goths and the Romans whose logic has already been set in motion'. Although the conflict is initially posed as one between the barbarous Goths and the civilized Romans, the two sides, both internally riven, act like cracked mirrors of each other whose fragments increasingly interpenetrate until, at the end of the play, they form what Loomba calls, citing Philip C. Kolin, a 'Rainbow Coalition', like 'those multi-racial, multi-ethnic groups found in contemporary society'.[18] But this rainbow excludes the colour black: Goths and Romans are at their closest in their sense of distance from Aaron, especially in his scandalous relationship with Tamora. In regard to this relationship, ideas of blackness merge with the figure of the 'lusty widow'. Even though Tamora may not be a widow, she is certainly without a husband and has three sons. To an early modern audience, Loomba suggests, 'Tamora's sexuality is especially threatening because she is a powerful older woman' who effectively menaces 'a social order which decrees that women should be subordinate to fathers and husbands'.[19] Her relationship with Aaron compounds this threat with a perceived racial one. As Loomba puts it: *'Titus Andronicus*, along with many others of Shakespeare's plays, registers the way in which emergent ideologies of race complicate feudal alliances and warfare, and it does so obliquely by aligning dangerous femininity with blackness.'[20]

Moreover, the alliance of 'dangerous femininity with blackness' produces its outward and visible sign, a baby boy who is 'the only interracial child in Shakespeare's plays'. He is not welcomed into the world. The nurse calls him a 'devil' and a 'joyless, dismal, black, and sorrowful issue' who is 'as loathsome as a toad' (4.2.66, 68, 69). She passes on to Aaron Tamora's command that he 'christen it with thy dagger's point' (4.2. 72) – that is, kill it, an order approved by Tamora's sons, Chiron and Demetrius: the former declares '[i]t shall not live' and the latter offers 'to broach the tadpole on my rapier's point'. Aaron, however, bad though he usually may be, resists, asking them '[w]ill you kill your brother?' But Demetrius says '[b]y this [baby], our mother is forever shamed' and Chiron observes 'Rome will despise her for this foul escape ['sexual transgression']' (4.2.114, 115). Later, Lucius calls the child 'the base fruit of his [Aaron's] burning lust' (5.1.43) and orders him to be hanged, but when Aaron offers a full confession in exchange for his child's life, Lucius agrees to 'swear by [his] god' to Aaron's stipulations that Lucius will 'save my boy [...] nourish, and bring him up' (5.1.87, 85). At the end of the play, Lucius has not reneged on this promise, though we know nothing of the boy's fate, perhaps because, as Loomba says, the 'interracial child' is 'so disturbing an idea that the play cannot discuss his fate or place in a cleaned up Rome'. But Aaron is partly rehabilitated by his defence of the child and this defence is also a defence of his colour, even if in a patriarchal perspective: 'for him, as much as for the white Romans, race is indeed lineage'.[21]

Loomba's reading of *Titus*, and of the other tragedies she considers, demonstrates the fruitfulness of an approach that brings together copious reference to Shakespeare's texts, discourse analysis, historical investigation and postcolonial perspectives. *Shakespeare, Race, and Colonialism* shows in specific detail how Shakespeare both is and is not our contemporary. The same is true of the two ecocritical approaches we will now consider: the first is Gabriel Egan's collection *Green Shakespeare*.

Gabriel Egan

In his introduction to *Green Shakespeare: From Ecopolitics to Ecocriticism* (2006), Gabriel Egan contends that the rejection of 'critical analogies from nature' by leftish critics like Terry Eagleton (b.1943) blinds them to 'the radical potential of an ecological approach to Shakespeare'.[22] Writing in 2004–5, Egan sees the book we discussed in Chapter 8 of this Guide, Jonathan Dollimore's *Radical Tragedy* (1984), as inaugurating a dominant movement in Shakespeare criticism that eschews 'the desire for unity' and celebrates 'the dispersed, the indefinite, the contradictory, the de-centred'.[23] Egan agrees that in Shakespeare the idea of nature is 'at times [...] irreducibly ideological' but argues that at other times the plays deploy a 'sense of what is truly natural' and 'characterize the behaviours and relationships as violations of nature's principles', drawing 'analogies between human society and the wider cosmic order'.[24]

Such analogies may serve 'to confound oppression precisely because they assume that the human subject is made of the same materials interacting in the same ways as are found in nature'.[25] As one example, Egan takes, from *Coriolanus*, Menenius' plea to the play's titular hero:

> ■ O, my son, my son! Thou art preparing fire for us: look thee, here's water to quench it. [*He weeps*] I was hardly moved to come to thee, but being assured none but myself could move thee, I have been blown out of our gates with sighs, and conjure thee to pardon Rome, and thy petitionary countrymen. (5.2.74–80) □

Undoubtedly, Egan concedes, Menenius can be manipulative; but the microcosmic/macrocosmic correspondence still obtains: a 'man's tears *are* the same as the rains that might quench a fire [...] and a city, conceived as a place and a group of men, *can* exhale like a man does'. Shakespeare employs analogies between the human body and the body politic, the social and political structure, 'to examine how things that happen on the macrocosmic scale (classes, societies, cities) are related to those that happen on the microcosmic, and attempts to poetically reimagine human collectivities as biologically cohesive unities pervade his work'.[26]

Egan's reading of *Lear* argues that the play offers, at the outset, two opposed views of the sources of human nature and behaviour. One is Gloucester's astrological superstition, which holds that '[t]hese late eclipses in the sun and moon portend no good to us' (1.2.82) and that, although 'the wisdom of nature ['human reason / natural science'] can reason it thus and thus, yet nature finds itself scourged by the sequent effects ['subsequent events']'. In other words, reason may doubt astrological influence, but the effects of that influence are, for Gloucester, plain to see. The opposing view is Edmund's rationalism, which wittily dismisses astrological ideas of the stars and planets shaping human beings and their actions:

> ■ This is the excellent foppery of the world, that when we are sick in fortune – often the surfeits of our own behaviour – we make guilty of our

disasters the sun, the moon and stars, as if were villains on necessity, fools by heavenly compulsion, knaves, thieves and treachers ['traitors'] by spherical predominance, drunkards, liars and adulterers by an enforced obedience of planetary influence, and all that we are evil in, by a divine thrusting on: an admirable evasion of whoremaster man, to lay his goatish disposition on the charge of a star! My father compounded with my mother under the dragon's tail and my nativity was under Ursa Major ['(constellation of) the Great Bear'], so that it follows I am rough and lecherous. I should have been that I am had the maidenliest star in the firmament twinkled on my bastardizing. (1.2.93–103) □

As Egan points out, however, Edmund has already provided another explanation for why he is as he is – that, as with all illegitimate children, more intensity went into his conception:

■ [...] Why brand they us
  With base? With baseness? Bastardy? Base, base?
  Who in the lusty stealth of nature take
  More composition and fierce quality ['a more complex creation and more vigorous disposition']
  Than doth within a dull, stale, tired bed,
  Go to th'creating a whole tribe of fops
  Got 'tween a sleep and wake. (1.2.9–15) □

Both Edmund's appeal to nature and Gloucester's to the stars lack cognitive respectability in the twenty-first century (though both are still parts of popular belief-systems). But, Egan contends, 'these ideas differ only in the scale of the forces that are considered dominant', with Gloucester's cosmic causation contrasting with Edmund's local and supposedly natural one. The contest between them 'is not really between rationalism and superstition but between competing rationalisms, for what else is astrology but a form of hyper-rationalism that insists upon explanations for everything?'[27]

Egan finds that *Lear* 'periodically returns to this opening debate between different explanations for human personality'. Kent, for example, says: '[i]t is the stars / The stars above us govern our conditions / Else one self mate and mate could not beget / Such different issues' (Q2, 208–11, RSC Shakespeare p. 2079). But the play does not vindicate Edmund's rationalism over this astrological belief and indeed eschews any definite explanation of human nature and behaviour.

The main action of *Lear* builds up to the storm. Egan points out that, in the theatrical conventions of the time, the advent of a storm on stage, with appropriate effects of thunder and lightning, presaged a 'theophany – the dramatic appearance of a god'.[28] But the play refuses to conform to this convention. It thus challenges what Egan calls the 'temptation to personalize nature, to see an agency where there is only a meteorological phenomenon'[29]. But while the play rejects the microcosmic/macrocosmic correspondence between the anger of the gods and the tumults in Lear's life, it stresses another such correspondence: as Egan puts it, 'the weather is a version of the storm in Lear's mind'.[30]

Egan points to further examples of playing with theatrical conventions in *Lear*. When Edgar describes the ascent to Dover Cliff, it is at first uncertain, if we imagine watching the play without any prior knowledge of it, whether his words should function as the kind of verbal scene setting that occurs elsewhere in Shakespeare. When Northumberland says in *Richard II*: 'I am a stranger here in Gloucestershire. / These high wild hills and rough uneven ways / Draws out our miles, and makes them wearisome' (2.3.3–5), we are intended to believe, within the fiction of the play, that the characters really are in Gloucestershire. So when Edgar says the ground he and Gloucester are climbing is '[h]orrible steep' and that the sound of the sea is audible, it may be that Edgar is offering a true description and that Gloucester's scepticism – '[m]ethinks the ground is even' (4.5.3) – is due, as Edgar suggests, to the fact that '[his] other senses grow imperfect / By [his] eyes' anguish' (4.5.4, 3, 6–7). Edgar's account of the view from the cliff top could increase the belief that he is providing a verbal evocation of what is supposed to be, within the theatrical illusion, an actual setting. But just as the expectation that the storm presages the appearance of a god is unfulfilled, so is the expectation that the lines are descriptive of what is supposed to be, within the play's imaginary world, a real place. A final subversion of expectation in *Lear* is the death of Cordelia, who might conventionally be expected, when her father carries her on to the stage, to recover, as she did in earlier *Lear* stories in drama, poetry and prose, and as she was made to do in Nahum Tate's influential adaptation of the play.

Egan challenges the Christian, humanist and cultural materialist readings of *Lear* in which, in one way or another, suffering brings knowledge of Christian truths, humanist values or an oppressive social order. In the course of his argument, he cites a passage that could seem, as he acknowledges, to reinforce the suffering-brings-knowledge view, when Lear says:

■ When the rain came to wet me once and the wind to make me chatter, when the thunder would not peace at my bidding, there I found 'em, there I smelt 'em out. Go to, they are not men o'their words: they told me I was everything: 'tis a lie, I am not ague-proof. (4.5.108–12) □

But, Egan points out, Lear is inaccurate to imply he bade the thunder to stop when in fact he encouraged it:

■ And thou, all-shaking thunder,
  Strike flat the thick rotundity o'th'world!
  Crack nature's moulds, all germens ['seeds'] spill at once
  That make ingrateful man! (3.2.6–9) □

Lear's inversion of his original exhortation to the storm does not support the claim that he has gained true knowledge through suffering, certainly not of himself. Instead, Egan suggests, his self-exposure to the elements looks more like 'a melodramatic gesture' that turns his suffering body into a message to his enemies which Egan summarizes thus: 'Look what your lies misled me to do [...] and see by how much nature is stronger than man'. This is not to say that Lear does not become mad or suffer but that these experiences do not significantly enhance his knowledge in the ways that a Christian, humanist or cultural materialist reading might suggest.

Lear, Egan claims, 'does indeed offer an ideological critique', but it does so 'by bringing the means of presentation into the critique'[31] in the ways discussed above: that is, by confounding the theatrical conventions in which thunder announces the appearance of a god and in which the description of places (such as the ascent to Dover Cliff and the view from the top) is supposed to indicate actual settings within the dramatic fiction. The play thus 'presents something rather more experientially disquieting that forces attention upon an urgent question about the weather' which Lear puts to Edgar in his Poor Tom guise: 'what is the cause of thunder?' (3.4.129). Egan observes that '[i]n the Globe playhouse in 1605, as across the globe today, the cause of unseasonal weather is not divine and not mysterious, it is human action'.[32]

Egan also addresses the question of Lear decking himself with flowers. This might be seen as a form of what we would today call self-medication, an instinctive use of, in the Gentleman's words, 'many simples operative ['effective medicinal herbs'], whose power / Will close the eye of anguish' (4.3.14–15). Cordelia describes Lear as:

■ Crowned with rank fumitory and furrow weeds,
  With burdocks, hemlock, nettles, cuckoo-flowers,
  Darnel, and all the idle weeds that grow
  In our sustaining corn. (4.3.3–6) □

Egan cites and paraphrases the account of the supposedly curative properties of these herbs in Frank McCombie's 'Garlands in Hamlet and King Lear' (1981): fumitor was used for scabs and furrow-weeds for fresh wounds; hemlock was an anaesthetic and nettles an anti-venom; cuckoo-flowers were used for skin blemishes and darnel for sores and ulcers.[33] But Egan is sceptical of a medicinal interpretation of this passage, pointing out that 'fashioning plants into a garland is a peculiar way to receive their benefits'.[34] He contends that they take on a different and far more potent body of connotations if we link them with a passage from a speech by the Duke of Burgundy in *Henry V* which uses such plants to indicate what happens when people turn from cultivating the land to wielding the sword: because peace 'hath from France too long been chased' (5.2.38):

■ [...] her fallow leas ['unploughed arable fields']
The *darnel, hemlock* and rank *fumitory*
Doth root upon, while that the coulter ['blade on a plough'] rusts
That should deracinate ['uproot'] such savagery.
The even mead [...]
Wanting the scythe, withal uncorrected, rank,
Conceives by idleness and nothing teems
But hateful *docks*, rough *thistles*, kecksies ['dry hollow stems', e.g., cow parsley], *burs* [...] (5.2.45–8, 50–2, Egan's emphasis) □

Seen in this perspective, Egan suggests, Lear's garland 'might be an anticipation of the evil of war between France and England'. This is not to deny the possible medicinal properties of the plants but to illustrate that nature may signify differently according to its contexts. To say this is not, however, to reduce nature to a mere ideological construction. As the storm suggests, nature is more intractable than that. But it is legitimate to propose not only analogies, but also causal links, between natural forces (like the weather) and human beings. Nature can affect human thought, feeling and behaviour, and human thought, feeling and behaviour can affect nature. *Lear* suggests such links by means of the macrocosm/microcosm analogy.

Egan demonstrates how an ecocritical perspective that combines historical scholarship, attention to Shakespeare's texts, and presentism can generate fresh interpretations that call on both macrocosmic/microcosmic analogies and theatrical conventions. A second, later example of ecocritism applied to Shakespeare is found in Simon C. Estok's book, which we will explore in the next section.

Simon C. Estok

Simon C. Estok's *Ecocriticism and Shakespeare: Reading Ecophobia in Shakespeare's Plays* (2011) argues that the concept of 'ecophobia' is crucial to an ecocritical practice that 'encompasses feminism, queer theory, critical racial theory, food studies, cultural anthropology, ecopsychology, post-structuralism and deconstruction' and 'theoretically informed' historicism.[35] Estok defines 'ecophobia' as 'an irrational and groundless fear or hatred of the natural world, as present and subtle in our daily lives and literature as homophobia and racism and sexism'.[36] Estok locates the object of this fear as the unpredictability of nature (there is a likeness here to Cleanth Brooks' interpretation of the 'babe' in *Macbeth* as symbolizing the uncontrollable future, discussed in Chapter 6 of this Guide). This unpredictability, he contends, 'seems key in so much of what is so integral to "nature"': the imagined unpredictability of sexual minorities (*Coriolanus*), of the witches (*Macbeth*), of Moors (in *Othello* and *Titus Andronicus*) and of women (in all the tragedies). Estock asserts that, 'in each case, "nature" is fused with all of the fear and loathing that results when imagined unpredictability prevails in the drama'.[37]

Estok's discussion of *Coriolanus* considers the issue raised by Jason Edwards that was discussed in the previous chapter of this Guide: the relationship between Coriolanus and Aufidius. Whatever the exact nature of that relationship, Estok contends, 'the space of their love itself [...] is a dangerous one, an uninhabitable space, a space neither of heterosexual marriage nor of same-sex friendship, a contemptible space somewhere between Rome and Corioles, a space that cannot be voiced without revulsion'. The play, Estok argues, 'generates precisely such a revulsion' towards its hero, which culminates 'in his expulsion'; this revulsion is not homophobic in the twenty-first-century sense but is based on 'the seventeenth-century contempt of a sexuality that is linked with inconsistency and slippery turns', with 'disorder and unpre-dictability'.[38]

Coriolanus represents this 'disorder and unpredictability', this queer-ness that cannot be pinned down as sodomy or, in a more modern idiom, homosexuality. Sicinus calls him 'a disease that must be cut away', Menenius likens him to a 'limb' with a 'disease' and a 'gangrened' foot, and Brutus speaks of him as having a contagious 'infection' that could '[s]pread further' (3.1.349, 362, 366–7). In the last act, the cry goes up: 'Tear him to pieces!' (5.6.138). According to Estok, '[n]ature abhors the queer in this play'. Coriolanus says '[t]ell me not wherein I seem unnat-ural' (5.3.92–3) because, Estok claims, 'he knows'. Cominius describes Coriolanus as leading the Volscians 'like a thing / Made by some other deity than nature', even if this deity 'shapes men better' than nature (4.6.109–11). Estok sums up Coriolanus' position thus: he is 'expend-able precisely because his individuality, accentuated by his suspect and certainly minority sexual position, puts him in direct conflict with the community that expects his leadership'.[39]

Estok is aware that, in using the term 'individuality', he may be perpetrating an anachronism. In an endnote, he cites Peter Stallybrass's essay 'Shakespeare, the Individual and the Text' (1992), which explores the uses of the term 'individual' in the seventeenth century, pointing out that Shakespeare never employed it, [40] and quotes the contention of Raymond Williams (1921–88) in *Keywords* (1976; 1983) that '[i]ndividual originally mean[t] indivisible. That now sounds like a paradox. "Individual" stresses a distinction from others; "indivisible" a necessary connection'.[41] The individuality of Coriolanus, in the modern sense, is fragile and divided. Estok argues that the play presents its titular hero 'as the effect of both nurture *and* nature, and it is the struggle between the two to produce him that initiates and sustains the drama'. *Coriolanus* shows that 'the production of the subject is also the production of the natural world'. Nature is 'always conceptualized *through* people, through subjects, is always the product of specific social and historical situations, is always, in a word, *constructed*'. But this does not make human subjects dominant over nature or nature a mere product of culture: instead, 'the social is *embedded* in the natural'. Coriolanus himself wants a clear boundary between nature and nurture but cannot achieve this because he is 'an agonistic effect of both *essence* and *ideology*'.[42] Estok agrees with Jonathan Dollimore's *Radical Tragedy*, in its account of *Coriolanus* discussed in Chapter 8 of this Guide, that '[e]ssential egotism [is] the ideological underpinning of class antagonism' and a 'complex function of social relations'.[43] But Estok also charges that it goes against the text of the play to claim, as Dollimore also does, that Coriolanus is 'the ideological effect of powers antecedent to and independent of him'.[44] This claim assumes that Coriolanus is wholly an effect of ideology; but, if he were, there would be no problem; it is precisely because he is not wholly such an effect that he is inwardly and disablingly fissured.

Coriolanus embodies an ecophobic response to a nature that speaks to him of weakness and is crammed with plebeians. He asks diseases to visit themselves on them, compares them to a 'herd' and 'souls of geese' and calls them more cowardly than apes:

■ All the contagion of the south light on you,
    You shames of Rome! You herd of – boils of plagues
    Plaster you o'er, that you may be abhorred
    Further than seen, and one infect another
    Against the wind a mile: you souls of geese
    That bear the shapes of men, how have you run
    From slaves that apes would beat! (1.4.35–41) □

Later Coriolanus denounces the plebeians in terms which make them part of what Estok calls 'a demonized environment that looms waiting to reclaim geographical and ontological spaces',[45] the spaces of being as well as place.

> ■ You common cry of curs, whose breath I hate
>   As reek o'th'rotten fens: whose loves I prize
>   As the dead carcasses of unburied men
>   That do corrupt my air: I banish you [...] (3.3.144–7) □

For Coriolanus, the plebeians are, Estok asserts, 'the very disorder of nature, the imagined chaos that lies outside of human society and culture'.[46] But Coriolanus' denunciations, in Estok's view, 'suggest both an awareness of and insecurity about his embodiedness, fragmentation and isolation' and 'force[...] a focus on his body', which 'becomes the site of confusion of natural and unnatural, a commodity unfit for both social and natural economies, and thus disposable'. Coriolanus' body 'is disciplined and tortured, manicured and maimed, the object of this ecophobic fury'.[47]

In effect, the body of Coriolanus becomes his voice, speaking for him because he cannot do so adequately with his tongue. Though eloquent in his denunciation of the plebeians, he cannot easily speak directly of himself or listen to others speak of him. He says that often, 'when blows have made me stay, I fled from words' (2.2.62), and listening threatens his identity. As his inner crisis grows, he says, '[a]nother word, Menenius, I will not hear thee speak' (5.2.78–9) and tells Aufidius that '[f]resh embassies and suits, / Nor from the state nor private friends, hereafter / Will I lend ear to' (5.3.18–19). He never listens to the plebeians and his eventual attention to his mother's words puts him at perhaps lethal risk, as he tells her:

> ■ You have won a happy victory to Rome.
>   But for your son, believe it, O, believe it,
>   Most dangerously you have with him prevailed,
>   If not most mortal to him. (5.3.198–201) □

Estok sees no integration at the end of *Coriolanus*: the 'surgical divisions in the land and society', which constitute 'an implicit and running theme in the play', not only still exist but are also 'exacerbated'. Nature in *Coriolanus* is 'a construct', 'the space and origin' of 'a viciously punitive source of authority', 'against which Coriolanus cannot be "author of himself" [5.3.37]'. It is 'a space of weeds, out of which Coriolanus is plucked and undone' and which 'cannot tolerate either the fierce individualism that so tragically characterizes Coriolanus or the position of sexual minority into which he finally thinks he will have the consolation of escaping'. In the play, a 'very dangerous and consuming nature' is inescapable and finally wins.[48]

Coriolanus exemplifies an ecophobia that is evident elsewhere in Shakespeare's plays and in the early modern era more generally: a fear of nature, a desire to control it, that culminates in the Enlightenment urge to dominate nature that carries through to our own time. If, on one level, Coriolanus' tragedy is his 'fierce individualism', on a broader level the tragic element in the play is the ecophobia that pits human beings against nature. Estok does not deny that there are also 'biophilic' or 'ecophilic' (life- or nature-loving) elements of 'wonder' and 'joy' in the attitudes of Shakespeare and the early modern period more generally to nature;[49] but the ecophobic aspect is important in shaping the modern world.

In a coda to his book, Estok reiterates the 'fundamental difference between ecocritical readings of Shakespeare' and the many volumes of valuable scholarship and criticism produced over time about 'representations of nature in Shakespeare'. Moreover, 'a defining focus of ecocriticism is central to each and every chapter' of his book – 'an emphasis on the real, the material world' we experience daily 'when we walk outside'. We 'reconstruct' this world 'through discourse' but it 'nevertheless exists before our discursive constructions of it' and will continue to do so after our individual and perhaps collective departure from it. But there is a further question: 'why, if we are really concerned about the environment, we should bother with Shakespeare – [it] seems at best a bit of a stretch to connect this old dead guy with current *environmental* crises'. Why not take up some more direct form of environmental activism? Estok does not aim to answer this question but 'to suggest possibilities and to open doors'. He does not claim that '[e]cocriticism and the paradigm of ecophobia' can provide 'all the answers' but affirms that they 'can help us enormously in moving toward them'. He also asserts that ecophobia is 'certainly not the only ethical paradigm Shakespeare represents', and in the next chapter we engage with other philosophical and ethical concerns in Shakespeare, as explored in the work of Stanley Cavell, Jacques Derrida, A. D. Nuttall and Donald R. Wehrs.

CHAPTER ELEVEN

Philosophy and Ethics

Shakespeare's tragedies operate on similar terrain to that of philosophy and this is evident in their critical history, their attraction for philosophers (Hegel) or those inclined to metaphysical speculation (Coleridge). Key later twentieth-century critical movements, such as poststructuralism and deconstruction, tended to demote Shakespeare philosophically, proceeding as if he were to be understood in terms of other, supposedly superior forms of philosophical, linguistic, psychoanalytical and political knowledge. But the tragedies continued to attract those who did not see them as cognitively inferior – for example, professional philosophers (Stanley Cavell) or literary critics with some philosophical expertise (A. D. Nuttall). This chapter considers key philosophical readings of Shakespeare's tragedies and the ways in which those tragedies themselves may be thought of as philosophizing. We start with Stanley Cavell.

Stanley Cavell

Stanley Cavell's *Disowning Knowledge in Seven Plays of Shakespeare* (2003) collects essays from 1976 to 1992–3. In his Introduction to the updated edition, Cavell outlines his 'intuition' that Shakespeare's 'great tragedies in the first years of the seventeenth century' anticipate the coming of scepticism a generation before the French philosopher and mathematician René Descartes (1596–1650) offered a philosophical account of the sceptical position in his *Meditations on First Philosophy* (first pubd 1641 in Latin; 1647 in French).[1] By 'scepticism' here Cavell means doubt about 'whether I know with certainty of the existence of the external world and of myself and others in it'. Descartes' own answer to this doubt was that God provides the ground of our knowledge of the external world, of oneself and of others, that, as Cavell puts it, God assures 'the general matching of the world with human ideas of it'.[2] But, Cavell argues, Descartes' clear arguments about the need for God to provide such grounding for our knowledge means that doubt about God's existence shakes the very basis of such knowledge.

137

In Cavell's perspective, a Shakespeare tragedy is 'obedient to a sceptical structure' but, conversely, scepticism, as a philosophical position, bears 'its own marks of a tragic structure'. A Shakespearean tragedy, he suggests, 'is itself an interpretation of what scepticism is itself an interpretation of'[3] – that is, such a tragedy is a dramatic interpretation of the universe as lacking any grounds for firm knowledge, which correlates with the tragic element in scepticism's explicit philosophical interpretation of the universe as lacking any grounds for firm knowledge. The 'doubt' of scepticism is, for Cavell, 'motivated [...] by a (displaced) denial, by a self-consuming disappointment that seeks world-consuming revenge'.[4] What Cavell calls 'the extreme precipitousness of Lear's story, the velocity of the banishments and of the consequences of the banishments, figured the precipitousness of scepticism's banishment of the world'[5] and 'Lear's "avoidance" of Cordelia is an instance of the annihilation inherent in the sceptical problematic'.[6]

Othello epitomizes 'the logic, the emotion, and the scene of scepticism'. The logic of scepticism is that of 'If I know anything, I know this'. It is evident when, in response to Brabantio's admonition that Desdemona 'has deceived her father, and may thee', Othello responds 'My life upon her faith!' (1.3.311, 312); it shows itself again when Othello later asserts '[...] when I love thee not, / Chaos is come again' (3.3.101–2). The 'emotion' of scepticism is 'the structure' of Othello's feelings 'as he is hauled back and forth across the keel of his love'. The 'scene' of scepticism is 'the pervasive air of the language and action of [*Othello*] as one in which Othello's mind continuously outstrips reality, dissolves it in trance or dream or in the beauty or ugliness of his incantatory imagination'.[7]

Othello, Cavell suggests, 'is the most romantic of Shakespeare's heroes'. When Desdemona says, early in the play, 'I saw Othello's visage in his mind' (1.3.267), she means, according to Cavell, that she sees his face, his image, as he sees it from within himself and that she understands his blackness, as he does, as 'the colour of a romantic hero', a person of 'purity' who has what Othello himself calls a 'perfect ['unblemished, guiltless'] soul' (1.2.34).[8] Desdemona suits such a hero; as Cavell puts it, Othello's 'perfection is now opened toward hers'. Othello's lines about 'what he feels he has lost in losing Desdemona's confirmation' show, for Cavell, his 'absolute stake in his purity, and its confirmation in hers':[9]

■ [...] My name, that was as fresh
   As Dian's visage [the face of Diana, ancient 'Roman goddess of chastity
   and the moon'], is now begrimed and black
   As mine own face. (3.3.427–9) □

Othello can now no longer see his reputation as equivalent to Diana's face, as he once saw it, and as Desdemona once saw it when she 'saw

Othello's visage in his mind'. He now sees his reputation in Iago's mind. In losing Desdemona's capacity to confirm his self-image, he loses his old imaginative power and thus 'his grasp of his own nature'; 'he no longer has the same voice in his history' and exchanges Desdemona's imagination for Iago's.[10] But Cavell suggests that this exchange, however bad it may seem, enables Othello to avoid another and worse exchange.

Othello's marriage is that of 'a romantic hero and a Christian man'. In his latter role, marriage involves two key ideas: that two people become one flesh and that, in St Paul's words, it is better to marry than burn. Both these ideas entail an acceptance of imperfection. Othello declares: 'But that I love the gentle Desdemona, / I would not my unhousèd free condition / Put into circumscription and confine / For the sea's worth' (1.2.27–30).

Cavell highlights the point that the opening scene of the play unfolds 'while Othello and Desdemona are in their bridal bed'. As Iago says to Brabantio: 'Even now, now, very now, an old black ram / Is tupping ['mounting sexually'] your white ewe' (1.1.92–3). In starting 'with a sexual scene denied our sight', *Othello* 'opens exactly as a normal comedy closes, as if turning comedy inside out'.[11] In both Venice (1.2) and Cyprus (2.3), Othello appears from his bedroom, as 'though an appearance from the place of sex and dreams is what gives him the power to stop an armed fight with a word and a gesture'.[12] Cavell suggests that 'the thing *denied our sight* throughout the opening scene' is what the last scene of the play shows: 'the scene of murder'.[13]

In turning to this scene, Cavell cites the opening lines of Othello's speech as he prepares to kill Desdemona:

■ It is the cause ['offence / reason for action'], it is the cause, my soul:
  Let me not name it to you, you chaste stars:
  It is the cause. Yet I'll not shed her blood,
  Nor scar that whiter skin of hers than snow,
  And smooth as monumental alabaster:
  Yet she must die, else she'll betray more men.
  Put out the light, and then put out the light. (5.2.1–7) □

Cavell feels the 'mysteries', 'privacies' and 'magniloquence' of these lines are serving 'some massive denial'. Although 'Othello must mean that he is acting impersonally', 'the words are those of a man in a trance, in a dream state, fighting not to awaken'. We should not assume that we know Desdemona better than Othello knows her, thus turning him, as Cavell nicely puts it, into 'some kind of exotic, gorgeous, superstitious lunkhead' – which is pretty much Iago's view of him. Somewhere, Cavell contends, Othello '*knows*' Iago's accusations against Desdemona are untrue. This is evident in the speed with which he recognizes the truth when Emilia tells him about the handkerchief – hardly conclusive disproof, any more than it was conclusive proof earlier, of Desdemona's infidelity. It is not, Cavell asserts, that Othello 'recognizes the truth too late', but that 'he recognizes it when he is ready to' – 'in this case when its burden is dead'. Othello *wanted* to believe Iago; he needed the poison he devoured. He could better tolerate 'the idea of Desdemona as an adulterous whore [...] than the idea of her as chaste'.[14]

Cavell considers the way in which, in the lines just quoted, Othello petrifies Desdemona through imagery, turning her into stone with a simile: 'smooth as monumental alabaster' (5.2.5). It is an image, Cavell thinks, which 'denies that he scarred her and shed her blood' and thus denies, simultaneously, 'that he has taken her virginity and that she has died of him'. Cavell argues that the 'whole scene of murder is built on the concept of sexual intercourse or orgasm as a dying', evident when Othello says to Desdemona '[t]hou art on thy death-bed' and she replies '[a]y, but not yet to die' (5.2.59–60). This is the bed on which she would 'die', in the sexual but not the mortal sense, in the immediate future.

Nonetheless, Desdemona has anticipated that this may be her last night. She has asked Emilia to '[l]ay on my bed my wedding sheets' (4.2.115), asked her '[i]f I do die before, prithee shroud me / In one of these same sheets' (4.3.24–50), and sung the song about the weeping maiden, scorned by her lover, singing by a sycamore ['pun on "sick amour"'] tree and repeating the refrain 'Sing willow' (4.3.42–54). Her preparation of the bed sets the stage for Othello to implement Iago's instructions, which Othello has already approved: '[d]o it not with poison: strangle her in her bed, even the bed she hath contaminated' / 'Good, good: the justice of it pleases' (4.1.198–200).

Cavell sums up 'the torture of logic' in Othello's mind in the following way: 'Either I shed her blood and scarred her or I did not. If I did not then she was not a virgin and this is a stain upon me. If I did then she is no longer a virgin. Either way I am contaminated.'[15] Othello has been, Cavell suggests, '[s]urprised to find that [Desdemona] is flesh and blood', since this means they are, being married, one flesh, and he is thus flesh and blood too. But Desdemona sees that Othello 'is not identical with his mind', the mind in which he sees himself as a pure hero. 'He cannot forgive Desdemona for existing, for being separate from him, outside, beyond command, commanding, her captain's captain.'[16]

Insofar as this is the case, it may seem to challenge the idea that Othello embodies the problem of scepticism. As Cavell declares, 'Othello certainly knows that Desdemona exists!'[17] But this 'is precisely the possibility that tortures him'. For Cavell, Othello's 'professions of scepticism over [Desdemona's] faithfulness are a cover story for a deeper conviction; a terrible doubt covering a yet more terrible certainty, an unstatable certainty'. Scepticism, which questions what grounds we can have for knowing that the external world, other people and other minds exist, emerges, according to Cavell, from 'the attempt to convert the human condition, the condition of humanity, into an intellectual difficulty, a riddle' – 'to convert metaphysical finitude into intellectual lack'. Cavell thus arrives at a kind of definition of tragedy as:

■ the place we are not allowed to escape the consequences, or price, of this cover: that the failure to acknowledge a best case of the other is a denial of that other, presaging the death of the other [...] and the death of our capacity to acknowledge as such, the turning of our hearts to stone, or their bursting.[18] □

Cavell's reading of *Othello*, as of the other Shakespeare tragedies he considers, is fascinating but depends on several large leaps: that scepticism is what he diagnoses it to be, 'an attempt to convert the human condition [...] into an intellectual difficulty' and a denial of the imperfect otherness of others and thus of one's own imperfection; that scepticism is produced by and generates extreme emotions – the banishment of the world and of others; that scepticism, as a philosophy, shows the signs of tragedy and informs the structures of tragedy; that Shakespeare's tragedies can be interpreted in terms of this idea of scepticism. All these are open to question but, in Cavell's work, they are combined with intricate and insightful interpretations that show the capacity of Shakespeare's tragedies not only to bear the weight of philosophical argument but also to *make* philosophical arguments while still remaining poetic dramas. We now turn to the engagement of the French deconstructionist philosopher Jacques Derrida (1930–2004) with a Shakespeare tragedy: *Hamlet*.

Jacques Derrida

Jacques Derrida's *Specters of Marx: The State of the Debt, the Work of Mourning and the New International* (1993) originated in his opening lecture at an international colloquium 'Whither Marxism?' on 22 and 23 April 1993 – that is, not in any centrally Shakespearean context. But the epigraph to his first chapter is a quotation from *Hamlet*:

■ HAMLET Swear.
  GHOST Swear. [*They swear*]
  HAMLET Rest, rest, perturbed spirit! – So, gentlemen,
  With all my love I do commend me to you:
  And what so poor a man as Hamlet is
  May do t'express his love and friending to you,

> God willing, shall not lack. Let us go in together:
> And still your fingers on your lips, I pray.
> The time is out of joint: O, cursèd spite
> That ever I was born to set it right!
> Nay, come, let's go together. (1.5.197–207) ☐

In his first pages Derrida makes an extraordinary link between the famous spectre invoked in the first sentence of the exordium of Marx and Engels's *Communist Manifesto* (1848) – 'A spectre is haunting Europe – the spectre of Communism'[19] – and the ghost that appears on the Elsinore battlements at the start of *Hamlet*. In the Manifesto, as in *Hamlet*, whose protagonist is 'the Prince of a rotten State', 'everything begins with the appearance of a spectre' – or, '[m]ore precisely, by the *waiting* for this apparition'. Or, rather, for 'a reapparition of the spectre as apparition for the first time in the play'.[20] Initially, the spectre is called 'this thing':

> ■ MARCELLUS   What, has this thing appeared again tonight?
>   BARNARDO   I have seen nothing. (1.1.25–6) ☐

Marcellus and Barnardo have seen the 'thing' twice – it is '[w]hat we two nights have seen' (1.1.38) – but it has not yet appeared on stage and, at this point, cannot be seen when Marcellus speaks of it. The sceptical Horatio is, as Derrida puts it, there 'to adjust speech to sight' and 'serve as third party and witness':[21] as Marcellus says, 'if again this apparition come, / He [Horatio] may approve our eyes and speak to it' (1.1.32–3).

When the ghost does appear, Marcellus urges Horatio to address it, assuming his studies give him some special capacity to do so – 'Thou art a scholar; speak to it, Horatio' (1.1.48). Marcellus then goes further, urging Horatio, in Derrida's paraphrase, to 'interrogate it, to question the Thing [still referred to by the third-person neuter pronoun] that it still is'[22]: 'Question it, Horatio' (1.1.52). Horatio does so:

> ■ What art thou that usurp'st this time of night
> Together with that fair and warlike form
> In which the majesty of buried Denmark
> Did sometimes march? By heaven I charge thee speak! (1.1.53–6) ☐

But the ghost – perhaps 'offended', as Barnardo suggests – 'stalks away', in Marcellus' words, and makes no response to Horatio's reiterated demands: 'Stay! Speak, speak! I charge thee, speak!' (1.1.57, 58, 59). By charging the apparition to speak, Derrida asserts, 'Horatio wants to inspect, stabilize, *arrest* the spectre in its speech'.[23] When it reappears once more, Horatio cries 'stay and speak!' (1.1.130). They try to strike it, but, as Marcellus realizes, 'it is as the air invulnerable' (1.1.138), and exits unscathed.

Derrida points in the ghost to what he calls a *'visor effect'*: 'we do not see who looks at us' – or rather, we may see them, but we do not see them looking. On one level, the ghost, once it (re)appears, is very visible. As Barnardo says, it is '[i]n the same figure like the king that's dead'; when he asks, '[l]ooks it not like the King?' Horatio replies: '[m]ost like'. Soon after it disappears, Marcellus asks Horatio, '[i]s it not like the king?' and Horatio replies, '[a]s thou art to thyself' (1.1.48, 49, 50, 67–8). The ghost looks like the king but clad for war: '[s]uch was the very armour he had on / When he th'ambitious Norway combated' (1.1.69–70). His face is not wholly obscured since his frown is visible – '[s]o frowned he once when, in an angry parle, / He smote the steeled pole-axe on the ice' (1.1.71–2). But, literally or metaphorically, he is wearing a helmet with a visor through which he can see but is not in any full sense seen. Even if the visor is raised, its effect is still there and perhaps even heightened: the visor can always come down. 'To feel ourselves seen by a look which it will always be impossible to cross, that is the *visor effect* on the basis of which we inherit from the law.'[24]

Horatio tells Hamlet of the appearance of a 'figure like your father, / Armed at all points exactly, cap-à-pie ['from head to foot']' (1.2.202–3). The stress on the ghost being armed and armoured recurs soon after, at the start of Hamlet's dialogue with Marcellus and Barnardo:

■ HAMLET   Armed, say you?
MARCELLUS *and* BARNADO   Armed, my lord.
HAMLET   From top to toe?
MARCELLUS *and* BARNARDO   My lord, from head to foot. (1.2.233–6) □

Hamlet then gets to the head and moves towards the face and its expression, as if, Derrida suggests, he hopes the ghost might not have revealed his identity:

■ HAMLET   Then saw you not his face?
HORATIO   Oh yes, my lord, he wore his beaver ['visor of a helmet'] up.
(1.2.237–8) □

Even so, his identity remains uncertain: as Hamlet says in his soliloquy after his conference with the players: '[t]he spirit that I have seen / May be the devil, and the devil hath power / T'assume a pleasing shape' (2.2.530–3), even his father's shape (not that this is wholly 'pleasing' to Hamlet).

Derrida makes a link between the rhyme in the famous closing couplet of this soliloquy – 'The play's the thing / Wherein I'll catch the conscience of the king' (2.2.536–7) – and the idea of the spectre as a 'thing', the term Marcellus uses, as we have just seen, before its reappearance. The rhyme suggests both the identity and difference of 'king' and 'thing', and could also apply both to a ghost and a living king. Here Derrida draws on the idea explored in the classic book *The King's Two Bodies* (1957) by the German medieval historian Ernst Kantorowicz (1895–1963). This idea, which emerged in the late Middle Ages and continued into the early modern era, held that a king – in life, not in death – has two bodies, a mortal body and an immortal body that is the supernatural embodiment of the realm over which he reigns. When the mortal body dies, the next king incorporates the immortal body – hence the apparent paradox of the cry: 'The King is Dead! Long Live the King!' Thus the king, in his mortal body, becomes a thing, the incarnation of an immortal body, 'precisely where he separates from his [mortal] body, which, however, does not leave him'. The king must 'have *more than one* body [...] in order to reign, and, first of all, to inherit royal dignity, whether by crime or election'.[25] Derrida cites Hamlet's response to Rosencrantz and Guildenstern in regard to the whereabouts of Polonius' body:

■ ROSENCRANTZ   My lord, you must tell us where the body is, and go with us to the king.
HAMLET   The body is with the king, but the king is not with the body. The king is a thing –
GUILDENSTERN   A thing, my lord?
HAMLET   Of nothing. (4.1.22–5) □

In *Hamlet*, the location of the king's immortal body is a key problem. Is it in Claudius, the usurper who has nonetheless been duly crowned king? Is it, potentially, in young Hamlet himself, waiting only on Hamlet's killing of Claudius to be actualized? Or is it still in some sense in old Hamlet, his father, perfidiously robbed of his life and throne and forced to walk the night?

According to Derrida, the 'Thing' that haunts the Elsinore battlements in the armour and with the face of Hamlet's father has three elements. One is that of mourning, and this involves trying to give the bodily remains of a dead person a solid if inert being, first by identifying them and then by giving them a definite location. This is, in a sense, to lay the ghost, to put the dead person in a safe place. Hamlet's first question to the gravedigger is '[w]hose grave's this, sirrah?' and although the gravedigger initially claims it as his own – in the sense that he is digging it – Hamlet eventually comes to learn that it is Ophelia's and – as discussed in the section on René Girard in Chapter 7 of this Guide – it becomes the place of his struggle with Laertes, as if the two young men are already staking their claims to occupy grave-space (interestingly, none of the other corpses mentioned before the slaughter at the end of the play – old Hamlet, old Fortinbras (killed by old Hamlet), Polonius, Rosencrantz and Guildenstern – has a grave that actually figures in the play: no one marks their burial place and provides a definite location for mourning).

A second component of the 'Thing', in Derrida's perspective, is that it reminds us that language is necessary to speak of generations of the dead, whether they are seen as skulls or spirits. The spectre on the battlements does not at first speak, but it is spoken about; it does speak to Hamlet, both on the battlements and later in the Queen's bedroom, but its existence – and the existence of the dead person it seems to represent, if doubtfully – is perpetuated by those who speak *of* it. When the singing gravedigger carelessly throws up a skull from the grave, Hamlet remarks: 'That skull had a tongue in it and could sing once' (5.1.57), stressing the skull's absence of speech and the perpetuation of its once living occupant (who turns out to be Yorick) in his own utterance.

A third component of the 'Thing', the spectre, is that it *'works, whether it transforms or transforms itself, poses or decomposes itself'*. The spectre works on, has an effect on, those who see it, who hear of it, who act or do not act upon what they may interpret to be its promptings. This is the case with the spectre of old Hamlet, the spectre of Marxism or indeed the 'Thing' which is a spectre of anything else, all of which may 'whisper to those in the present to *follow* a ghost'.[26] But where and whither? Is it not paradoxical to follow a ghost (from the past) into the future? And does not following a ghost also mean being followed (haunted) by it? As Derrida puts it:

> ■ What does it mean to follow a ghost? And what if this came down to being followed by it, always persecuted perhaps by the very chase we are leading? Here again what seems to be out front, the future, comes back in advance from the past, from the back. 'Something is rotten in the state of Denmark' declares Marcellus, at the point at which Hamlet is preparing, precisely, to *follow* the ghost ('I'll follow thee' [1.4.68]). And he too will soon ask him 'Whither?'. 'Where wilt thou lead me? Speak; I'll go no further. / [GHOST] Mark me […] I am thy father's spirit' [1.5.1–2, 13].[27] □

In *Specters of Marx*, Derrida goes on to mount a rich exploration of mourning and haunting, or what he calls a 'hauntology' ['une hantologie'], a 'logic of haunting' that is 'not merely larger and more powerful than an ontology or a thinking of Being [*une pensée de l'être*]' but that harbours 'within itself, but like circumscribed places or particular effects, eschatology and teleology themselves'.[28] This exploration goes far beyond, but returns to, *Hamlet* and also has implications for other Shakespearean tragedies. As Derrida puts it: 'a spectre is also a *revenant*. One cannot control its comings and goings because it *begins by coming back* [*il commence par revenir*]. Think as well of Macbeth, and remember the spectre of Caesar.' In this last sentence, Derrida hints at how his ideas may be developed in relation to *Macbeth* or *Julius Caesar*. But in *Specters of Marx* it is, above all, the tragedy of *Hamlet* that haunts the Derridean battlements, that provides the grand template for the spectres that haunt the castles of human culture, and that, for good and ill, work on their inhabitants. Derrida is certainly not deconstructing the status of *Hamlet* but re-inforcing its position, in his own terms, as a universally significant work. A. D. Nuttall would have agreed about the universal significance of *Hamlet* but had little time for Derrida. In *Shakespeare the Thinker*, he also considers the philosophical dimensions of the tragedies, but he does not confine himself to Hamlet and comes from a different perspective.

A. D. Nuttall

A. D. Nuttall's *Shakespeare the Thinker* (2007) argues that Shakespeare was a dramatist, not a systematic philosopher, but that there are moments at which his plays stage major encounters with philosophical issues. One especially interesting philosophical area Nuttall explores is the dramatization – and criticism – of Stoicism in *Julius Caesar* and *Hamlet*, and the anticipations of empiricism and scepticism in the latter play. In his account of *Caesar*, an important focus is Brutus' soliloquy in which he seeks to justify, in advance, Caesar's assassination:

■ It must be by his death: and for my part,
I know no personal cause to spurn at him
But for the general. He would be crowned:
How that might change his nature, there's the question.
It is the bright day that brings forth the adder,
And that craves wary walking: crown him that,
And then I grant we put a sting in him,
That at his will he may do danger with.
Th'abuse of greatness is when it disjoins
Remorse from power: and to speak truth of Caesar,
I have not known when his affections swayed
More than his reason. But 'tis a common proof
That lowliness is young ambition's ladder
Whereto the climber upward turns his face,
But when he once attains the upmost round,
He then unto the ladder turns his back,
Looks in the clouds, scorning the base degrees
By which he did ascend: so Caesar may;
Then, lest he may, prevent. And since the quarrel

Will bear no colour for the thing he is,
Fashion it thus: that what he is, augmented,
Would run to these and these extremities:
And therefore think him as a serpent's egg
Which hatched, would as his kind grow mischievous,
And kill him in the shell. (2.1.10–34) □

Nuttall observes how in this soliloquy, Brutus, with 'donnish scrupu-lousness',[29] seeks out flaws in his own position and then looks for faults in the case against his position. Though Brutus is often said to be ration-alizing in this speech, Nuttall argues that this is only true if we take 'rationalizing' to mean 'assuming by an act of will a certain rational manner, to persuade oneself that one is behaving well and that all this will look all right when viewed in retrospect'. Nuttall acknowledges that 'the sense of doubleness, of the fact that an attitude has been assumed, does permeate the speech' and suggests that this may account for the view – erroneous, in his judgement – that Brutus is rationalizing in the course of it. But the 'root of our unease' with the speech, Nuttall sug-gests, 'is a sense that Brutus is contriving to forget or erase actuality'.[30] In his soliloquy, 'the careful assertion of moral reasoning, in itself noble, has somehow come adrift'. Nuttall even finds in the speech 'a streak of self-satisfaction, an obscure interior equivalent to the public pride of the statuesque Stoic'.[31]

In *Caesar*, Nuttall maintains, Shakespeare criticizes Stoicism, implying that 'it is a philosophy pathologically subject to degeneration into [a] detachment' which is not that of 'the Olympian observer' but of 'the frightened fugitive [...] hiding from an over-rich and hurt-ful universe'. A lesser writer than Shakespeare who 'had seen so deeply into the unacknowledged evasions at the heart of Stoicism' would have given us 'a contemptible Brutus'. But Shakespeare, Nuttall asserts, still presents Brutus as a genuinely honourable man whose doubts, as expressed in the soliloquy quoted above, are also honourable and who is accurately, unironically elegized by Mark Antony at the end of the play as 'the noblest Roman of them all' (5.5.73). Although Brutus' stoicism will later lead him to repress his feelings about his wife's death, his 'love for his wife and his grief at her death', which he 'is proud to be able to repress, actually redeem him as a human being' – and as 'Brutus is redeemed, Stoicism is damned'.[32]

Shakespeare's implied criticism of Stoicism in the portrayal of Brutus finds its strange reflection, Nuttall suggests, in the play's implicit criticism of Antony's 'sinister ability not to repress but to foment extrav-agant emotion',[33] most notably in what Nuttall sees as 'the greatest oration in the English language' over Caesar's body.[34] For example, to refute the charge that Caesar aspired to the power of a monarch, Antony says:

■ You all did see, that on the Lupercal,
I thrice presented him a kingly crown,
Which he did thrice refuse. Was this ambition? (3.2.92–4) □

Casca, however, has earlier given a different account, in prose, of the same event:

■ I saw Mark Antony offer him a crown – yet 'twas not a crown neither, 'twas one of these coronets – and as I told you, he put it by once: but for all that, to my thinking, he would fain have had it. Then he offered it to him again, then he put it by again: but to my thinking, he was very loath to lay his fingers off it. And then he offered it the third time; he put it the third time by, and still as he refused it, the rabblement hooted, and clapped their chopped [chapped, roughened] hands, and threw up their sweaty night-caps, and uttered such a deal of stinking breath because Caesar refused the crown that it had almost choked Caesar, for he swooned and fell down at it. (1.2.239–47) □

According to Casca, as Nuttall summarizes it, 'Caesar did indeed refuse the crown three times, but he did so, seemingly, *with increasing reluctance* and fainted at the last refusal'. But Antony's rhetoric turns this reluctance into a wholehearted refusal that contradicts the underlying sense that Rome and Caesar were indeed moving towards monarchy. Antony's rhetoric and the enthusiastic responses it arouses suggest that 'the Roman world as a whole is a place of malfunctioning emotion' in which 'love is an ill-nourished, undeveloped thing', either 'crushed by Stoic repression' or 'rhetorically manipulated and converted into aggression'.[35]

Moving on to *Hamlet*, Nuttall points out that this play, which followed hard on *Julius Caesar*, refers back to it several times. In the Second Quarto, Horatio says:

■ In the most high and palmy state of Rome.
A little ere the mightiest Julius [Caesar] fell,
The graves stood tenantless and the sheeted dead
Did squeak and gibber in the Roman streets: (Q2, 6–9, RSC Shakespeare p. 2000) □

In the play scene Polonius says that when he was at university: 'I did enact Julius Caesar: I was killed i'th'Capitol: Brutus killed me' (3.2.86). In the graveyard scene, Hamlet says: 'Imperial Caesar, dead and turned to clay, / Might stop a hole to keep the wind away' (5.1.161–2).

On the philosophical level, Stoicism 'spills over from *Julius Caesar* into *Hamlet* and becomes a subjective nightmare'.[36] *Hamlet* closely follows the 'slow process of subjectivization' of Stoicism, in which a supposedly anti-emotional philosophy turns, 'as the impersonal, rational cosmos fades', into 'a curious internal excitement'.[37] Horatio seems to be Hamlet's ideal of Stoicism. In the play scene Hamlet calls him 'one, in suffering all, that suffers nothing, / A man that fortune's buffets and rewards / Hath ta'en with equal thanks', a 'man that is not passion's slave' (3.2.51–3, 57). And Horatio describes himself, in the extremity of the last act, as 'more an antique Roman than a Dane' (5.2.288), prepared to follow Hamlet into death by drinking the last dregs from the poisoned cup. But Stoic sentiments from Hamlet's own lips take on a different force. As an example, Nuttall cites Hamlet's remark to Rosencrantz and Guildenstern: 'there is nothing either good or bad, but thinking makes it so' (2.2.244–5). Nuttall acknowledges that this is, in Shakespeare's time, a commonplace statement originating in Stoic philosophy, but contends that, voiced by Hamlet, it opens up the possibility of ethical relativism: that good or bad are not fixed but can change according to the view a particular society or individual takes of them.

The classical Stoic detached himself from the codes of any specific society. But Hamlet is more deeply alone. As Nuttall puts it, Hamlet 'has been ordered by a dead man to become a bearer of death and, in consequence, to die himself'.[38] (The phrasing here partly recalls G. Wilson Knight's observation, quoted in Chapter 6 of this Guide, that Hamlet is 'the ambassador of death walking amid life'.[39]) Hamlet 'is cut off [...] from sexuality and procreation' and thus 'must turn on Ophelia and repel her from his tainted, shadowy presence'.[40]

Hamlet does not only approach ethical relativism; he also opens up the possibility of epistemological relativism, of doubting whether there are grounds for knowing that anything exists. This is the kind of scepticism Stanley Cavell explores in relation to Shakespeare's tragedies, as we saw in the first section of this chapter. Nuttall cites Hamlet's remark: 'O God, I could be bounded in a nutshell, and count myself a king of infinite space, were it not that I have bad dreams' (2.2.247–8). The apparent limitations of the physical world can be transcended within the mind – thus calling the existence of the physical world into question – but that transcendence is checked, not by the material reality of the physical world (its spatial boundaries, for instance) but by bad dreams which – if they are bad dreams about, say, the rotten state of Denmark or indeed about the human condition – may be real. As Nuttall points out, empiricism, 'the philosophy [...] that all knowledge is founded on sensory experience, was to become the dominant mode in the course of the seventeenth century, after Shakespeare's death' and a familiar empiricist conundrum is 'How do I know that I'm not dreaming?'. Indeed,

Nuttall asserts, this conundrum is 'the point at which empiricism can mutate into its apparent opposite, scepticism'[41] – if sensory experience cannot tell you that you are not dreaming, what your senses perceive as reality may be a dream. Nuttall likens empiricism's mutation into its apparent opposite to a similar process in Stoicism. 'Just as Stoicism, for all its insistence on reason, held the seeds of a strange subjectivism, so empiricism, though it begins by sounding thoroughly down to earth, had in it that which could foster immaterialist idealism'.[42]

Nuttall demonstrates that Shakespeare's tragedies raise, engage with and anticipate key movements in Western philosophy – for example, Stoicism, empiricism and scepticism. We move on to an essay by Donald R. Wehrs that considers Shakespeare's tragedies in light of both early modern neurophysiology and twenty-first-century neuroscience.

Donald R. Wehrs

Donald R. Wehrs' essay, 'Moral Physiology, Ethical Prototypes and the Denaturing of Sense in Shakespearean Tragedy' (2006), contends that Shakespearean tragedy shows 'patterns of feeling and thought that lock otherwise admirable characters into asocial consistencies, preventing affective [emotional] intuitions from modifying self-understanding and judgement'. Such patterns are alien to 'the moral physiology' derived from classical writers such as Cicero, Plutarch and Lucian and popularized by the great early modern Dutch scholar Desiderius Erasmus (?1467–1536). Modern cognitive science, though a diverse field, has 'consistently yielded results' that support the key claims of early modern moral physiology.[43] Wehrs sums up the key tenets of moral physiology thus:

> ■ [R]eason and emotion presuppose and enrich one another [...] habitual practices modify states of being [...] moral deliberation hinges upon a cultivated, continuous interplay of right feeling and right thinking [...] that depends upon concrete images or patterns of excellence, prototypes, that impress and reinforce themselves upon us through experience [...] maternal relations [are important] in forming such models or images.[44] □

Like Nuttall, Wehrs sees *Julius Caesar* as a criticism of Stoicism but contends that, in this respect, it is not unusual in the early modern period. The play is distinctive, rather, as 'a dramatization of how embodiment works against dissociation'.[45] What Wehrs calls 'somatically transmitted ethical sense' – that is, moral sense transmitted through the body – binds 'images to memory to emotion schemas rooted in ethical prototypes'. Brutus has tried to dissociate his consciousness from such 'emotion schemas', and thus 'disastrously underestimates the influence of personal passions and loyalties'. The oration of Brutus after Caesar's death 'renders Caesar into a succession of abstractions', whereas 'Antony's incessantly calls attention to the body':[46] 'Look, in this place ran Cassius' dagger through: / See what a rent the envious Casca made' (3.2.171–2). As Wehrs puts it, the 'material spectacle of the body works against Brutus's dematerializing, dissociative discourse'. Antony's 'unscrupulous rhetoric' is effective because 'Caesar's bloodied corpse moves the crowd by recalling them to gratitude (*pietas*) toward one likened variously to the father or mother of the nation'.[47]

Wehrs argues that 'the sensory images associated with Caesar's assassination violate a sense of gratitude integral to corporeal subjectivity' – that is, to a sense of self located in one's body – and awaken 'a "natural" call to pity that commands us to become "like a mother" to the Other's broken, bleeding body'. Because of this, these images cannot be separated from emotion and understood as 'sacrifice' or 'purgation'. The body rejects the assassination at a level on which feelings and ethics are inextricably intertwined. This is as true of the conspirators as of anyone. Brutus and Cassius are beaten not so much on the battlefield as by their feeling that they have been ungrateful and that the gods have decreed their deaths. Mistakenly believing that Titinius, an officer in his army, has been captured by the enemy, Cassius orders his bondman, Pindarus, to stab him (Cassius) and his last words are: 'Caesar, thou art revenged, / Even with the sword that killed thee' (5.3.46–7). Titinius returns wearing a laurel wreath of victory but kills himself when he finds Cassius dead, and Brutus, seeing their bodies, says: 'O Julius Caesar, thou art mighty yet / Thy spirit walks abroad and turns our swords / In our own proper ['very own'] entrails' (5.3.99–101). Brutus will follow Cassius and Titinius into self-slaughter, aiming to 'resolve himself, through the ultimate self-fashioning and dissociative gesture of suicide, into the kind of unmoving, abstract "spirit" or idea he sought to make of Caesar'.[48]

In *Hamlet*, the resistance of nature to 'the blunting of sense' is so strong that 'moral physiology' takes revenge upon the splitting of 'cognition, and thus identity, from somatic ethical responsiveness'.[49] If the process of knowing (cognition), and one's sense of self (identity), are separated from the body's inherent moral reactions (somatic ethical responsiveness) then, in accordance with the propositions of both early modern moral physiology and modern cognitive science, nature will resist the consequent sensory constriction and the ethically sensitive body will strike back. The play starts by asserting the reality of the ghost against Horatio's incredulousness; Barnardo says to Horatio: '[a]nd let us once again assail your ears, / That are so fortified against our story' (1.1.36–7). Barnardo's imagery here ('assail', 'fortified') links Horatio's 'philosophy' with the wish for fortification against troubling notions. Wehrs takes this as an example of how early modern thought adopts a key project of ancient Greek philosophy, in which concepts supposedly fortify human beings against the assaults of chance and feeling. But in *Hamlet*, Wehrs argues, it is necessary to hear those things which assail fortified ears, and in the play these issue from the voice of a dead but not quite silent father whose words subvert a new regime, that of Claudius, which dissociates 'consciousness from emotion schemas' so as to drain the Danish court of vigour, freshness, depth and fruition: as Hamlet says in his first soliloquy, '[h]ow weary, stale, flat and unprofitable / Seem to me all the uses of this world!' (1.2.133–4). Wehrs sees the source of this perception as the behaviour of Gertrude in her rapid remarriage: as Hamlet says later in the same soliloquy: '[a] beast that wants discourse of reason / Would have mourned longer' (1.2.150–1). Wehrs' indictment of Gertrude runs thus:

> ■ By casting radical doubt upon the solidity of any 'referential process' linking sound and sense, image and emotion, memory and identity, and thus casting doubt upon any basis for gratitude towards herself, Gertrude puts into question whether there is anything in the 'world' [1.2.134] into which she has brought Hamlet that is worthy of gratitude.[50] □

In an endnote, Wehrs mentions the essay '*Hamlet* – the "Mona Lisa" of Literature' (1995) by Jacqueline Rose (b.1949), which highlights the way in which Gertrude has been made to take the blame for the failures of both *Hamlet* and Hamlet[51] – Rose's title comes from T. S. Eliot's statement in 'Hamlet and His Problems' (1919), discussed in Chapter 4 of this Guide: 'Hamlet is the *Mona Lisa* of Literature'.[52] Wehrs implies, however, that his own account of Gertrude is not sexist 'because feminine-maternal bonds are so crucial to the affective and rational lives of people of both sexes [that] the consequences of their violation or denial are the stuff of tragedy'.[53] What Hamlet sees as Gertrude's breach of the 'feminine-maternal' bond has resulted in a world that is, to his perception, emptied of emotional and ethical cultivation: 'an unweeded garden / That grows to seed: things rank and gross in nature / Possess it merely' (1.2.135–7). In this context, the ghost provides an injection of energy; it 'breaks up the "stale, flat" [1.2.133] early modern world presided over by banal cultural fathers, Claudius and Polonius, by giving substance to Hamlet's most nightmarish suspicions, and thus revitalizes ethical registers of significance'. The apparition 'imposes a task' – to 'set [...] right' the 'time [that] is out of joint' (2.1.205, 206) – which 'confers upon the son an identity commensurate with that of the archaic, heroic father'.[54] But, according to Wehrs, Hamlet distrusts the ghost for two reasons: its adjurations chime in too closely with his own aversion to

Claudius' regime, and its theatricality in offering him an antidote to inertia – the assumption of the role of avenger – raises the suspicion that its performance may be a concealed lure to death or madness.

Suspicious of the ghost's theatricality, Hamlet devises a theatrical way in which to test its words – the play that will 'catch the conscience of the king' (2.2.537). This plan comes at the end of a soliloquy that has earlier dwelt on the comparison between an actor who offers a fictional display of passion and Hamlet's incapacity to offer a real one:

> ■ Is it not monstrous that this player here,
> But in a fiction, in a dream of passion,
> Could force his soul so to his whole conceit ['imagination']
> That from her working all his visage wanned ['paled'],
> Tears in his eyes, distraction in's aspect ['expression/glance'],
> A broken voice, and his whole function suiting
> With forms to his conceit ['all of his natural powers furnishing actions to match
> his imaginings']? And all for nothing! (2.2.482–8) □

Wehrs suggests that this part of Hamlet's soliloquy shows the Prince's grasp of how acting is a performance that entails a bodily display which, within specific theatrical conventions, signals psychological content – for example, the audience assumes that an actor crying onstage is to be understood as in distress (unless other bodily signs and/or words within the performance suggest his tears are assumed). By employing this link between body and feeling, Wehrs argues, actors 'make art recall and thus reactivate the work of mothers and maternal nature' in creating a kind of 'dialogue' between knowledge and feeling, the verbal and non-verbal, which provides the basis of possible meaning. Hamlet's play will deploy this kind of 'dialogue'-creation – which will include actual words as well as a dumb-show – to try to waken Claudius from his ethical slumbers, to 'tent ['probe (as one would a wound)'] him to the quick' (2.2.529).

Hamlet also tries to tent his mother to the quick with his words in the bedroom scene, asking her to abandon gestures and listen to him: 'Leave wringing of your hands [...] / And let me wring your heart, for so I shall, / If it be made of penetrable stuff, / If damnèd custom have not brazed it so / That it is proof and bulwark against sense ['fortified against feeling']' (3.4.39–43). Wehrs does not deny the bullying and hysterical aspects of Hamlet in this encounter but asserts that, in wishing that words would 'wring [a] heart' – would impact upon 'penetrable stuff', a subjectivity located in a body – the Prince seeks to 'perform the redemptive work that Erasmus assigns to speech' and, by an emotional and ethical response, to shatter the 'damned custom' of a self-construction indifferent to social bonds. Hamlet's 'words like daggers enter in [Gertrude's] ears' (3.4.96) partly to counteract Claudius' mendacity that has 'fortified' queenly and courtly ears against embodied ethical calls. His verbal assaults upon Gertrude, vicious though they may be, have a benign aim: to make her reconnect body, morality and consciousness. In light of Wehrs' view, Hamlet is partly right when he justifies his appalling behaviour by saying 'I must be cruel, only to be kind' (3.4.176). But, as 'the complexities of the rest of the play indicate, Hamlet's ability to affirm and appeal to embodied ethical subjectivity does not resolve tragic conflict, but establishes its context'.[55]

Wehrs' linkage of early modern thought about the body and the emotions with twenty-first-century cognitive science is an intriguing and by no means implausible one – though as well as appearing to validate early modern thought scientifically it could, conversely, cast doubt on cognitive science as more ideological than objective. Most fascinatingly, Wehrs' approach seems to revive, in semi-scientific form, an idea that looked as though it had been decisively discarded in later twentieth-century literary criticism: that of the 'dissociation of sensibility' promulgated by T. S. Eliot in 1921 (discussed in Chapter 4 of this Guide). Its recurrence in Wehrs could be regarded as an example of 'the return of the repressed', not necessarily in a psychoanalytical sense but as a more general cultural phenomenon. Another 'return of the repressed' was the re-emergence, in the late twentieth and the twenty-first century, of an interest in Shakespeare and religion after the materialist emphases that had come to dominate in the 1980s. This 'religious turn' in relation to tragedy is the topic of our final chapter, where we consider innovative and thought-provoking work by Julia Reinhard Lupton, Stephen Greenblatt and Gillian Woods.

CHAPTER TWELVE

Religions and Reformations

In the materialist readings of Shakespearean tragedy that predominated from the 1980s, there was a tendency to rewrite religion in terms of its social and political effects, its production of assent or subversion, and to set aside any idea of religion as a self-sufficient force, or spirituality as a valid mode of experience in its own right. But later decades have seen a 'religious turn' in Shakespeare studies, and early modern studies more generally, that can be separated into two main strands. One strand is related to the transition from an idea of society based on divine right to an idea of society based on economic and social contracts. In pursuing this strand, critics have drawn on the concept of 'political theology' developed by the German thinker Carl Schmitt (1888–1985). As Donald Hammill and Julia Reinhard Lupton explain in the introduction to their collection *Political Theology and Early Modernity* (2012), 'political theology' is 'not the same as religion' but 'a form of questioning that arises precisely when religion is no longer a dominant explanatory or life mode, either historically (as in [the] Reformation) or existentially (as doubt, scepticism, or boredom)'.[1] The second strand is concerned with religious discourses and institutions in Shakespeare's time that are in the process of change due to the Reformation, and the possible social, psychological and theatrical effects of this change. We begin by considering the first strand in the work of Julia Reinhard Lupton.

Julia Reinhard Lupton

There are two key terms in the title of Julia Reinhard Lupton's book *Citizen-Saints: Shakespeare and Political Theology* (2005). The first term, 'citizen-saints', joins together two apparently opposed words: the citizen is one who subdues their outsiderish inclinations to the requirements of a particular society; the saint is one who seeks a sacred space outside any society. Lupton conjoins them in order to suggest that they are linked as well as opposed and that the full transition between them is unachieved. As Lupton puts it, the 'citizen-saint is [a] centaur, a hybrid between sacred and secular forms of community and hence at home in neither'.[2] But this hybrid may anticipate a desirable shape of things to come. 'The phrase [*citizen-saint*],' Lupton suggests, 'also designates and indeed calls forth a positive ethical potential in a retooled conception of both citizenship and religious fellowship that would exist beyond the limited fields of national and sectarian belonging that each has been used to defend.'[3]

The other term in Lupton's title, 'political theology', refers to the mixing of political and religious ideas, for example in the notion of the divine right of kings. The phrase 'political theology' goes back a long way – Lupton instances its use in the *Theological-Political Tractatus* (1677) of the seventeenth-century Dutch philosopher Baruch Spinoza (1632–77) – but in the twentieth and twenty-first centuries it is most strongly linked with Carl Schmitt, the conservative Catholic legal, political and constitutional thinker who seems to have been an unrepentant supporter of the Nazis but whose work has influenced thinkers of both left and right. His short book *Political Theology: Four Chapters on the Concept of Sovereignty* (1922) was important to Ernst Kantorowicz's study *The King's Two Bodies* (discussed in the previous chapter of this Guide).

Recent Shakespearean and early modern criticism has used the concept of political theology in addressing what Lupton calls 'the strange hybridization of political and religious thinking' in the early modern era. As examples of this kind of criticism, Lupton cites Richard Halpern's *Shakespeare among the Moderns* (1997) and Debora Shuger's *Political Theologies in Shakespeare's England* (2001). Lupton locates her own book in this strand of research but directs its attention 'to the corpus of citizens implied by political theology rather than its gallery of dead kings', to 'figures who dwell in the suburbs of sovereignty' and to 'the always-emergent future implied by [the] sacred tropes of fellowship [of political theology] rather than the termination of its mythic past on the public stage of deposition and regicide'.[4]

In her reading of *Othello,* Lupton detects a 'fundamental religious ambiguity' in the play; Othello is a Christian convert and thus eligible to be a Venetian citizen; but it is unclear whether his conversion is 'from a pagan religion or from Islam'.[5] The latter provenance, of a well-established religion challenging the universal claims of Christianity and the particularity in the practices of Judaism, would, Lupton suggests, represent a greater danger. But the marriage of Othello to Desdemona is not primarily monstrous or scandalous: rather, Lupton propounds, it exemplifies 'the extension of the Christian message from European Gentiles to all the nations of the world';[6] it stands as 'a mystic symbol of Gentile conversion'.[7] This 'Christian-humanist discourse', however, 'always operates as a *universalism minus the circumcised*, a set that excludes not the unconverted heathens of the New World', who appear open to conversion since they lack strong monotheistic allegiances, 'but rather the Jews and the Muslims'.[8] Christians, Jews and Muslims share religious texts, interpretative habits, theological principles, a claimed descent from Abraham, and the idea of a single God. But they can also come into bitter conflict.

In *Othello*, the Muslim presence is most evident in the shape of the Turks who threaten Venice; Othello's opposition to them serves to confirm his conversion as one who not only accepts but also protects Christianity. But the uncertainty about whether he was previously pagan or Muslim, the possibility that he may once have been the latter, potentially places Islam '*inside* Othello as the past he has abjured as well as *outside* Othello as the enemy he fights',[9] and means that, before his conversion, he was not *ante legem* – prior to the law, following a pagan creed that preceded or lay beyond it – but *sub lege*, under the law of a potent monotheism – resembling, in this respect, not only a Muslim, but also a Jew. Lupton focuses on a fragment of Othello's backstory in which he recalls how he told Brabantio, with Desdemona also listening, '[o]f being taken by the insolent foe / And sold to slavery, of my redemption thence' (1.3.151–2). The linking of 'slavery' and 'redemption' in the second line echoes, Lupton suggests, the Jews' journey from slavery to freedom in the Old Testament Book of Exodus and the interpretation of this, in a perspective derived from Paul, as the liberation from Judaic law into Christian grace. On the one hand, this body of allusion suggests the liberating aspect of Othello's conversion; on the other, it implies Othello converted from a prior position under the law, like a Muslim or Jew. Thus it opens the possibility of a regression (from a Christian viewpoint) to that prior position.

As Othello's marriage crisis quickly develops, regression does indeed seem to occur, either to barbarism or to the attitudes associated with a different monotheism. Othello's reprimand to the unruly soldiers in Act 2 anticipates the latter route:

■ Why, how now, ho! From whence ariseth this?
  Are we turned Turks, and to ourselves do that
  Which heaven hath forbid the Ottomites?
  For Christian shame, put by this barbarous brawl! (2.3.151–4) □

Lupton points out that the expression 'turning Turk' was common from the late medieval period and usually meant a Christian's opportunistic or enforced conversion to Islam. The irony of Othello's use of the phrase emerges as the tragedy of the play develops and he himself seems to be 'turning Turk'. As Lupton says, '"turning Turk" delineates a distinctive tragic trajectory that runs alongside the path of barbarization, paralleling, elaborating, and deviating from it'.[10] On the one hand, 'turning

Turk' may seem to connote the Venetians' descent into barbaric anarchy; but in fact Othello's point is that Turkish soldiers are more lawful than their Venetian counterparts, that the latter do to themselves what the former are forbidden by heaven to do. Here he invokes the image of a more rigorous monotheism than Christianity.

At the end of this scene, Iago looks back on his suggestion to Cassio that he make Desdemona his intermediary with Othello:

> ■ And then for her
> To win the Moor – were't to renounce his baptism,
> All seals and symbols of redeemed sin –
> His soul is so enfettered to her love
> That she may make, unmake, do what she list [...] (2.3.306–10) □

In these lines, Lupton asserts, 'Iago plots the tragic pattern of the play'.[11] Othello's love for Desdemona drives him, effectively, 'to renounce his baptism'. Lupton also homes in on the phrase *'seals and symbols* of redeemed sin', which she connects with St Paul's notion of circumcision as 'a sign or seal' of faith (Romans 4.11). Here Paul replaces circumcision with baptism as the act that seals the contract with God, thus also sealing off circumcision as a sign of the old law that Christ's gospel has both fulfilled and cancelled. By renouncing his baptism, Lupton suggests, Othello will come to embody, not the progress from law to grace, but a backsliding from grace to law, from baptism to circumcision, from, as Lupton puts it, 'a semiosis based on the fluid transparency of the *logos,* the spirit that gives life, to another based on the externality of written, bodily signs, the letter that kills'.[12]

Othello increasingly becomes 'a tragic parody of the Old Testament God', the Lord 'whose name is Jealous (Ex[odus] 34:14)'.[13] When he comes into the bedroom to kill Desdemona he positions himself as an impersonal agent of justice: 'It is the cause, it is the cause, my soul [...] It is the cause' (5.2.1, 3). He tries to persuade her to confess before she dies since this would confirm the rightness of the death sentence he has pronounced and enhance its authority by showing he had not deprived her of the chance to repent. Her denials of guilt, however, make it difficult for him to see the act as he had wanted to under the old law:

> ■ [T]hou dost stone my heart,
> And makes me call what I intend to do
> A murder, which I thought a sacrifice. (5.2.73–5) □

Othello's idea of 'sacrifice' links him with the old law while Desdemona's devotion represents the new idea of love and her death resembles that of Christ and the Christian saints. His killing of her thus re-enacts and symbolizes the replacement of the old law of vengeance with the new gospel of love.

Othello's last speech indicates his role in two cultural stories – 'paganization and Islamicization'.[14] The coexistence and overlapping of these two stories is highlighted, for Lupton, by the ambiguity of whether 'base' should be followed by 'Indian' or 'Judean' (line 390 below):

■ Soft you; a word or two before you go.
  I have done the state some service, and they know't –
  No more of that. I pray you, in your letters,
  When you shall these unlucky deeds relate,
  Speak of me as I am: nothing extenuate,
  Nor set down aught in malice. Then must you speak
  Of one that loved not wisely but too well:
  Of one not easily jealous, but being wrought,
  Perplexed in the extreme: of one whose hand
  Like the base Judean, threw a pearl away
  Richer than all his tribe: of one whose subdued eyes,
  Albeit unusèd to the melting mood,
  Drops tears as fast as the Arabian trees [myrrh trees which drip with the gum resin]
  Their medicinable gum. Set you down this,
  And say besides, that in Aleppo once,
  Where a malignant and a turbaned Turk
  Beat a Venetian and traduced the state,
  I took by th'throat the circumcisèd dog,
  And smote him, thus. [*Stabs himself*] (5.2.381–99) □

'Judean' is in the First Folio, and is the word used in the RSC Shakespeare, but 'Indian' (from the First Quarto) is more common. The term 'Indian' likens Othello to an exotic, pagan Indian, whose tears are compared to the trees that yield the myrrh which was one of the Wise Men's gifts at the birth of Christ; here Othello suggests his regression to paganism within a pained awareness of the Christian redemption that he has rejected through his backsliding. The term 'Judean', however, recalls not only the story of Judas but also that of Herod, the Judean king who ordered the execution of his wife Mariam because of his jealousy – a clear parallel with Othello and Desdemona. Lupton prefers the reading 'Indian' followed by 'Judean' in brackets to indicate that the latter functions as an *auxiliary narrative* to 'the broader tragedy of paganization' in *Othello*.

This 'auxiliary narrative leads into Othello's story of the killing of the Turk in Aleppo. The Turk is not only a generic exotic being; he is, precisely, 'circumcised', as Othello himself is, if he is a Muslim. As Lupton puts it:

■ The sword at once points outwards to circumcision as the trait identifying the object of his scorn, and reflexively returns it onto Othello's own body as the very means of death, as a final stroke that cuts off his life by turning the Turk into and onto himself. The suicide, then, not only murders the 'circumcisèd dog' that Othello has become, but is itself a kind of circumcision, a gesture that constitutes at once a means of social reinscription and a subjectivizing signature.[15] □

By this means, Lupton argues, Othello writes himself into Venetian history as a subject who has 'done the state some service' and resembles Mary Magdalene in having 'loved not wisely but too well'. 'In death, Othello becomes both saint and citizen, both true Christian and acknowledged member of the Venetian Republic.'[16]

Lupton's reading of *Othello* in terms of the concepts of the citizen-saint and of political theology is an insightful one which shows what may be gained by interpreting Shakespeare's tragedies in relation to the confluence, in the early modern era, of politics and three great religious movements – Christianity, Judaism and Islam. The next book we discuss, Stephen Greenblatt's *Hamlet in Purgatory* (2001), focuses on a theological and political breach within Christianity: the Reformation and its after-effects in Shakespeare's best-known tragedy.

Stephen Greenblatt

In *Hamlet in Purgatory*, Greenblatt focuses on the strangeness of the appearance, in *Hamlet*, of a ghost who says that he comes from purgatory – even though the idea of purgatory, and its associated practices, had supposedly been abolished by the English Reformation. The persistence of purgatory in Shakespeare's play suggests a continued need for ideas and methods that purported to connect the living and the dead – and after the Reformation, Greenblatt suggests, it was the theatre, rather than the church, that tried to meet this need. This leads him into a fascinating analysis of *Hamlet*.

The ghost of old Hamlet exhorts his son to vengeance: 'If thou didst ever thy dear father love – / […] Revenge his foul and most unnatural murder' (1.5.27, 29). But his last words to his son at this stage are 'remember me' (1.5.96), and it is the task of remembrance on which Hamlet broods:

■ Remember thee?
Ay, thou poor ghost, while memory holds a seat
In this distracted globe. Remember thee?

Yea, from the table of my memory
I'll wipe away all trivial fond records,
All saws ['sayings, maxims'] of books, all forms, all pressures past
That youth and observation copied there;
And thy commandment all alone shall live
Within the book and volume of my brain,
Unmixed with baser matter: (1.5.100–9) □

The ghost itself, Greenblatt suggests, can be seen as 'a kind of embodied memory'.[17] But as the play proceeds, Hamlet charges himself with forgetting, echoing the image of 'dullness' first used by the ghost when he says:

■ I find thee apt,
And duller shouldst thou be than the fat weed
That roots itself in ease on Lethe wharf,
Wouldst thou not stir in this. (1.5.36–9) □

Hamlet calls himself '[a] dull and muddy-mettled rascal' (2.2.498) and in a soliloquy in Q2 castigates his dullness: 'How all occasions do inform against me, / And spur my dull revenge' (Q2, 105–6, RSC Shakespeare p. 2002). But as Greenblatt points out, Hamlet does not act as though his *memory* of old Hamlet's death had been dulled, even if he can seem tardy in taking revenge. His 'antic disposition' (1.5.189) could indicate 'an *excess* of remembrance',[18] just as Ophelia's later distraction does. Greenblatt also observes that Hamlet's assumption of such a disposition fails to divert his uncle's attention from him; indeed, it has the opposite effect, drawing attention to Hamlet and prompting Claudius to summon Rosencrantz and Guildenstern to the court.

Hamlet's 'dullness' in taking revenge is due above all to his suspicion that the ghost may be malicious: '[t]he spirit that I have seen / May be the devil' (2.2.530–1), as he says when giving his reason for getting the actors to put on the play. But Claudius' reaction to the play seems to confirm the ghost's veracity, if not his identity: 'I'll take the ghost's word for a thousand pound' (3.2.247). Almost immediately afterwards, given the opportunity to kill Claudius while he is at prayer, Hamlet desists because he does not want to despatch his uncle 'in the purging of his soul' (3.3.88) but to kill him while he is engaged in an activity '[t]hat has no relish of salvation in't' (3.3.95). In his mother's bedroom, he momentarily thinks he may have done just this when he stabs a figure whom he assumes to be Claudius engaged in the activity, not one that smacks of salvation, of hiding and eavesdropping behind the arras. Greenblatt contends that this briefly allies Hamlet with young Fortinbras, whose 'unimprovèd mettle hot and full' (1.1.106) spurs him to violence to reclaim the territory that old Hamlet won from old Fortinbras. We can also link it, Greenblatt suggests, to Laertes' later attempt to avenge his dead father, Polonius. In killing a figure whom he thinks to be his uncle, Hamlet appears to demonstrate his remembrance of his filial fidelity, as the ghost urged. But this is not backed up by the dialogue that follows. Hamlet urges his mother to look on his father's picture:

> ■ See, what a grace was seated on his brow:
> Hyperion's curls, the front of Jove himself,
> An eye like Mars to threaten or command,
> A station like the herald Mercury
> New lighted on a heaven-kissing hill,
> A combination and a form indeed
> Where every god did seem to set his seal
> To give the world assurance of a man:
> This was your husband. (3.4.62–70) □

Greenblatt doubts the commemorative efficacy of what he calls 'this perfervid eulogy'. While 'the metamorphosis of a particular man into a painted combination of classical deities' might seem like the kind of '[p]ious remembrance' that takes the form of 'intense idealization', it 'might alternatively be viewed as a characteristic way of forgetting'.[19] Moreover, the description is prologue to his disgusted portrayal of his mother's lovemaking with his uncle:

> ■ Nay, but to live
> In the rank sweat of an enseamèd bed,
> Stewed in corruption, honeying and making love
> Over the nasty sty – (3.4.91–4) □

These potent but putrid images seem to block off pious memories of his father and this could be, Greenblatt suggests, why the ghost reappears as Hamlet vehemently denounces his uncle:

> ■ HAMLET   A murderer and a villain,
>   A slave that is not twentieth part the tithe
>   Of your precedent lord, a vice of kings,
>   A cutpurse of the empire and the rule,
>   That from a shelf the precious diadem stole,
>   And put it in his pocket – !
> GERTRUDE   No more!
>   *Enter Ghost*
> HAMLET   A king of shreds and patches – (3.4.98–105) □

Greenblatt makes the interesting point that Q1 has the ghost, not in his armour, but in his nightgown, making him 'a figure not of the battlements nor of the throne room, but of the closet or the bedroom'.[20] It is also possible, Greenblatt suggests, that an audience who remembered the idea of purgatory might find that the change from dark armour to light night-gown 'would lightly echo those multiple hauntings in which spirits from Purgatory displayed their progressive purification by a gradual whitening of their robes'.[21]

The ghost, in imperative mode, commands that young Hamlet continue to remember and explains the reason for his appearance:

■ Do not forget: this visitation
   Is but to whet thy almost blunted purpose. (3.4.112–13) □

Hamlet's previous behaviour – his staging of the play, his refusal to kill Claudius in a situation that might send the latter to heaven, and his killing of Polonius under the impression that he is Claudius engaged in an act of concealment and eavesdropping that 'has no relish of salvation in't' (3.3.95) – does not necessarily demonstrate that his purpose is 'almost blunted'; rather, he could be acting intelligently to ensure his father's command was properly and fully carried out. But it could be that his father's other command – 'Remember me' – is fading. Whereas Hamlet, Barnardo, Marcellus and Horatio all see the ghost in the first act, only Hamlet sees it now. In a way, its vanishing has already begun. The bedroom scene is the last appearance of the ghost in the play and he is rarely referred to again in words. In Q2 Hamlet does berate himself for '[b]estial oblivion, or some craven scruple / Of thinking too precisely on th'event' (following 4.3.9.113–14, RSC Shakespeare p. 2002) and compares himself unfavourably with young Fortinbras, leading his army into battle against Denmark:

■ How stand I then,
   That have a father killed, a mother stained,
   Excitements of my reason and my blood,
   And let all sleep [...] (following 4.3.9, 129–33, RSC Shakespeare
   p. 2002) □

In one further reference back, Greenblatt points out 'a small but telling difference': in Act 5, Hamlet describes Claudius as '[h]e that hath killed my king and whored my mother' (5.2.69). The use of the term 'king' instead of 'father' is an instance of how, in the part of the play that follows the ghost's last appearance, 'the remembrance of the dead has become depersonalized'.[22]

Even at the end of the play, where it might seem most appropriate, there is no mention of the king and father whose murder has triggered the tragic process. Hamlet does not reveal the reasons for his final actions or announce his uncle's guilt. Laertes says '[t]he king, the king's to blame' (5.2.265), but he is not laying the blame on Claudius for killing old Hamlet or setting the tragedy in motion; rather his reference is more immediate: Claudius is to blame for poisoning the drink, meant for Hamlet, that killed Gertrude, and for envenoming the sword that will soon dispatch both Hamlet and himself. Laertes never learns of Claudius' murder of Hamlet's father. Hamlet stabs his 'murd'rous' uncle (5.2.270) and makes him drink the last dregs of the poisoned liquor, but the general cries of 'Treason! Treason!' (5.2.268) are directed towards Hamlet's killing of the King, or the poisoning of Gertrude and Hamlet, not towards Claudius' original crime. Hamlet himself, in forcing the venomous remains of the drink down his uncle's throat, speaks of his mother rather than his father: '[d]rink off this potion. Is thy union here? / Follow my mother' (5.2.271–2). As Greenblatt sums it up: '[a]t the moment that his command is finally fulfilled, old Hamlet has in effect been forgotten'.[23] It seems that Hamlet in his last moments may be about to speak of him and of Claudius' perfidy, but death intervenes:

> ■ You that look pale and tremble at this chance,
> That are but mutes or audience to this act,
> Had I but time – as this fell sergeant, death,
> Is strict in his arrest – O, I could tell you –
> But let it be. (5.2.280–4) □

Greenblatt points, however, to two ways in which Hamlet's father could be remembered. One is in the story that Horatio is urged to stay alive to tell:

> ■ If thou didst ever hold me in thy heart,
> Absent thee from felicity awhile,
> And in this harsh world draw thy breath in pain
> To tell my story. (5.2.294–7) □

This form of remembrance will not, however, have the quality of inner conviction that Hamlet could have given it; Horatio has seen the ghost but has never heard it speak. The second form of remembrance, however, is much more inward: Hamlet twice declares to Horatio 'I am dead' (5.2.279, 284) and this is exactly what a ghost might say. In these final moments, Greenblatt suggests, it 'is as if the spirit of Hamlet's father has not disappeared; it has been incorporated by his son'.[24]

A dominant strand in *Hamlet* is, Greenblatt contends, 'the disruption or poisoning of virtually all rituals for managing grief, allaying personal and collective anxiety, and restoring order'.[25] The poison flows from Claudius, who also adopts the orthodox Protestant position in arguing that grieving of the kind that the idea of purgatory used to allay is unnecessary:

> ■ to persever
> In obstinate condolement is a course
> Of impious stubbornness: 'tis unmanly grief:
> It shows a will most incorrect to heaven,
> A heart unfortified, a mind impatient,
> An understanding simple and unschooled. (1.2.92–7) □

But these impeccable Protestant sentiments, Greenblatt points out, come from the lips of the play's chief villain. And the ghost could have urged his son to revenge without mentioning his purgatorial provenance. This is to not to say Shakespeare, or his plays, are crypto-Catholic, but that he made dramatic use of the materials thrown up by the Reformation in a way that turned the theatre itself into a substitute for vanishing Catholic doctrine and ritual. The Catholic Church had developed a potent technique for dealing with the dead in the idea and rituals of purgatory; the Reformation outlawed this technique but, in Greenblatt's view, could not eliminate 'the longings and fears that Catholic doctrine had focused and exploited'. So, in a post-Reformation context, 'the space of Purgatory becomes the space of the stage where old Hamlet's ghost is doomed for a certain term to walk the night' – a term that has lasted 400-odd years and helped to form a cult of the dead which Shakespeare's audiences continue to observe.[26]

The question of the survival of Catholic ideas and practices in Shakespeare's tragedies is taken up in Gillian Woods' book, *Shakespeare's Unreformed Fictions* (2013), which we will explore next.

Gillian Woods

Gillian Woods' *Shakespeare's Unreformed Fictions* explores how 'unreformed' elements of Roman Catholicism lose their doctrinal definition in the post-Reformation era but enter into Shakespeare's plays in a variety of sometimes contradictory ways and contribute to the playful and profound exploration of ethical dilemmas and the issues of belief that both drama and faith pose, especially in those times. Among the tragedies, Woods focuses on *King Lear*, taking up the link, earlier explored by Stephen Greenblatt in *Shakespearean Negotiations* (see Chapter 8 of this Guide), between the play and Samuel Harsnett's *Declaration of Egregious Popish Impostures* (1603).

Shakespeare in *Lear*, Woods suggests, treats as tragedy the theme of possession that Harsnett had satirized as mock-tragicomedy. This generic shift also breaks with past English drama, including Shakespeare's own – both *The Comedy of Errors* and *Twelfth Night* show recovery from supposed possession in a comic light. The use of the tragic genre for *Lear* creates a 'sympathizing context' within which the play 'dramatizes possession and exorcism to question the alterity of the other'. In *Lear*, 'demonic rhetoric not only registers the depravity of the human condition [...] but also opens out new possibilities for social relationships in the midst of that corruption and rethinks the relationship between fiction and ethics'.[27]

This demonic rhetoric emerges from and in relation to Edgar. When he declares 'Edgar I nothing am' (2.2.177), he means, on one level, that he will disguise himself to escape arrest for allegedly plotting his father's murder; but he also, as Woods puts it, 'announces an utter loss of self, or at least the form of self that was once "Edgar"'.[28] Taking on the identity of a possessed vagrant, however, enables him to utter aspects of himself that would have been censored in his courtly discourse. It also enables him to assume and explore otherness.

In addition to its deployment of demonic rhetoric, *Lear* depicts the suffering human body. Harsnett's *Declaration* uses hunting imagery to satirize what it portrays as the behaviour of lecherous exorcising priests avid to view and violate female flesh and to symbolize a wider political threat to England as a Protestant nation. But Harsnett establishes a distance between the reader and the human bodies that are the prey of the alleged priestly hunters. The experience of bodies that *Lear* offers the audience is quite different. It is much more sparing in its use of hunting imagery and is rather 'overwhelmed by a sense of predation itself: children attack fathers, brother pursues brother, and sister kills sister'.[29] The subjective experience of the suffering body, ignored by Harsnett, is stressed by Shakespeare. *Lear* 'functions as a kind of living autopsy that strips back the flesh to reveal not merely the physical but also the metaphysical essence of the human'.[30]

There is also a key difference in the attitudes to fiction of the *Declaration* and of *Lear*. The *Declaration* purports to expose dramatic fiction as manipulative and mendacious illusion; *Lear* 'rehabilitates dramatic fiction as an authentic space to confront existential terror and a moral place to explore the limits of ethics'.[31] Edgar plays a role as Poor Tom, and other roles, but there is no 'revelation scene' to fix those roles as deceptive in contrast to the 'real' Edgar: Edgar's roles and his reality blur and blend. *Lear* is set in the past (even when it was first performed) but subverts chronology and historical distance. 'The tragic fiction presents inescapable pain that is always true.'[32]

Lear also, Woods asserts, 'reclaims fiction and theatre as ethical experiences'. This is most evident in the 'Dover Cliff' scene, where Edgar says: '[w]hy I do trifle thus with his despair / Is done to cure it' (4.5.40–1).

Woods sees 'Edgar's theatrical exorcism' (which could itself seem rather cruel) as 'an act of compassion that helps re-solder what Gloucester had earlier called, in general terms, the "bond cracked 'twixt son and father"' (1.2.86–7). This contrasts with Harsnett's *Declaration*, which 'characterizes exorcism as mere theatre and therefore sinful'; *Lear* 'recasts theatre as exorcism that is salvific'. Woods draws attention to Edgar's fluidity in role-playing in this sequence of the play: he 'plays himself, a possessed beggar, a dispossessing exorcist, a demon, and a shocked viewer'.[33] The 'real' Edgar is never revealed but not because he is concealed; these differing facets are what he is and they are essential to his performance of a 'theatrical exorcism' that is 'an expression of love that affirms faith in humanity':[34] as Edgar says to his father: '[t]hy life's a miracle' (4.5.65).

Woods also finds redemption at the end of *Lear*. Cordelia's suffering wholly absorbs the old man, whereas both Hamlet and Othello, as we saw earlier in this chapter, look beyond their own deaths to the stories they want told about them; even Romeo writes an explanatory letter to his father. Lear, bound up in his daughter's story, 'experiences a pity [for Cordelia] so strong as to be fatal'.[35] Woods takes this as an extreme example of the 'moving of affection and passion'[36] which, for Harsnett, is the aim of tragedy. The fictionality of the scene does not mitigate the pain it portrays but reveals the different sort of truth that fiction provides.

Woods also sees 'ethical progress' in the final scene. Lear started the play wanting others to perform his script; at the end, he is 'desperate to hear his daughter's *own* voice'. His daughter's suffering has made him 'recognize the selfhood of the other'.[37] The 'intractable tragedy' of *Lear* 'is that the profound kinship it identifies is rooted in agonized deprivation'. It is a tragedy that makes 'ethical demands on its audience' and its vision, 'even as it meditates on the self, recognizes and restores kinship with the other'.[38] This high claim for *Lear* reaffirms the status of Shakespearean tragedy in the twenty-first century.

Conclusion

We have come to the end of a long journey – from 1693 to 2013 – and seen many sights, heard many voices, on the way. But the end is also a beginning. The range and variety of the criticism we have considered shows that there can be no final destination in the exploration of Shakespeare's tragedies; they have the capacity, inherent in their richness of language and their engagement with fundamental themes, to go on generating new meanings for fresh audiences. This is not to say that the new meanings necessarily drive out the old ones, even though it is inevitable, and salutary, that some critical innovators take on the role of magicians who aim to make their predecessors vanish in a puff of stale smoke. But when the smoke clears, the predecessors, if they are any good, are still there and can always come forward again to take a bow – as this Guide has aimed to show. The new meanings may amplify and reanimate the old meanings and the old meanings may pose invigorating questions to the new ones. Moreover, the new meanings in time will become old ones, assimilated to that great conversation around Shakespeare in which it is, at best, a joy and a challenge to participate. We participate by continuing the critical journey.

In the twenty-first century, an era of radical unpredictability when the very bases of human life, from the weather to the genetic code, are revealing unexpected configurations, this critical journey could go in many directions, but there are four potential windows at which we might point our cursors. One, both leading on and departing from the last chapter of this Guide, is the approach to spirituality in Shakespeare that Ewan Fernie outlines in his introduction to his essay collection *Spiritual Shakespeares* (2005). Rejecting the embarrassment that materialist critics allegedly feel when encountering spiritual experiences in Shakespeare, this book 'treats Shakespearean spirituality as a distinctive, inalienable and challenging dimension of the plays' that is illuminable by, but irreducible to, 'any established theory or theology'.[1] Fernie argues, moreover, that 'a fresh consideration of spirituality might reinvigorate and strengthen politically progressive materialist criticism'.[2] In his own essay on *Hamlet* in the same volume, he advocates 'presentism', which he defines as 'a deliberate strategy of interpreting texts in relation to current affairs',[3] rather than 'reading Shakespeare historically' – it is the latter approach that Julia Reinhard Lupton, Stephen Greenblatt and Gillian Woods all, in their respective ways, take in the last chapter of this Guide, though each of them implies the importance of Shakespeare for living in and understanding the present. Fernie does not deny the value of readings that stress Shakespeare's historical difference, but affirms that 'our primary and most urgent responsibility is to the present'. He advocates 'a form of presentism more deliberately attuned to the challenging strangeness of literature', which is a matter not only of 'historical alterity but also of the extra, unforeseeable difference literature makes to history'. His essay 'analyses the strange spirituality of the last act of *Hamlet* as a striking epitome of literary difference that speaks powerfully and provocatively in favour of a complete commitment to the present'.[4]

A second possible window to future explorations of Shakespeare's tragedies is the relationship between those tragedies and the early modern stirrings of what we now call science. For example, Valerie Traub's essay, 'The Nature of Norms in Early Modern England: Anatomy, Cartography, *King Lear*' (2009), argues that 'in the pre-disciplinary organization of knowledge of the late sixteenth and early seventeenth centuries, when separate fields of expertise had yet to be firmly demarcated', texts now deemed '"literary" comprise a mode of discourse that, while structured through distinct rhetorical forms, nonetheless exists within, partakes of, and contributes to the same epistemological domain in which scientific values, procedures, and logics were being developed';[5] she asks 'what access does *King Lear* provide regarding the role played by anatomy and cartography in contributing to novel structures of thought?'[6] Other Shakespeare tragedies might also provide access to questions about the contribution of early modern proto-scientific notions and practices to new and developing structures and organizations of thought.

A third potential window is that of the representation of the domestic space and life in Shakespeare's tragedies. For instance, in *At Home in Shakespeare's Tragedies* (2010), Geraldo U. de Sousa (b.1952), affirms that 'in Shakespeare's tragedies, house and home remain a focal point of concern, especially as they intersect the public domain',[7] and explores 'Shakespeare's narrative and dramatic constructions of physical yet always virtual and *imagined* domestic surroundings in *King Lear, Othello, Hamlet* and *Macbeth*'.[8]

A fourth and fuzzier window is suggested by Tom Standage's book *Writing on the Wall: Social Media – The First 2,000 Years* (2013). Standage explores 'the historical antecedents of today's social media'[9] by examining 'a series of social-media systems that arose in very different times and places', from ancient Rome to modern America, but that 'are linked by the common thread that they are based on the person-to-person sharing of information'.[10] Standage only mentions Shakespeare once, with reference to his distribution of his 'sugard sonnets among his private friends', as Francis Meres (1565–1647) put it in his *Palladis Tamia: Wit's Treasury* (1598).[11] But *Writing on the Wall* sparks off wider reflections.

Suppose we thought of Shakespeare's tragedies as a social medium which involves the sharing and transmission of dramatic structures, poetry and perceptions between author, co-author, actors, audiences, scholars and critics in both space and time, in the Globe and across the globe, in history and in the present? Suppose, further, that we considered the possibilities of using that medium as a way to talk both about Shakespeare's tragedies and the personal and public tragedies that beset us now? Might this yield new interpretations of Shakespeare's tragedies and new resources for encountering the actual individual and collective tragedies that mark the past and present? Might Shakespeare's tragedies serve as the space of a social sharing in which we can deepen our grasp of the understanding of tragedy as both a literary genre and an existential reality? If so, this may help to realize a promise inherent in the experience of Shakespeare's tragedies themselves, which are unsparing in their rendering of human pain and folly but potentially liberating in their intensity, a paradox captured in the lines of W. B. Yeats (1865–1939), continuing the conversation with Shakespeare in the poem 'Lapis Lazuli': 'Heaven blazing into the head: / Tragedy wrought to its uttermost'.[12]

Notes

INTRODUCTION

1. William Shakespeare, *The Complete Works*, The Oxford Shakespeare, ed. Stanley Wells and Gary Taylor (Oxford: Oxford University Press, 1988). *The History of King Lear: The Quarto Text*, pp. 909–41; *The Tragedy of King Lear: The Folio Text*, pp. 943–74.
2. William Shakespeare, *Tragedies*, The Norton Shakespeare, based on the Oxford edition, ed. Stephen Greenblatt (New York and London: W. W. Norton, 1997). *The History of King Lear: The Quarto Text*, pp. 546–700 (even pages only); *The Tragedy of King Lear: The Folio Text*, pp. 547–701 (odd pages only); *King Lear: A Conflated Text*, pp. 707–81.
3. Kenneth Muir, *Shakespeare's Tragic Sequence* (London: Hutchinson, 1972), p. 12.
4. Tom McAlindon, 'What is a Shakespearean Tragedy?', in Claire McEachern (ed.), *The Cambridge Companion to Shakespearean Tragedy* (Cambridge: Cambridge University Press, 2002), p. 1.
5. Colin Burrow, 'What Is a Shakespearean Tragedy?', in Claire McEachern (ed.), *The Cambridge Companion to Shakespearean Tragedy*, 2nd edn (Cambridge: Cambridge University Press, 2013), pp. 1–23. No specific reason for McAlindon's excision is supplied and his name does not occur in this edition. Muir's *Shakespeare's Tragic Sequence* is listed in the bibliography (p. 296) but not otherwise cited.
6. See Sarah Dewar-Watson, *Tragedy*, Palgrave Macmillan Readers' Guides to Essential Criticism series (London and Basingstoke: Palgrave Macmillan, 2014).

CHAPTER ONE: THE AUGUSTANS

1. Ben Jonson, 'To the memory of my beloved, the AUTHOR Master William Shakespeare and what he hath left us', in William Shakespeare, *The Complete Works*, The RSC Shakespeare, ed. Jonathan Bate and Eric Rasmussen (Basingstoke: Palgrave Macmillan, 2007), pp. 61–2.
2. John Milton, 'L'Allegro', in *Complete Shorter Poems*, ed. John Carey, Longman Annotated English Poets series, fourth impression with corrections 1981, seventh impression (London and New York: Longman, 1989), pp. 130–9.
3. Thomas Rymer, *The Tragedies of the Last Age Consider'd and Examin'd* (1678; available 1677). And *A Short View of Tragedy* (1693, ed. Arthur Freeman, The English Stage: Attack and Defense 1577–1730 series (New York and London: Garland, 1974). *Short View*, p. 111. (In this edition, the pagination restarts at page 1 for the main text of *Short View*.)
4. Rymer, *Short View*, p. 111.
5. Rymer, *Short View*, pp. 111–12.
6. Rymer, *Short View*, pp. 139, 140.
7. T. S. Eliot, 'Hamlet' (1919), in *Selected Essays*, 2nd edn (London: Faber and Faber, 1932), p. 141, n.1.
8. John Dryden, 'The Grounds of Criticism in Tragedy' [Preface to *Troilus and Cressida* (1679)], in *Dramatic Poesy and Other Essays*, Everyman's Library no. 568 (London: J. M. Dent, 1939), p. 141.
9. Dryden, 'Grounds of Criticism', pp. 141–2.

10. T. S. Dorsch (ed. and trans.), *Classical Literary Criticism*: *Aristotle:* On the Art of Poetry; *Horace:* On the Art of Poetry; *Longinus*: On the Sublime, Penguin Classics series (Harmondsworth: Penguin, 1984), p. 121.

11. Dryden, 'Grounds of Criticism', p. 142.

12. John Dennis, 'On the Genius and Writings of Shakespeare' (1712), in D. Nicol Smith (ed.), *Eighteenth Century Essays on Shakespeare* (Glasgow: James Maclehose and Sons, 1903), p. 83. Available online at: http://www.gutenberg.org/files/30227/30227-h/30227-h.html.

13. Dennis, 'On the Genius', p. 99.

14. Dennis, 'On the Genius', p. 83.

15. Dennis, 'On the Genius', p. 84.

16. Dennis, 'On the Genius', p. 84.

17. Dennis, 'On the Genius', p. 84.

18. Dennis, 'On the Genius', p. 84.

19. Dennis, 'On the Genius', p. 85.

20. Dennis, 'On the Genius', p. 85.

21. Dennis, 'On the Genius', p. 88.

22. Rymer, *Tragedies of the Last Age*, p. 26.

23. Dennis, 'On the Genius', p. 88.

24. Samuel Johnson, 'Preface' to *The Plays of William Shakespeare*, in Samuel Johnson, *The Major Works*, ed. Donald Greene, World's Classics series (Oxford: Oxford University Press, 2000), p. 423.

25. Johnson, 'Preface', pp. 423–4.

26. Johnson, 'Preface', p. 424.

27. Johnson, 'Preface', p. 424.

28. Johnson, 'Preface', p. 424.

29. Johnson, 'Preface', p. 425.

30. Erin Sullivan, 'Anti-Bardolatry through the Ages, or, Why Voltaire, Tolstoy, Shaw and Wittgenstein didn't like Shakespeare', *Opticon1826* 2 (1 April 2007). Available online at: http://www.ucl.ac.uk/opticon1826/archive/issue2/VfPA_H_Shakespeare.pdf.
    Sullivan gives his source as qtd. in Theodore Besterman, introduction to *Voltaire on Shakespeare* (Geneva: Institut et Musée Voltaire, 1967), pp. 16, 19.

31. Johnson, 'Preface', p. 425.

32. Johnson, 'Preface', p. 425.

33. Johnson, 'Preface', p. 428.

34. Johnson, 'Preface', p. 428.

35. Johnson, 'Preface', pp. 428–9.

36. Johnson, 'Preface', p. 429.

CHAPTER TWO: THE ROMANTICS

1. Lord Byron, *Don Juan*, ed. T. G. Steffan, E. Steffan and W. W. Pratt, Penguin English Poets series (Harmondsworth: Penguin, 1973), p. 97.

2. Jane Austen, *Mansfield Park*, Penguin English Library (Harmondsworth: Penguin, 1975), p. 335.

3. Samuel Taylor Coleridge, *Lectures and Notes on Shakespeare and Other Dramatists*, World's Classics series no. 363 (London: Humphrey Milford; Oxford University Press, 1931), pp. 175–6.

4. August von Wilhelm Schlegel, *Lectures on Dramatic Art and Literature*, trans. John Black (Project Gutenberg: EBook #7148, 2003), p. 538.

5. Schlegel, *Lectures*, p. 539.

6. Schlegel, *Lectures*, p. 542.

7. For an excellent account of the critical response (including Schlegel's) to *Romeo and Juliet* from the late sixteenth to the early twenty-first century, see Gillian Woods,

Shakespeare: Romeo and Juliet: *A Reader's Guide to Essential Criticism*, Palgrave Macmillan Readers' Guides series (Basingstoke and New York: Palgrave Macmillan, 2013).

8. Schlegel, *Lectures*, p. 590.
9. Schlegel, *Lectures*, p. 592.
10. Schlegel, *Lectures*, p. 594.
11. Schlegel, *Lectures*, pp. 594–5.
12. Schlegel, *Lectures*, p. 595.
13. Schlegel, *Lectures*, p. 596.
14. Schlegel, *Lectures*, p. 596.
15. Schlegel, *Lectures*, p. 597.
16. Schlegel, *Lectures*, p. 597n.
17. Schlegel, *Lectures*, p. 598.
18. Schlegel, *Lectures*, p. 599.
19. Schlegel, *Lectures*, p. 602.
20. Schlegel, *Lectures*, p. 603.
21. Schlegel, *Lectures*, p. 605.
22. Schlegel, *Lectures*, pp. 605–6.
23. Schlegel, *Lectures*, p. 608.
24. William Hazlitt, *Characters of Shakespeare's Plays*, World's Classics series no. 205 (London: Humphrey Milford: Oxford University Press, 1916), p. 12.
25. Hazlitt, *Characters*, p. 12.
26. Hazlitt, *Characters*, p. 35.
27. Hazlitt, *Characters*, pp. 86–7.
28. Hazlitt, *Characters*, p. 88.
29. Hazlitt, *Characters*, p. 44.
30. Hazlitt, *Characters*, p. 45.
31. Hazlitt, *Characters*, p. 125.
32. Hazlitt, *Characters*, p. 128.
33. Hazlitt, *Characters*, p. 141.
34. Qtd. Hazlitt, *Characters*, p. 145. See Charles Lamb, 'On the Tragedies of Shakspeare [*sic*], considered with reference to their fitness for Stage Representation', in D. Nicol Smith (ed.), *Shakespeare Criticism: A Selection: 1623–1840*, World's Classics series no. 212 (London: Oxford University Press, 1916), p. 206.
35. Hazlitt, *Characters*, p. 146.
36. Coleridge, *Lectures and Notes*, p. 179.
37. Coleridge, *Lectures and Notes*, p. 180.
38. Coleridge, *Lectures and Notes*, p. 193.
39. Coleridge, *Lectures and Notes*, p. 208.
40. Coleridge, *Lectures and Notes*, p. 186.
41. Coleridge, *Lectures and Notes*, p. 205.
42. Coleridge, *Lectures and Notes*, p. 225.
43. Coleridge, *Lectures and Notes*, p. 227.
44. Coleridge, *Lectures and Notes*, p. 228.
45. Coleridge, *Lectures and Notes*, p. 233.
46. Coleridge, *Lectures and Notes*, p. 234.
47. Coleridge, *Lectures and Notes*, p. 160.
48. Coleridge, *Lectures and Notes*, p. 170.

CHAPTER THREE: THE VICTORIANS

1. See, however, chapter 2 of Robert Sawyer, *Victorian Appropriations of Shakespeare* (Madison, NJ: Fairleigh Dickinson University Press, 2003) for a positive assessment of Swinburne as a Shakespeare critic.

2. Edward Dowden, *Shakspere [sic]: A Critical Study of His Mind and Art*, 15th edn (London: Kegan Paul, Trench, Trübner, ?1918), p. 98.

3. Dowden, *A Critical Study*, p. 100.

4. Dowden, *A Critical Study*, p. 126.

5. Dowden, *A Critical Study*, p. 129.

6. Dowden, *A Critical Study*, p. 132.

7. G[eorg] G[ottfried] Gervinus, *Shakespeare Commentaries*, trans. 'under the author's superintendence' by F[rances] E[lizabeth] Bunnètt, new edn, revised (London: Smith, Elder, 1877), p. 615.

8. Gervinus, *Shakespeare Commentaries*, pp. 615–16.

9. Gervinus, *Shakespeare Commentaries*, p. 616.

10. George Brandes, *William Shakespeare*, no trans. given, new impression revised with two appendices (London: William Heinemann, 1920), p. 378.

11. Brandes, *William Shakespeare*, p. 421.

12. Brandes, *William Shakespeare*, p. 422.

13. Brandes, *William Shakespeare*, p. 448.

14. Brandes, *William Shakespeare*, p. 449.

15. Brandes, *William Shakespeare*, p. 460.

CHAPTER FOUR: CHARACTER AND CORRELATIVE

1. A. C. Bradley, *Shakespearean Tragedy: Lectures on* Hamlet, Othello, King Lear, Macbeth. St Martin's Library (London: Macmillan, 1957). Aristotle is mentioned on p. 10 and in a footnote on p. 15.

2. Bradley, *Shakespearean Tragedy*. Hegel is mentioned on p. 10 in the main text and a footnote, and on p. 291 in a footnote. The p. 10 footnote refers the reader to Bradley's 'Hegel's Theory of Tragedy'. This is included in Bradley's *Oxford Lectures on Poetry* (London and Basingstoke: Macmillan St Martin's Press, 1970), pp. 68–95.

3. Bradley, *Shakespearean Tragedy*, p. 1.

4. Bradley, *Shakespearean Tragedy*, p. 2.

5. Bradley, *Shakespearean Tragedy*, pp. 2–3.

6. See The RSC Shakespeare [hereafter RSC], ed. Jonathan Bate and Eric Rasmussen (Basingstoke: Macmillan, 2007), p. 63, where the Catalogue (contents page) of the First Folio is reproduced and shows *Cymbeline, King of Britain* in the last of its entries under 'Tragedies'. *Troilus and Cressida* is missing because a copy of it did not arrive until after the printing of the preliminary pages, but it was included 'between the histories and the tragedies' (p. 1456).

7. Bradley, *Shakespearean Tragedy*, p. 3.

8. Bradley, *Shakespearean Tragedy*, p. 7.

9. Bradley, *Shakespearean Tragedy*, p. 9.

10. Bradley, *Shakespearean Tragedy*, p. 13.

11. Bradley, *Shakespearean Tragedy*, p. 15.

12. Bradley, *Shakespearean Tragedy*, p.16.

13. Bradley, *Shakespearean Tragedy*, p. 29.

14. Bradley, *Shakespearean Tragedy*, p. 70.

15. Bradley, *Shakespearean Tragedy*, p. 86.

16. Bradley, *Shakespearean Tragedy*, p.102.

17. Bradley, *Shakespearean Tragedy*, p. 91.

18. Bradley, *Shakespearean Tragedy*, p. 143.

19. Bradley, *Shakespearean Tragedy*, p. 150.

20. Bradley, *Shakespearean Tragedy*, p. 151.

21. Bradley, *Shakespearean Tragedy*, p. 164. 'And loved him, with that love which was her doom' is how the line runs in Alfred, Lord Tennyson, *Lancelot and Elaine*, in *Poems and*

Plays, Oxford Standard Authors, ed. T. Herbert Warren, revd and enlgd Frederick Page (London, Oxford, New York: Oxford University Press, 1975), p. 372.

22. Bradley, *Shakespearean Tragedy*, p.166.
23. Bradley, *Shakespearean Tragedy*, p. 189.
24. Bradley, *Shakespearean Tragedy*, p. 193.
25. Bradley, *Shakespearean Tragedy*, p. 228.
26. Bradley, *Shakespearean Tragedy*, p. 235.
27. Bradley, *Shakespearean Tragedy*, p. 217.
28. Qtd Bradley, *Shakespearean Tragedy*, p. 220.
29. Bradley, *Shakespearean Tragedy*, p. 218.
30. Bradley, *Shakespearean Tragedy*, p. 278.
31. Bradley, *Shakespearean Tragedy*, p. 279.
32. Bradley, *Shakespearean Tragedy*, p. 280.
33. Bradley, *Shakespearean Tragedy*, p. 281.
34. Bradley, *Shakespearean Tragedy*, p. 280.
35. Bradley, *Shakespearean Tragedy*, p. 281.
36. Bradley, *Shakespearean Tragedy*, p. 295.
37. Bradley, *Shakespearean Tragedy*, p. 296.
38. T. S. Eliot, 'Hamlet and His Problems' (1919) in *The Sacred Wood: Essays on Poetry and Criticism* (London: Methuen, 1972), p. 95.
39. Eliot, 'Hamlet and His Problems', p. 96.
40. Eliot, 'Hamlet and His Problems', p. 97.
41. Eliot, 'Hamlet and His Problems', p. 98.
42. Eliot, 'Hamlet and His Problems', p. 99.
43. Eliot, 'Hamlet and His Problems', p. 100.
44. John J. Duffy, 'T. S. Eliot's Objective Correlative: A New England Commonplace', *New England Quarterly*, 42:1 (Mar. 1969), 108–15.
45. Eliot, 'Hamlet and His Problems', p. 100.
46. Eliot, 'Hamlet and His Problems', p. 101.
47. Eliot, 'Hamlet and His Problems', p. 101.
48. Eliot, 'Hamlet and His Problems', p. 103.

CHAPTER FIVE: PSYCHOANALYSIS AND DESIRE

1. Sigmund Freud, *The Interpretation of Dreams*, Pelican Freud Library series vol. 4, trans. James Strachey, ed. James Strachey, assd Alan Tyson, revd Angela Richards (Harmondsworth: Penguin, 1977), p. 366.
2. Freud, *Interpretation of Dreams*, p. 367.
3. George Brandes, *William Shakespeare*, no trans. given, new impression revd with two appendices (London: William Heinemann, 1920), p. 341. 'He had lost his father, his earliest friend and guardian, whose honour and reputation lay so near to his heart [...] he had doubtless sat by the death-bed of the little Hamnet [...] All the years of his youth, spent at his father's side, revived in Shakespeare's mind, memories flocked in upon him, the fundamental relation between son and father preoccupied his thoughts, and he fell to brooding over filial love and filial reverence.
   In the same year *Hamlet* began to take shape in Shakespeare's imagination.'
4. Freud, *Interpretation of Dreams*, p. 368.
5. Sigmund Freud, 'Some Character-Types Met With in Psycho-Analytical Work', in John Strachey and Anna Freud (eds), *The Complete Psychological Works of Sigmund Freud*, vol. 14, 1914–1916 (London: The Hogarth Press and the Institute of Psycho–Analysis, 1957), p. 320.
6. RSC glosses (p. 1906) that 'He has no children' 'refers either to Macbeth or to Malcolm'.
7. Freud, 'Some Character-Types', p. 321.

8. Freud, 'Some Character-Types', p. 319.

9. Freud, 'Some Character-Types', p. 321.

10. Freud, 'Some Character-Types', p. 323.

11. Freud, 'Some Character-Types', p. 324.

12. Ernest Jones, *Hamlet and Oedipus* (Garden City, NY: Doubleday Anchor Books, 1954), pp. 20–1.

13. Jones, *Hamlet and Oedipus*, p. 21.

14. Jones, *Hamlet and Oedipus*, p. 22.

15. Paget's original statement: 'She says, as all such patients do, "I cannot"; it looks like "I will not"; but it is "I cannot will".' Qtd in Jon Stone, Jo Perthen and Alan J. Carson, 'REVIEW. 'A Leg to Stand On' by Oliver Sacks: a Unique Autobiographical Account of Functional Paralysis', *Journal of Neurology, Neuroscience and Psychiatry*, 83:9 (2012), 866. Available at: http://jnnp.bmj.com/content/83/9/864.full.pdf+html. Accessed 11 Mar. 2014. Stone et al. give source on p. 867 n.6 as: James Paget, 'Nervous Mimicry', in Stephen Paget (ed.), *Selected Essays and Addresses by Sir James Paget* (London and New York: Longmans, Green and Co, 1873), [n.p.]

16. Jones, *Hamlet and Oedipus*, p. 59.

17. Jones, *Hamlet and Oedipus*, p. 91.

18. Jones, *Hamlet and Oedipus*, p. 92.

19. Jones, *Hamlet and Oedipus*, p. 95.

20. Jones, *Hamlet and Oedipus*, p. 96 n.25.

21. Jones, *Hamlet and Oedipus*, p. 97.

22. Jones, *Hamlet and Oedipus*, p. 109.

23. Jones, *Hamlet and Oedipus*, p. 112.

24. Jones, *Hamlet and Oedipus*, p. 113.

25. Jones, *Hamlet and Oedipus*, p. 139.

26. Jones, *Hamlet and Oedipus*, p. 140.

27. T. J. B. Spencer (ed.), *Shakespeare's Plutarch: The Lives of Julius Caesar, Brutus, Marcus Antonius, and Coriolanus in the translation of Sir Thomas North* [1535–1604] (London: Penguin, 1964), p. 106. That Shakespeare was aware of the rumour that Brutus was Caesar's illegitimate son is suggested in *Henry VI 2* when Suffolk says: 'Brutus's bastard hand / Stabbed Julius Caesar' (4.2.138–9).

28. Jones, *Hamlet and Oedipus*, p. 141.

29. Jacques Lacan, 'Sept Leçons sur *Hamlet*', in *Le Séminaire de Jacques Lacan Livre VI*, ed. Jacques-Alain Miller, Champ Freudien series (Paris: Editions Martinière, 2013), pp. 342–3.

30. Lacan, 'Sept Leçons sur *Hamlet*', p. 343.

31. Lacan, 'Sept Leçons sur *Hamlet*', p. 332.

32. Lacan, 'Sept Leçons sur *Hamlet*', p. 365.

33. Lacan, 'Sept Leçons sur *Hamlet*', p. 392.

34. Lacan, 'Sept Leçons sur *Hamlet*', p. 393.

35. Lacan, 'Sept Leçons sur *Hamlet*', p. 367.

36. Lacan, 'Sept Leçons sur *Hamlet*', p. 364.

37. Lacan, 'Sept Leçons sur *Hamlet*', p. 380.

38. Lacan, 'Sept Leçons sur *Hamlet*', p. 381.

39. Lacan records his disappointment at consulting the *New English Dictionary* and finding no mention of what Shakespeare meant by 'dead men's fingers' ('Sept Leçons sur *Hamlet*', p. 381). In '*Hamlet*: Ophelia's Long Purples', *Shakespeare Quarterly*, 29:3 (Summer 1978), Karl P. Wentersdorf argues that the flower in question may be *Arum maculatum* – wild arum or cuckoo-pint – and that, while there is no evidence that these were ever called 'dead-men's fingers', the name 'seems more appropriate to *Arum maculatum* than to *Orchis mascula*, partly because the Arum's phallic spadix [spike of minute flowers] is surrounded by a partly open whitish sheath that can be thought of as a shroud,

and partly because the term "finger" can be a euphemism for the phallus' (p. 416). Wentersdorf gives the example of Thersites' commentary on Diomed and Cressida in *Troilus and Cressida*: 'How the devil Luxury, with his fat rump and potato-finger, tickles these together! Fry, lechery, fry!' (5.2.62–3). RSC glosses 'potato-finger' as 'large penis/ fat finger (also suggestive as a digit that ['tickles'] sexually' (p. 1522). Wentersdorf's suggestion would support Lacan's interpretation.

40. The word 'mandragora' occurs in *Othello* when Iago says: '[n]ot poppy, nor mandragora, / Nor all the drowsy syrups of the world / Shall ever medicine thee to that sweet sleep / Which thou owed'st [owned] yesterday' (3.3.366–9). It features in *Antony and Cleopatra* when the Egyptian queen says, 'give me to drink mandragora [...] [t]hat I might sleep out this great gap of time / My Antony is away' (1.5.4, 6–7).

41. Lacan, 'Sept Leçons sur *Hamlet*', p. 381.

42. Lacan, 'Sept Leçons sur *Hamlet*', p. 342.

43. Lacan, 'Sept Leçons sur *Hamlet*', p. 306.

44. Freud, 'Some Character-Types', p. 366.

45. Lacan, 'Sept Leçons sur *Hamlet*', p. 306.

CHAPTER SIX: IMAGERY AND FORM

1. G. Wilson Knight, *The Wheel of Fire: Interpretations of Shakespearian Tragedy with Three New Essays*, University Paperbacks series (London: Methuen, 1960), p. 1.

2. Knight, *Wheel of Fire*, p. 2.

3. Knight, *Wheel of Fire*, p. 3.

4. Knight, *Wheel of Fire*, p. 6.

5. Knight, *Wheel of Fire*, p. 7.

6. Knight, *Wheel of Fire*, pp. 7–8.

7. Knight, *Wheel of Fire*, p. 8.

8. Knight, *Wheel of Fire*, p. 9.

9. Knight, *Wheel of Fire*, p. 11.

10. Knight, *Wheel of Fire*, p. 11.

11. Knight, *Wheel of Fire*, p. 14.

12. Knight, *Wheel of Fire*, p. 15.

13. Knight, *Wheel of Fire*, p. 14.

14. Knight, *Wheel of Fire*, p. 26.

15. Knight, *Wheel of Fire*, p. 29.

16. Knight, *Wheel of Fire*, p. 27.

17. Knight, *Wheel of Fire*, p. 29.

18. Knight, *Wheel of Fire*, p. 30.

19. Knight, *Wheel of Fire*, p. 32.

20. Knight, *Wheel of Fire*, p. 34.

21. Knight, *Wheel of Fire*, p. 32.

22. Knight, *Wheel of Fire*, p. 32.

23. Knight, *Wheel of Fire*, p. 100.

24. Knight, *Wheel of Fire*, p. 101.

25. Knight, *Wheel of Fire*, p. 102.

26. See F. R. Leavis, 'Literary Criticism and Philosophy' (orig. pubd *Scrutiny* (Mar.–Jun. 1937), in *The Common Pursuit* ([1962] Harmondsworth: Penguin, 1978), pp. 211–22.

27. L. C. Knights, 'Preface' to *Explorations: Essays in Criticism Mainly on the Literature of the Seventeenth Century* (Harmondsworth: Penguin in association with Chatto & Windus, 1964), p. 11.

28. L. C. Knights, 'How Many Children Had Lady Macbeth? An Essay in the Theory and Practice of Shakespeare Criticism' [1933], in L. C. Knights, *Explorations* (1964), p. 13.

29. Knights, 'How Many Children', p. 15.

30. See T. S. Eliot, 'The Metaphysical Poets', in *Selected Essays* (London: Faber and Faber, 1932), pp. 281–91, esp. pp. 287–8:'[t]he poets of the seventeenth century, the successors of the dramatists of the sixteenth, possessed a mechanism of sensibility which could devour any kind of experience […] In the seventeenth century a dissociation of sensibility set in, from which we have never recovered.'
31. Knights, 'How Many Children', p. 16.
32. Knights, 'How Many Children', p. 16.
33. Knights, 'How Many Children', p. 18.
34. Knights, 'How Many Children', p. 28.
35. Knights, 'How Many Children', p. 29.
36. Knights, 'How Many Children', p. 41.
37. Knights, 'How Many Children', p. 29.
38. Knights, 'How Many Children', p. 30.
39. Knights, 'How Many Children', p. 31.
40. Knights, 'How Many Children', p. 31.
41. Knights, 'How Many Children', p. 39.
42. Knights, 'How Many Children', p. 40.
43. Knights, 'How Many Children', p. 41.
44. Knights, 'How Many Children', p. 42.
45. Knights, 'How Many Children', p. 44.
46. Knights, 'How Many Children', p. 45.
47. Knights, 'How Many Children', p. 46.
48. Knights, 'How Many Children', p. 47.
49. Katharine Cooke, *A. C. Bradley and His Influence in Twentieth-Century Shakespeare Criticism* (Oxford: Clarendon Press at Oxford University Press, 1972), p. 128. Cf. A. C. Bradley, *Shakespearean Tragedy*, St Martin's Library (London: Macmillan, 1957): Shakespeare 'has produced a tragedy utterly unlike [*King Lear*], not much less great as a dramatic poem, and as a drama superior' (p. 327).
50. Knights, 'How Many Children', p. 45.
51. Knights, 'How Many Children', p. 41.
52. L. C. Knights, 'Prince Hamlet', in L. C. Knights, *Explorations: Essays in Criticism Mainly on the Literature of the Seventeenth Century* (Harmondsworth: Penguin in association with Chatto & Windus, 1964), p. 76.
53. Knights, 'Prince Hamlet', p. 80.
54. Knights, 'Prince Hamlet', p. 86.
55. Knights, 'Prince Hamlet', pp. 86–7.
56. Knights, 'Prince Hamlet', p. 87.
57. Knights, 'Prince Hamlet', p. 83.
58. Caroline F. E. Spurgeon, *Shakespeare's Imagery and What It Tells Us* (Cambridge: Cambridge University Press, 1990), p. 8.
59. Spurgeon, *Shakespeare's Imagery*, p. 5.
60. Spurgeon, *Shakespeare's Imagery*, pp. 344–5.
61. G. Wilson Knight, *The Imperial Theme: Further Interpretations of Shakespeare's Tragedies Including the Roman* Plays (London: Methuen, 1961), p. 130.
62. Spurgeon, *Shakespeare's Imagery*, p. 310.
63. Spurgeon, *Shakespeare's Imagery*, p. 310.
64. Spurgeon, *Shakespeare's Imagery*, p. 316.
65. Spurgeon, *Shakespeare's Imagery*, p. 317.
66. Spurgeon, *Shakespeare's Imagery*, p. 318.
67. Spurgeon, *Shakespeare's Imagery*, pp. 318–19.
68. Spurgeon, *Shakespeare's Imagery*, p. 335.
69. Spurgeon, *Shakespeare's Imagery*, p. 336.
70. Spurgeon, *Shakespeare's Imagery*, p. 336.

71. Spurgeon, *Shakespeare's Imagery*, p. 339.
72. Spurgeon, *Shakespeare's Imagery*, p. 325.
73. Spurgeon, *Shakespeare's Imagery*, p. 327.
74. Cleanth Brooks, 'The Naked Babe and the Cloak of Manliness', in *The Well Wrought Urn: Studies in the Structure of Poetry* (London: Denis Dobson, 1949), p. 30.
75. Brooks, 'The Naked Babe', p. 33.
76. Brooks, 'The Naked Babe', p. 34.
77. Brooks, 'The Naked Babe', p. 36.
78. Brooks, 'The Naked Babe', p. 37.
79. Brooks, 'The Naked Babe', p. 42.
80. Brooks, 'The Naked Babe', pp. 42–3.
81. Brooks, 'The Naked Babe', p. 38.
82. Brooks, 'The Naked Babe', p. 41.
83. Oscar James Campbell, 'Shakespeare and the "New Critics"', in James G. McManaway, Giles E. Dawson and Edwin E. Willoughby (eds), *Joseph Quincy Adams Memorial Studies* (Washington: Folger Shakespeare Library, 1948), pp. 89–90. For a fuller account of Campbell's riposte and a discussion of Helen Gardner's challenge to Brooks, see Nicolas Tredell, *Shakespeare: Macbeth: A Reader's Guide to Essential Criticism* (Basingstoke and New York: Palgrave Macmillan, 2006), pp. 78–83.

CHAPTER SEVEN: ARCHETYPE AND ABSURDITY

1. Northrop Frye, *Fools of Time: Studies in Shakespearean Tragedy*, Alexander Lectures, 1966 (Toronto, Buffalo, London: University of Toronto Press, 1967), p. 16.
2. Frye, *Fools of Time*, p. 17.
3. Frye, *Fools of Time*, p. 33.
4. Frye, *Fools of Time*, p. 6.
5. Frye, *Fools of Time*, p. 29.
6. Frye, *Fools of Time*, p. 48.
7. Frye, *Fools of Time*, p. 47.
8. Frye, *Fools of Time*, p. 47.
9. Frye, *Fools of Time*, p. 49.
10. Frye, *Fools of Time*, p. 70.
11. Frye, *Fools of Time*, pp. 71–2.
12. Frye, *Fools of Time*, p. 72.
13. Frye, *Fools of Time*, p. 73.
14. Frye, *Fools of Time*, p. 117.
15. Peter Brook, 'Preface' to Jan Kott, *Shakespeare Our Contemporary*, trans. Boleslaw Taborski, 2nd edn, University Paperbacks series (London: Methuen, 1967), p. ix.
16. Brook, 'Preface', p. x.
17. Jan Kott, *Shakespeare Our Contemporary*, trans. Boleslaw Taborski, 2nd edn, University Paperbacks series (London: Methuen, 1967), p. 52.
18. Kott, *Shakespeare Our Contemporary*, p. 55.
19. Kott, *Shakespeare Our Contemporary*, p. 59.
20. Kott, *Shakespeare Our Contemporary*, p. 55.
21. Qtd Kott, *Shakespeare Our Contemporary*, p. 85. See Samuel Taylor Coleridge, *Lectures and Notes on Shakespeare and Other Dramatists*, World's Classics series no. 363 (London: Humphrey Milford; Oxford University Press, 1931), p. 228.
22. Qtd Kott, *Shakespeare Our Contemporary*, p. 228. See William Hazlitt, *Characters of Shakespeare's Plays*, World's Classics series no. 205 (London: Humphrey Milford: Oxford University Press, 1916), p. 45.
23. Kott, *Shakespeare Our Contemporary*, p. 86.

24. Kott, *Shakespeare Our Contemporary*, p. 87.
25. Kott, *Shakespeare Our Contemporary*, p. 99.
26. Kott, *Shakespeare Our Contemporary*, p. 99.
27. Kott, *Shakespeare Our Contemporary*, p. 92.
28. Kott, *Shakespeare Our Contemporary*, p. 99.
29. Kott, *Shakespeare Our Contemporary*, p. 104.
30. Kott, *Shakespeare Our Contemporary*, p. 113.
31. Kott, *Shakespeare Our Contemporary*, p. 115.
32. Kott, *Shakespeare Our Contemporary*, p. 116.
33. Kott, *Shakespeare Our Contemporary*, pp. 120, 121.
34. Marjorie Garber, *Shakespeare and Modern Culture* (New York: Pantheon, 2008), p. 256.
35. Kott, *Shakespeare Our Contemporary*, pp. 125, 128.
36. René Girard, *A Theatre of Envy: William Shakespeare*, 2nd edn (Leominster, Herefordshire: Gracewing; New Malden, Surrey: Inigo Enterprises, 2000), p. 3.
37. Girard, *Theatre of Envy*, p. 161.
38. Girard, *Theatre of Envy*, p. 164.
39. Girard, *Theatre of Envy*, p. 165.
40. Girard, *Theatre of Envy*, p. 6.
41. Girard, *Theatre of Envy*, p. 5.
42. Girard, *Theatre of Envy*, p. 195.
43. Girard, *Theatre of Envy*, p. 185.
44. Girard, *Theatre of Envy*, p. 191.
45. Girard, *Theatre of Envy*, p. 223.
46. Girard, *Theatre of Envy*, p, 226.
47. Naomi Conn Liebler, *Shakespeare's Festive Tragedy: The Ritual Foundations of Genre* (London and New York: Routledge, 1995), p. 1.
48. Liebler, *Shakespeare's Festive Tragedy*, p. 13.
49. Liebler, *Shakespeare's Festive Tragedy*, p. 13.
50. Liebler, *Shakespeare's Festive Tragedy*, p. 13.
51. Liebler, *Shakespeare's Festive Tragedy*, p. 23.
52. Liebler, *Shakespeare's Festive Tragedy*, p. 23.
53. Liebler, *Shakespeare's Festive Tragedy*, p. 17. Liebler's quotes are from René Girard, *Violence and the Sacred*, trans. Patrick Gregory (Baltimore, MD: Johns Hopkins University Press, 1977), pp. 99, 46.
54. Liebler, *Shakespeare's Festive Tragedy*, p. 17.
55. Liebler, *Shakespeare's Festive Tragedy*, p. 20.
56. Liebler, *Shakespeare's Festive Tragedy*, pp. 20–1.
57. Liebler, *Shakespeare's Festive Tragedy*, p. 35.
58. Liebler, *Shakespeare's Festive Tragedy*, p. 196.
59. Liebler, *Shakespeare's Festive Tragedy*, p. 197.
60. Liebler, *Shakespeare's Festive Tragedy*, p. 205.
61. Liebler, *Shakespeare's Festive Tragedy*, p. 206.
62. Liebler, *Shakespeare's Festive Tragedy*, p. 219.
63. L. C. Knights, 'How Many Children Had Lady Macbeth? An Essay in the Theory and Practice of Shakespearean Interpretation', *Explorations: Essays in Criticism Mainly on the Literature of the Seventeenth Century* ([1946] Harmondsworth: Penguin in association with Chatto & Windus, 1964), p. 40.
64. Liebler, *Shakespeare's Festive Tragedy*, p. 222.
65. Knights, 'How Many Children', p. 47.
66. Liebler, *Shakespeare's Festive Tragedy*, p. 222.
67. Liebler, *Shakespeare's Festive Tragedy*, p. 17.
68. The term is from Antony Easthope, *British Post-Structuralism since 1968* (London and New York: Routledge, 1988).

CHAPTER EIGHT: HISTORY AND SUBJECTIVITY

1. Stephen Greenblatt, *Shakespearean Negotiations: The Circulation of Social Energy in Renaissance England* (Oxford: Clarendon Press at Oxford University Press, 1990), p. 116.
2. Greenblatt, *Shakespearean Negotiations*, p. 117.
3. Greenblatt, *Shakespearean Negotiations*, p. 117.
4. Greenblatt, *Shakespearean Negotiations*, p. 118.
5. Greenblatt, *Shakespearean Negotiations*, p. 118.
6. Greenblatt, *Shakespearean Negotiations*, p. 119.
7. Greenblatt, *Shakespearean Negotiations*, p. 119.
8. Greenblatt, *Shakespearean Negotiations*, p. 120.
9. Greenblatt, *Shakespearean Negotiations*, p. 120.
10. Qtd Greenblatt, *Shakespearean Negotiations*, pp. 120–1.
11. Greenblatt, *Shakespearean Negotiations*, p. 121.
12. Greenblatt, *Shakespearean Negotiations*, p. 122.
13. Greenblatt, *Shakespearean Negotiations*, p. 122.
14. Greenblatt, *Shakespearean Negotiations*, pp. 123–4.
15. Greenblatt, *Shakespearean Negotiations*, p. 128.
16. Leonard Tennenhouse, *Power on Display: The Politics of Shakespeare's Genres* (New York and London: Methuen, 1986), p. 112.
17. Tennenhouse, *Power on Display*, p. 114.
18. Tennenhouse, *Power on Display*, p. 124.
19. William Hazlitt, *Characters of Shakespeare's Plays*, World's Classics series no. 205 (London: Humphrey Milford; Oxford University Press, 1916), p. 45.
20. Jan Kott, *Shakespeare Our Contemporary*, trans. Boleslaw Taborski, 2nd edn, University Paperbacks series (London: Methuen, 1967), p. 86.
21. Tennenhouse, *Power on Display*, p. 135.
22. Tennenhouse, *Power on Display*, p. 140.
23. Tennenhouse, *Power on Display*, p. 141.
24. Tennenhouse, *Power on Display*, p. 143.
25. Tennenhouse, *Power on Display*, p. 146.
26. Jonathan Dollimore, *Radical Tragedy: Religion, Ideology and Power in the Drama of Shakespeare and His Contemporaries* (Brighton: Harvester, 1984), p. 3.
27. Dollimore, *Radical Tragedy*, p. 4.
28. Dollimore, *Radical Tragedy*, p. 8.
29. Dollimore, *Radical Tragedy*, p. 202.
30. Dollimore, *Radical Tragedy*, p. 203.
31. Dollimore, *Radical Tragedy*, p. 204.
32. Dollimore, *Radical Tragedy*, pp. 205–6.
33. Dollimore, *Radical Tragedy*, p. 215.
34. Dollimore, *Radical Tragedy*, p. 216.
35. Dollimore, *Radical Tragedy*, p. 217.
36. Dollimore, *Radical Tragedy*, p. 222.
37. Dollimore, *Radical Tragedy*, p. 224.
38. Dollimore, *Radical Tragedy*, p. 228.
39. Qtd Dollimore, *Radical Tragedy*, p. 229. Dollimore gives his source as: Brian Vickers, *Shakespeare: Coriolanus*, Studies in English Literature series no. 58 (London: Edward Arnold, 1966), p. 59.
40. Dollimore, *Radical Tragedy*, p. 229.
41. Dollimore, *Radical Tragedy*, pp. 229–30.
42. Catherine Belsey, *The Subject of Tragedy: Identity and Difference in Renaissance Drama* (London and New York: Routledge, 1985), p. ix.
43. Belsey, *The Subject of Tragedy*, p. 8.
44. Belsey, *The Subject of Tragedy*, p. 41.

45. Belsey, *The Subject of Tragedy*, p. 41.
46. Belsey, *The Subject of Tragedy*, p. 42.
47. Belsey, *The Subject of Tragedy*, p. 47.
48. Belsey, *The Subject of Tragedy*, p. 47.
49. Belsey, *The Subject of Tragedy*, p. 183.
50. Belsey, *The Subject of Tragedy*, p. 184.
51. Belsey, *The Subject of Tragedy*, p. 184.

CHAPTER NINE: GENDER AND SEXUALITY

1. Janet Adelman, *Suffocating Mothers: Fantasies of Maternal Origin in Shakespeare's Plays*, Hamlet *to* The Tempest (New York and London: Routledge, 1992), p. 2.
2. Adelman, *Suffocating Mothers*, p. 11.
3. Adelman, *Suffocating Mothers*, pp. 12–13.
4. Adelman, *Suffocating Mothers*, p. 16.
5. Adelman, *Suffocating Mothers*, p. 17.
6. Adelman, *Suffocating Mothers*, p. 30.
7. Adelman, *Suffocating Mothers*, p. 64.
8. Adelman, *Suffocating Mothers*, p. 67.
9. Adelman, *Suffocating Mothers*, pp. 67–8.
10. Adelman, *Suffocating Mothers*, p. 68.
11. Adelman, *Suffocating Mothers*, p. 68.
12. Adelman, *Suffocating Mothers*, p. 68.
13. Adelman, *Suffocating Mothers*, p. 69.
14. Adelman, *Suffocating Mothers*, p. 75. For an account of Adelman's interpretation of *Macbeth* in *Suffering Mothers*, see Nicolas Tredell, *Shakespeare:* Macbeth: *A Reader's Guide to Essential Criticism*, Palgrave Macmillan Readers' Guides to Essential Criticism series (Basingstoke and New York: Palgrave Macmillan, 2006), pp. 138–42.
15. Adelman, *Suffocating Mothers*, p. 104.
16. Adelman, *Suffocating Mothers*, p. 106.
17. Adelman, *Suffocating Mothers*, p. 108.
18. Adelman, *Suffocating Mothers*, p. 109.
19. Adelman, *Suffocating Mothers*, p. 110.
20. Adelman, *Suffocating Mothers*, p. 128.
21. Adelman, *Suffocating Mothers*, p. 128.
22. Philippa Berry, *Shakespeare's Feminine Endings: Disfiguring Death in the Tragedies*, Feminist Readings of Shakespeare series (London and New York: Routledge, 1999), p. 1.
23. Berry, *Shakespeare's Feminine Endings*, p. 5.
24. Berry, *Shakespeare's Feminine Endings*, p. 23.
25. Berry, *Shakespeare's Feminine Endings*, p. 26.
26. The term 'handkerchief occurs five times in 3.3, in lines 339, 340, 341, 475, 481; six times in 3.4, in lines 50, 56, 93, 96, 100, 105; nine times in 4.1, in lines 12, 20, 24, 43 (twice), 47, 153, 159, 173; and six times in 5.2, in lines 55, 72, 76, 245, 256, 360. The term 'napkin' occurs three times in 3.3, in lines 320, 323 and 357.
27. Berry, *Shakespeare's Feminine Endings*, p. 95.
28. Berry, *Shakespeare's Feminine Endings*, p. 95.
29. Berry, *Shakespeare's Feminine Endings*, p. 101.
30. Berry, *Shakespeare's Feminine Endings*, p. 103.
31. Berry, *Shakespeare's Feminine Endings*, p. 119.
32. Berry, *Shakespeare's Feminine Endings*, p. 120.
33. Berry, *Shakespeare's Feminine Endings*, p. 120.
34. Coppélia Kahn, *Roman Shakespeare: Warriors, Wounds and Women*, Feminist Readings of Shakespeare series (London and New York: Routledge, 1997), p. 1.

35. For an account of Kahn's interpretation of *Macbeth* in *Man's Estate*, see Tredell, *Shakespeare*, pp. 130–5.

36. Kahn, *Roman Shakespeare*, p. 2.

37. Kahn, *Roman Shakespeare*, p. 15.

38. Kahn, *Roman Shakespeare*, p. 17.

39. Kahn, *Roman Shakespeare*, p. 90.

40. Kahn, *Roman Shakespeare*, p. 101.

41. Kahn, *Roman Shakespeare*, p. 103.

42. Kahn, *Roman Shakespeare*, p. 105.

43. Kahn, *Roman Shakespeare*, p. 105.

44. Madhavi Menon (ed.), 'Introduction: Queer Shakes', in Madhavi Menon (ed.), *Shakesqueer: A Queer Companion to the Complete Works of Shakespeare* (Durham and London: Duke University Press, 2011), p. 9.

45. Jason Edwards, '"Tell Me Not Wherein I Seem Unnatural": Queer Meditations on *Coriolanus* in the Time of War', in Menon, *Shakesqueer*, p. 80.

46. Edwards, '"Tell Me Not"', p. 81. In his endnote (p. 88, n3) at the end of his essay, Edwards raises the question of who was responsible for the 'Coriol/anus' joke, of course instancing Jonathan Goldberg's 'The Anus in *Coriolanus*' (1994), and also finding premonitory hints in *The Body Embarrassed* (1993) by Gail Kern Paster (b.1944) and *Language as Symbolic Action* (1966) by Kenneth Burke (1897–1993). But an earlier begetter was surely Cole Porter (1891–1964), who makes the joke in the song 'Brush Up Your Shakespeare', sung by the gangsters Lippy and Slug, in his musical *Kiss Me, Kate* (first performed 1948). It is significant, however, given Porter's own concealed gayness, that he transfers it into what was then an acceptable jocular advocacy of violence against women who resist male advances: '[i]f she says your behaviour is heinous / Kick her right in the Coriolanus'.

47. Edwards, '"Tell Me Not"', p. 83.

48. Edwards, '"Tell Me Not"', p. 83, attributes these lines to Cominius, addressing Coriolanus, whereas in fact they are spoken by Coriolanus addressing Cominius.

49. Edwards, '"Tell Me Not"', p. 83, calls the speech from which these lines come a 'soliloquy' but it is addressed to Coriolanus (possibly with silent servants in the background) and it can be inferred that when Aufidius says 'here I clip / The anvil of my sword' (4.5.106–7), he physically embraces Coriolanus.

50. Edwards, '"Tell Me Not"', p. 83.

51. Edwards, '"Tell Me Not"', p. 84.

52. Edwards, '"Tell Me Not"', p. 85.

53. Edwards, '"Tell Me Not"', p. 86.

CHAPTER TEN: ETHNICITY AND ECOLOGY

1. Margo Hendricks, 'Surveying "Race" in Shakespeare', in Catherine M. S. Alexander and Stanley Wells (eds), *Shakespeare and Race* (Cambridge: Cambridge University Press, 2000), p. 1.

2. Hendricks, 'Surveying "Race" in Shakespeare', p. 20.

3. Barbara Everett, '"Spanish" Othello: the Making of Shakespeare's Moor', in Alexander and Wells, *Shakespeare and Race*, p. 67.

4. Everett, '"Spanish" Othello', p. 68.

5. Qtd Everett, '"Spanish" Othello', p. 68.

6. Everett, '"Spanish" Othello', p. 69.

7. Everett, '"Spanish" Othello', p. 71.

8. Everett, '"Spanish" Othello', p. 71.

9. Everett, '"Spanish" Othello', p. 74.

10. Everett, '"Spanish" Othello', p. 75.

11. Everett, '"Spanish" Othello', pp. 76–7.

12. Ania Loomba, *Shakespeare, Race, and Colonialism*, Oxford Shakespeare Topics series (Oxford: Oxford University Press, 2002), p. 76.

13. Samuel Taylor Coleridge, *Lectures and Notes on Shakespeare and Other Dramatists*, World's Classics series no. 363 (London: Humphrey Milford; Oxford University Press, 1931), p. 228.

14. Loomba, *Shakespeare, Race, and Colonialism*, p. 78.

15. Loomba, *Shakespeare, Race, and Colonialism*, p. 79.

16. Loomba, *Shakespeare, Race, and Colonialism*, p. 81.

17. Loomba, *Shakespeare, Race, and Colonialism*, p. 82.

18. Loomba, *Shakespeare, Race, and Colonialism*, p. 83; p. 175, n.7 gives her source as: Philip C. Kolin, '"Lucius, the Severely Flawed Redeemer of *Titus Andronicus*": A Reply', *Connotations*, 7:1 (1997/8), 95–6.

19. Loomba, *Shakespeare, Race, and Colonialism*, p. 86.

20. Loomba, *Shakespeare, Race, and Colonialism*, p. 89.

21. Loomba, *Shakespeare, Race, and Colonialism*, p. 90.

22. Gabriel Egan, *Green Shakespeare: From Ecopolitics to Ecocriticism*, Accents on Shakespeare series (London and New York: Routledge, 2006), p. 10.

23. Egan, *Green Shakespeare*, p. 12.

24. Egan, *Green Shakespeare*, p. 16.

25. Egan, *Green Shakespeare*, p. 63.

26. Egan, *Green Shakespeare*, p. 63.

27. Egan, *Green Shakespeare*, p. 135.

28. Egan, *Green Shakespeare*, p. 138.

29. Egan, *Green Shakespeare*, p. 139.

30. Egan, *Green Shakespeare*, p. 144.

31. Egan, *Green Shakespeare*, p. 144.

32. Egan, *Green Shakespeare*, p. 145.

33. Egan, *Green Shakespeare*, pp. 146–7.

34. Egan, *Green Shakespeare*, p. 147. Egan gives his source as: Frank McCombie, 'Garlands in *Hamlet* and *King Lear*', *Notes and Queries*, 226 (1981), 132–4.

35. Simon C. Estok, *Ecocriticism and Shakespeare: Reading Ecophobia in Shakespeare's Plays*, Literatures, Cultures, and the Environment series (New York: Palgrave Macmillan, 2011), p.12.

36. Estok, *Ecocriticism and Shakespeare*, p. 4.

37. Estok, *Ecocriticism and Shakespeare*, p. 5.

38. Estok, *Ecocriticism and Shakespeare*, p. 35.

39. Estok, *Ecocriticism and Shakespeare*, p. 3.

40. Estok, *Ecocriticism and Shakespeare*, pp. 135–6, n.4. Estok gives his source as: Peter Stallybrass, 'Shakespeare, the Individual, and the Text', in Laurence Grossberg, Cary Nelson and Paula Treichler (eds), *Cultural Studies* (New York and London: Routledge, 1992), pp. 593–4.

41. Qtd Estok, *Ecocriticism and Shakespeare*, p. 136, n.4. Estok gives his source as: 'cited by Stallybrass [(1992), p.] 594'. Quote here taken directly from Raymond Williams, *Keywords: A Vocabulary of Culture and Society*, revd and expanded edn (London: Fontana, 1988), p. 161.

42. Estok, *Ecocriticism and Shakespeare*, p. 40.

43. Jonathan Dollimore, *Radical Tragedy: Religion, Ideology and Power in the Drama of Shakespeare and his Contemporaries* (Brighton: Harvester, 1984), p. 222.

44. Dollimore, *Radical Tragedy*, p. 118.

45. Estok, *Ecocriticism and Shakespeare*, p. 45.

46. Estok, *Ecocriticism and Shakespeare*, p. 46.

47. Estok, *Ecocriticism and Shakespeare*, pp. 45–6.

48. Estok, *Ecocriticism and Shakespeare*, p. 47.
49. Estok, *Ecocriticism and Shakespeare*, pp. 44–5.

CHAPTER ELEVEN: PHILOSOPHY AND ETHICS

1. Stanley Cavell, *Disowning Knowledge in Seven Plays of Shakespeare*, updated edn (Cambridge: Cambridge University Press, 2003), p. 3.
2. Cavell, *Disowning Knowledge*, p. 11.
3. Cavell, *Disowning Knowledge*, pp. 5–6.
4. Cavell, *Disowning Knowledge*, p. 6.
5. Cavell, *Disowning Knowledge*, p. 5.
6. Cavell, *Disowning Knowledge*, p. 6.
7. Cavell, *Disowning Knowledge*, p. 128.
8. Cavell, *Disowning Knowledge*, p. 129.
9. Cavell, *Disowning Knowledge*, p. 130.
10. Cavell, *Disowning Knowledge*, p. 130.
11. Cavell, *Disowning Knowledge*, pp. 132–3.
12. Cavell, *Disowning Knowledge*, p. 131.
13. Cavell, *Disowning Knowledge*, p. 132.
14. Cavell, *Disowning Knowledge*, p. 133.
15. Cavell, *Disowning Knowledge*, p. 135.
16. Cavell, *Disowning Knowledge*, p. 136.
17. Cavell, *Disowning Knowledge*, p. 137.
18. Cavell, *Disowning Knowledge*, p. 138.
19. Karl Marx and Friedrich Engels, *The Communist Manifesto*, Penguin Books – Great Ideas series no. 13 (London: Penguin, 2004), p. 2.
20. Jacques Derrida, *Specters of Marx: The State of the Debt, the Work of Mourning and the New International*, trans. Peggy Kamuff, intro. Bernd Magnus and Stephen Cullenberg (New York and London: Routledge, 2006), Kindle edn, p. 2.
21. Derrida, *Specters of Marx*, p. 5.
22. Derrida, *Specters of Marx*, p.12.
23. Derrida, *Specters of Marx*, p. 13.
24. Derrida, *Specters of Marx*, p. 6.
25. Derrida, *Specters of Marx*, p. 8.
26. Derrida, *Specters of Marx*, p. 9.
27. Derrida, *Specters of Marx*, p. 9.
28. Derrida, *Specters of Marx*, p. 10.
29. A. D. Nuttall, *Shakespeare the Thinker* (New Haven, CT and London: Yale University Press, 2007), p. 180.
30. Nuttall, *Shakespeare the Thinker*, p. 183.
31. Nuttall, *Shakespeare the Thinker*, p. 184.
32. Nuttall, *Shakespeare the Thinker*, p. 185.
33. Nuttall, *Shakespeare the Thinker*, p. 188.
34. Nuttall, *Shakespeare the Thinker*, p. 186.
35. Nuttall, *Shakespeare the Thinker*, p. 188.
36. Nuttall, *Shakespeare the Thinker*, p. 192.
37. Nuttall, *Shakespeare the Thinker*, p. 193.
38. Nuttall, *Shakespeare the Thinker*, p. 194.
39. G. Wilson Knight, *The Wheel of Fire: Interpretations of Shakespearian Tragedy with Three New Essays*, University Paperbacks series (London: Methuen, 1960), p. 32.
40. Nuttall, *Shakespeare the Thinker*, p. 194.
41. Nuttall, *Shakespeare the Thinker*, p. 194.
42. Nuttall, *Shakespeare the Thinker*, pp. 194–5.

43. Donald R. Wehrs, 'Moral Physiology, Ethical Prototypes and the Denaturing of Sense in Shakespearean Tragedy', *College Literature*, 'Cognitive Shakespeare: Criticism and Theory in the Age of Neuroscience', 33:1 (Winter, 2006), 68.
44. Wehrs, 'Moral Physiology', p. 68.
45. Wehrs, 'Moral Physiology', pp. 76–7.
46. Wehrs, 'Moral Physiology', p. 78.
47. Wehrs, 'Moral Physiology', p. 79.
48. Wehrs, 'Moral Physiology', p. 79.
49. Wehrs, 'Moral Physiology', p. 79.
50. Wehrs, 'Moral Physiology', p. 80.
51. Wehrs gives his source as: Jacqueline Rose, '*Hamlet* – the "Mona Lisa" of Literature', in David Scott Kastan (ed.), *Critical Essays on Shakespeare's* Hamlet (New York: G. K. Hall, 1995), pp. 156–70. Also in Deborah E. Barker and Ivo Kamps (eds), *Shakespeare and Gender: A History* (London and New York: Verso, 1995), pp. 104–19; and Jacqueline Rose, *Sexuality in the Field of Vision* (London: Verso, 2005), pp. 123–40.
52. T. S. Eliot, 'Hamlet and His Problems' (1919), in *The Sacred Wood: Essays on Poetry and Criticism* (London: Methuen, 1972), p. 99.
53. Wehrs, 'Moral Physiology', pp. 86–7, n.29.
54. Wehrs, 'Moral Physiology', p. 80.
55. Wehrs, 'Moral Physiology', p. 83.

CHAPTER TWELVE: RELIGIONS AND REFORMATIONS

1. Graham Hammill and Julia Reinhard Lupton (eds), 'Introduction' to *Political Theology and Early Modernity* (Chicago and London: University of Chicago Press, 2012), p. 1.
2. Julia Reinhard Lupton, *Citizen-Saints: Shakespeare and Political Theology* (Chicago and London: University of Chicago Press, 2005), p. 4.
3. Lupton, *Citizen-Saints*, p. 4.
4. Lupton, *Citizen-Saints*, p. 5.
5. Lupton, *Citizen-Saints*, p. 105.
6. Lupton, *Citizen-Saints*, p. 109.
7. Lupton, *Citizen-Saints*, p. 110.
8. Lupton, *Citizen-Saints*, p. 111.
9. Lupton, *Citizen-Saints*, p. 112.
10. Lupton, *Citizen-Saints*, p. 114.
11. Lupton, *Citizen-Saints*, p. 115.
12. Lupton, *Citizen-Saints*, p.116.
13. Lupton, *Citizen-Saints*, p. 116.
14. Lupton, *Citizen-Saints*, p. 118.
15. Lupton, *Citizen-Saints*, p. 120.
16. Lupton, *Citizen-Saints*, p. 121.
17. Stephen Greenblatt, *Hamlet in Purgatory* (Princeton: Princeton University Press, 2001), p. 212.
18. Greenblatt, *Hamlet in Purgatory*, p. 218.
19. Greenblatt, *Hamlet in Purgatory*, p. 222.
20. Greenblatt, *Hamlet in Purgatory*, p. 222.
21. Greenblatt, *Hamlet in Purgatory*, p. 223.
22. Greenblatt, *Hamlet in Purgatory*, p. 226.
23. Greenblatt, *Hamlet in Purgatory*, p. 227.
24. Greenblatt, *Hamlet in Purgatory*, p. 229.
25. Greenblatt, *Hamlet in Purgatory*, p. 247.
26. Greenblatt, *Hamlet in Purgatory*, pp. 256–7.
27. Gillian Woods, *Shakespeare's Unreformed Fictions* (Oxford: Oxford University Press, 2013), p. 143.

28. Woods, *Shakespeare's Unreformed Fictions*, p. 145.
29. Woods, *Shakespeare's Unreformed Fictions*, p. 153.
30. Woods, *Shakespeare's Unreformed Fictions*, p. 154.
31. Woods, *Shakespeare's Unreformed Fictions*, p. 158.
32. Woods, *Shakespeare's Unreformed Fictions*, p. 163.
33. Woods, *Shakespeare's Unreformed Fictions*, p. 163.
34. Woods, *Shakespeare's Unreformed Fictions*, p. 164.
35. Woods, *Shakespeare's Unreformed Fictions*, p. 166.
36. Qtd Woods, *Shakespeare's Unreformed Fictions*, pp. 142, 166.
37. Woods, *Shakespeare's Unreformed Fictions*, p. 166.
38. Woods, *Shakespeare's Unreformed Fictions*, p. 167.

CONCLUSION

1. Ewan Fernie, 'Introduction' to *Spiritual Shakespeares*, Accents on Shakespeare series (London and New York: Routledge, 2005), p. 2.
2. Fernie, *Spiritual Shakespeares*, p. 3.
3. Fernie, *Spiritual Shakespeares*, p. 186.
4. Fernie, *Spiritual Shakespeares*, p. 187.
5. Valerie Traub, 'The Nature of Norms in Early Modern England: Anatomy, Cartography, *King Lear*', *South Central Review*, 26:1–2 (Winter & Spring 2009), 44.
6. Traub, 'The Nature of Norms', p. 45.
7. Geraldo U. de Sousa, *At Home in Shakespeare's Tragedies* (Farnham, Surrey; Burlington, VT: Ashgate, 2010), p. 9.
8. Sousa, *At Home*, p.10.
9. Tom Standage, *Writing on the Wall: Social Media – The First 2,000 Years* (London: Bloomsbury, 2013), p. 3.
10. Standage, *Writing on the Wall*, p. 4.
11. Standage, *Writing on the Wall*, p. 77. A facsimile of the pages (pp. 281–2) of Meres' *Palladis Tamia* on which the 'sugred sonnets' comment occurs is available online at: http://internetshakespeare.uvic.ca/Library/SLT/life/early%20maturity/meres.html.
12. W. B. Yeats, 'Lapis Lazuli', in *Collected Poems of W. B. Yeats* (London and Basingstoke: Macmillan, 1977), p. 338.

Select Bibliography

EDITIONS OF SHAKESPEARE

All Shakespeare quotations are from the RSC Shakespeare but reference has sometimes been made to the Oxford Shakespeare and Norton *Tragedies*.

Shakespeare, William. *The Complete Works*. The RSC Shakespeare, ed. Jonathan Bate and Eric Rasmussen. Basingstoke: Palgrave Macmillan, 2007.

Shakespeare, William. *The Complete Works*, The Oxford Shakespeare, ed. Stanley Wells and Gary Taylor. Oxford: Oxford University Press, 1988.

Shakespeare, William. *Tragedies*. The Norton Shakespeare, based on the Oxford edition, ed. Stephen Greenblatt. New York and London: W. W. Norton, 1997.

INTRODUCTION

Burrow, Colin. 'What Is a Shakespearean Tragedy?'. In *The Cambridge Companion to Shakespearean Tragedy*, ed. Claire McEachern. 2nd edn. Cambridge: Cambridge University Press, 2013, pp. 1–23.

Dewar-Watson, Sarah. *Tragedy: A Reader's Guide to Essential Criticism*. Palgrave Macmillan Readers' Guides to Essential Criticism series. London and Basingstoke: Palgrave Macmillan, 2014.

McAlindon, Tom. 'What Is a Shakespearean Tragedy?'. In *The Cambridge Companion to Shakespearean Tragedy*, ed. Claire McEachern. Cambridge: Cambridge University Press, 2002, pp. 1–22.

Muir, Kenneth. *Shakespeare's Tragic Sequence*. London: Hutchinson, 1972.

CHAPTER ONE: THE AUGUSTANS

Dennis, John. 'On the Genius and Writings of Shakespeare'. In *Eighteenth Century Essays on Shakespeare*, ed. D. Nicol Smith. Glasgow; James Maclehose and Sons, 1903, pp. 83–105. Available online at:
http://www.gutenberg.org/files/30227/30227-pdf.pdf.

Dorsch, T. S. (ed. and trans.). *Classical Literary Criticism: Aristotle:* On the Art of Poetry; *Horace:* On the Art of Poetry; *Longinus:* On the Sublime. Penguin Classics series. Harmondsworth: Penguin, 1984.

Dryden, John. 'The Grounds of Criticism in Tragedy' [Preface to *Troilus and Cressida* (1679)]. In *Dramatic Poesy and Other Essays*. Everyman's Library no. 568. London: J. M. Dent, 1939, pp. 126–45.

Eliot, T. S. 'Hamlet and His Problems' (1919). In *The Sacred Wood: Essays on Poetry and Criticism*. London: Methuen, 1972, pp. 95–103. Essay republished as 'Hamlet' (1919) in T. S. Eliot, *Selected Essays*, 2nd edn (London: Faber and Faber, 1932), pp. 141–6.

Johnson, Samuel. 'Preface' to *The Plays of William Shakespeare*. In Samuel Johnson, *The Major Works*, ed. Donald Greene. World's Classics series. Oxford: Oxford University Press, 2000, pp. 419–56.

Jonson, Ben. 'To the memory of my beloved, the AUTHOR Master William Shakespeare and what he hath left us'. In William Shakespeare, *The Complete Works*. The RSC Shakespeare, ed. Jonathan Bate and Eric Rasmussen. Basingstoke: Macmillan, 2007, pp. 61–2.

Milton, John. 'L'Allegro'. In *Complete Shorter Poems*, ed. John Carey. Longman Annotated English Poets series. Fourth impression with corrections 1981, seventh impression. London and New York: Longman, 1989, pp. 130–9.

Rymer, Thomas. *The Tragedies of the Last Age Consider'd and Examin'd* (1678; available 1677). And *A Short View of Tragedy* (1693, ed. Arthur Freeman). The English Stage: Attack and Defense 1577–1730 series. New York and London: Garland, 1974. In this edition, the pagination restarts at page 1 for the main text of *Short View*.

Smith, D. Nicol (ed.). *Eighteenth Century Essays on Shakespeare*. Glasgow: James Maclehose and Sons, 1903, pp. 83–105. Available online at: http://www.gutenberg.org/files/30227/30227-pdf.pdf.

Sullivan, Erin. 'Anti-Bardolatry through the Ages, or, Why Voltaire, Tolstoy, Shaw and Wittgenstein didn't like Shakespeare'. *Opticon1826*, 2 (1 April 2007), 9 pp. Available online at: http://www.ucl.ac.uk/opticon1826/archive/issue2/VfPA_H_Shakespeare.pdf.

CHAPTER TWO: THE ROMANTICS

Austen, Jane. *Mansfield Park*. Penguin English Library. Harmondsworth: Penguin, 1975.

Byron, Lord, George Gordon. *Don Juan*, ed. T. G. Steffan, E. Steffan and W. W. Pratt. Penguin English Poets series. Harmondsworth: Penguin, 1973.

Coleridge, Samuel Taylor. *Lectures and Notes on Shakespeare and Other Dramatists*. World's Classics series no. 363. London: Humphrey Milford; Oxford University Press, 1931.

Hazlitt, William. *Characters of Shakespeare's Plays*. World's Classics series no. 205. London: Humphrey Milford; Oxford University Press, 1916.

Lamb, Charles. 'On the Tragedies of Shakspeare [*sic*], considered with reference to their fitness for Stage Representation'. In *Shakespeare Criticism: A Selection: 1623–1840*, ed. D. Nicol Smith. World's Classics series no. 212. London: Oxford University Press, 1916.

Schlegel, August von Wilhelm. *Lectures on Dramatic Art and Literature*, trans. John Black. Project Gutenberg: EBook #7148, 2003.

Woods, Gillian. *Shakespeare: Romeo and Juliet: A Reader's Guide to Essential Criticism*. Palgrave Macmillan Readers' Guides series. Basingstoke and New York: Palgrave Macmillan, 2013.

CHAPTER THREE: THE VICTORIANS

Brandes, George. *William Shakespeare*, no trans. given, new impression revd. with two appendices. London: William Heinemann, 1920.

Dowden, Edward. *Shakspere: A Critical Study of His Mind and Art*. 15th edn. London: Kegan Paul, Trench, Trübner, ?1918.

Gervinus, G[eorg] G[ottfried]. *Shakespeare Commentaries*, trans. 'under the author's superintendence' by F[rances] E[lizabeth] Bunnètt, new edn, revd. London: Smith, Elder, 1877.

Sawyer, Robert. *Victorian Appropriations of Shakespeare*. Madison, NJ: Fairleigh Dickinson University Press, 2003.

CHAPTER FOUR: CHARACTER AND CORRELATIVE

Bradley, A. C. 'Hegel's Theory of Tragedy'. In *Oxford Lectures on Poetry*. London and Basingstoke: Macmillan St Martin's Press, 1970, pp. 68–95.

Bradley, A. C. *Shakespearean Tragedy: Lectures on* Hamlet, Othello, King Lear, Macbeth. St Martin's Library. London: Macmillan, 1957.

Duffy, John J. 'T. S. Eliot's Objective Correlative: A New England Commonplace'. *New England Quarterly*, 42:1 (Mar. 1969), 108–15.

Eliot, T. S. 'Hamlet and His Problems' (1919). In *The Sacred Wood: Essays on Poetry and Criticism*. London: Methuen, 1972, pp. 95–103. Essay republished as 'Hamlet (1919)' in T. S. Eliot, *Selected Essays*, 2nd edn. London: Faber and Faber, 1932, pp. 141–6.

Tennyson, Alfred Lord. *Lancelot and Elaine*. In *Idylls of the King*, in Tennyson, *Poems and Plays*, Oxford Standard Authors, ed. T. Herbert Warren, revd and enlgd Frederick Page. London, Oxford, New York: Oxford University Press, 1975, pp. 368–89.

CHAPTER FIVE: PSYCHOANALYSIS AND DESIRE

Freud, Sigmund. *The Interpretation of Dreams*, trans. James Strachey, revd Angela Richards. Pelican Freud Library, vol. 4. Harmondsworth: Penguin, 1977. German text available at: http://www.gutenberg.org/ebooks/40739.

Freud, Sigmund. 'Some Character-Types Met With in Psycho-Analytical Work'. In *The Complete Psychological Works of Sigmund Freud*, ed. John Strachey and Anna Freud. Vol. 14: 1914–1916. London: The Hogarth Press and the Institute of Psycho-Analysis, 1957, pp. 311–33. German text available at: http://www.gutenberg.org/ebooks/29101.

Jones, Ernest. *Hamlet and Oedipus*. Garden City, NY: Doubleday Anchor Books, 1954.

Lacan, Jacques. 'Sept Leçons sur *Hamlet*' ['Seven Lessons on *Hamlet*']. In *Le désir et son interpretation 1958–1959, Le séminaire de Jacques Lacan livre VI*, texte établi par Jacques-Alain Miller. Paris: Éditions de la Martinière, 2013, pp. 279–419.

Spencer, T. J. B. (ed.). *Shakespeare's Plutarch: The Lives of Julius Caesar, Brutus, Marcus Antonius, and Coriolanus in the translation of Sir Thomas North* [1535–1604]. London: Penguin, 1964.

Stone, Jon, Jo Perthen and Alan J. Carson. 'REVIEW. 'A Leg to Stand On' by Oliver Sacks: a Unique Autobiographical Account of Functional Paralysis'. *Journal of Neurology, Neuroscience and Psychiatry*, 83:9 (2012), 864–7. Available online at: http://jnnp.bmj.com/content/83/9/864.full.pdf+html.

Wentersdorf, Karl P. '*Hamlet*: Ophelia's Long Purples'. *Shakespeare Quarterly*, 29:3 (Summer 1978), 413–17.

CHAPTER SIX: IMAGERY AND FORM

Brooks, Cleanth. 'The Naked Babe and the Cloak of Manliness' (1946). Collected in Brooks, *The Well Wrought Urn: Studies in the Structure of Poetry*. New York: Reynal and Hitchcock, 1947, pp. 3–46.

Campbell, Oscar James. 'Shakespeare and the "New Critics"'. In *Joseph Quincy Adams Memorial Studies*, ed. James G. McManaway, Giles E. Dawson and Edwin E. Willoughby. Washington: Folger Shakespeare Library, 1948, pp. 81–96.

Cooke, Katharine. *A. C. Bradley and His Influence in Twentieth-Century Shakespeare Criticism*. Oxford: Clarendon Press at Oxford University Press, 1972.

Eliot, T. S. 'The Metaphysical Poets'. In *Selected Essays*. London: Faber and Faber, 1932, pp. 281–91.

Knight, G. Wilson. *The Imperial Theme: Further Interpretations of Shakespeare's Tragedies Including the Roman Plays*. University Paperbacks series. London: Methuen, 1961.

Knight, G. Wilson. *The Wheel of Fire: Interpretations of Shakespearean Tragedy with Three New Essays*. University Paperbacks series. London: Methuen, 1960.

Knights, L. C. *Explorations: Essays in Criticism Mainly on the Literature of the Seventeenth Century*. Harmondsworth: Penguin Books in association with Chatto & Windus, 1964.

Knights, L. C. 'How Many Children Had Lady Macbeth? An Essay in the Theory and Practice of Shakespearean Criticism'. Cambridge: Minority Press, 1933, collected in *Explorations: Essays in Criticism Mainly on the Literature of the Seventeenth Century*. Harmondsworth: Penguin Books in association with Chatto & Windus, 1964, pp. 13–50.

Knights, L. C. 'Preface' to *Explorations: Essays in Criticism Mainly on the Literature of the Seventeenth Century*. Harmondsworth: Penguin Books in association with Chatto & Windus, 1964, pp. 9–11.

Knights, L. C. 'Prince Hamlet'. In L. C. Knights, *Explorations: Essays in Criticism Mainly on the Literature of the Seventeenth Century*. Harmondsworth: Penguin in association with Chatto & Windus, 1964, pp. 76–87.

Leavis, F. R. 'Literary Criticism and Philosophy'. In F. R. Leavis, *The Common Pursuit*. Harmondsworth: Penguin, 1978, pp. 211–22.

Spurgeon, Caroline F. E. *Shakespeare's Imagery and What It Tells Us*. Cambridge: Cambridge University Press, 1990.

Tredell, Nicolas. *Shakespeare:* Macbeth: *A Reader's Guide to Essential Criticism.* Palgrave Macmillan Readers' Guides to Essential Criticism series. Basingstoke and New York: Palgrave Macmillan, 2006, pp. 78–83 (on Oscar James Campbell and Helen Gardner).

CHAPTER SEVEN: ARCHETYPE AND ABSURDITY

Brook, Peter. 'Preface' to Jan Kott, *Shakespeare Our Contemporary*, trans. Boleslaw Taborski. 2nd edn. University Paperbacks series. London: Methuen, 1967, pp. ix–xi.

Easthope, Antony. *British Post-Structuralism since 1968.* London and New York: Routledge, 1988.

Frye, Northrop. *Fools of Time: Studies in Shakespearean Tragedy.* Toronto: University of Toronto Press; London: Oxford University Press, 1967.

Garber, Marjorie. *Shakespeare and Modern Culture.* New York: Pantheon, 2008.

Girard, René. *A Theatre of Envy: William Shakespeare.* Oxford: Oxford University Press, 1991.

Girard, René. *Violence and the Sacred*, trans. Patrick Gregory. Baltimore, MD: Johns Hopkins University Press, 1977.

Kott, Jan, *Shakespeare Our Contemporary*, trans. Boleslaw Taborski. 2nd edn. University Paperbacks series. London: Methuen, 1967.

Liebler, Naomi Conn. *Shakespeare's Festive Tragedy: The Ritual Foundations of Genre.* London and New York: Routledge, 1995.

CHAPTER EIGHT: HISTORY AND SUBJECTIVITY

Belsey, Catherine. *The Subject of Tragedy: Identity and Difference in Renaissance Drama.* London and New York: Routledge, 1985.

Dollimore, Jonathan. *Radical Tragedy: Religion, Ideology and Power in the Drama of Shakespeare and His Contemporaries.* Brighton: Harvester, 1984; 2nd edn: New York and London: Harvester Wheatsheaf, 1989; 3rd edn: Durham, NC: Duke University Press, 2004; Basingstoke: Palgrave Macmillan, 2010.

Greenblatt, Stephen. *Shakespearean Negotiations: The Circulation of Social Energy in Renaissance England.* Oxford: Clarendon Press at Oxford University Press, 1990.

Tennenhouse, Leonard. *Power on Display: The Politics of Shakespeare's Genres.* New York and London: Methuen, 1986.

Vickers, Brian. *Shakespeare:* Coriolanus. Studies in English Literature series no. 58. London: Edward Arnold, 1966.

CHAPTER NINE: GENDER AND SEXUALITY

Adelman, Janet. *Suffocating Mothers: Fantasies of Maternal Origin in Shakespeare's Plays,* Hamlet *to* The Tempest. New York and London: Routledge, 1992.

Berry, Philippa. *Shakespeare's Feminine Endings: Disfiguring Death in the Tragedies.* Feminist Readings of Shakespeare series. London and New York: Routledge, 1999.

Edwards, Jason. '"Tell Me Not Wherein I Seem Unnatural": Queer Meditations on *Coriolanus* in the Time of War'. In *Shakesqueer: A Queer Companion to the Complete Works of Shakespeare*, ed. Madhavi Menon. Durham, NC and London: Duke University Press, 2011, pp. 80–8.

Kahn, Coppélia. *Roman Shakespeare: Warriors, Wounds and Women.* Feminist Readings of Shakespeare series. London and New York: Routledge, 1997.

Menon, Madhavi. 'Introduction: Queer Shakes' to Madhavi Menon (ed.), *Shakesqueer: A Queer Companion to the Complete Works of Shakespeare.* Durham, NC and London: Duke University Press, 2011, pp. 1–27.

Tredell, Nicolas. *Shakespeare:* Macbeth: *A Reader's Guide to Essential Criticism,* Palgrave Macmillan Readers' Guides to Essential Criticism series. Basingstoke and New York: Palgrave Macmillan, 2006, pp. 130–5 (on Khan), pp. 138–42 (on Adelman).

CHAPTER TEN: ETHNICITY AND ECOLOGY

Alexander, Catherine M. S., and Stanley Wells (eds). *Shakespeare and Race*. Cambridge: Cambridge University Press, 2000.

Egan, Gabriel. *Green Shakespeare: From Ecopolitics to Ecocriticism*. Accents on Shakespeare series. London and New York: Routledge, 2006.

Estok, Simon C. *Ecocriticism in Shakespeare: Reading Ecophobia in Shakespeare's Plays*. Literatures, Cultures, and the Environment series. New York: Palgrave Macmillan, 2011.

Everett, Barbara. '"Spanish" Othello: the Making of Shakespeare's Moor'. In *Shakespeare and Race*, ed. Catherine M. S. Alexander and Stanley Wells. Cambridge: Cambridge University Press, 2000, pp. 64–81.

Hendricks, Margo. 'Surveying "Race" in Shakespeare'. In *Shakespeare and Race*, pp. 1–22.

Loomba, Ania. *Shakespeare, Race, and Colonialism*. Oxford Shakespeare Topics series. Oxford: Oxford University Press, 2002.

McCombie, Frank. 'Garlands in *Hamlet* and *King Lear*'. *Notes and Queries*, 226 (1981), 132–4.

Stallybrass, Peter. 'Shakespeare, the Individual, and the Text'. In *Cultural Studies*, ed. Laurence Grossberg, Cary Nelson and Paula Treichler. New York and London: Routledge, 1992, pp. 593–612.

Williams, Raymond. *Keywords: A Vocabulary of Culture and Society*, revd and expanded edn. London: Fontana, 1988.

CHAPTER ELEVEN: PHILOSOPHY AND ETHICS

Cavell, Stanley. *Disowning Knowledge in Seven Plays of Shakespeare*, updated edn. Cambridge: Cambridge University Press, 2003.

Derrida, Jacques. *Specters of Marx: The State of the Debt, the Work of Mourning and the New International*, trans. Peggy Kamuf, intro. Bernd Magnus and Stephen Cullenberg. New York and London: Routledge, 2006. French text available at: http://ebookbrowsee. net/spectres-de-marx-jacques-derrida-pdf-d307050478.

Marx, Karl, and Friedrich Engels. *The Communist Manifesto*. Great Ideas series no. 13. London: Penguin, 2004.

Nuttall, A. D. *Shakespeare the Thinker*. New Haven, CT and London: Yale University Press, 2007.

Rose, Jacqueline. '*Hamlet* – the "Mona Lisa" of Literature'. In Jacqueline Rose, *Sexuality in the Field of Vision*. London: Verso, 2005, pp. 123–40.

Wehrs, Donald R. 'Moral Physiology, Ethical Prototypes and the Denaturing of Sense in Shakespearean Tragedy'. *College Literature*, 33:1 (Winter 2006), 67–92.

CHAPTER TWELVE: RELIGIONS AND REFORMATIONS

Greenblatt, Stephen. *Hamlet in Purgatory*. Princeton: Princeton University Press, 2001.

Hammill, Graham and Julia Reinhard Lupton (eds). 'Introduction' to *Political Theology and Early Modernity*. Chicago and London: University of Chicago Press, 2012, pp. 1–20.

Lupton, Julia Reinhard. *Citizen-Saints: Shakespeare and Political Theology*. Chicago and London: University of Chicago Press, 2005.

Woods, Gillian. *Shakespeare's Unreformed Fictions*. Oxford: Oxford University Press, 2013.

CONCLUSION

Fernie, Ewan (ed.). *Spiritual Shakespeares*. London and New York: Routledge, 2005.

Sousa, Geraldo U. de. *At Home in Shakespeare's Tragedies*. Farnham, Surrey; Burlington, VT: Ashgate, 2010.

Standage, Tom. *Writing on the Wall: Social Media – The First 2,000 Years*. London: Bloomsbury, 2013.

Traub, Valerie. 'The Nature of Norms in Early Modern England: Anatomy, Cartography, *King Lear*'. *South Central Review*, 26:1– 2 (Winter & Spring 2009), 42–81.

Yeats, William Butler. 'Lapis Lazuli'. In *Collected Poems of W. B. Yeats*. London and Basingstoke: Macmillan, 1977, pp. 338–9.

Index

Adelman, Janet, 100, 111, 114
  Suffocating Mothers: Fantasies of Maternal Origin in Shakespeare's Plays, 7
  on *Coriolanus*, 104
  on *Hamlet*, 101–3
  on *King Lear*, 104–6
  on *Macbeth*, 104
  on *Othello*, 103–4, 108
Aeschylus, 18
  Eumenides, 21
Alexander, Catherine M. S.
  Shakespeare and Race, 120
All's Well That Ends Well, 3
Allston, Washington
  Lectures on Art, 38
Angry Young Men, 68
Anne, Queen, 9
Antony and Cleopatra, 3, 16, 22, 32, 49, 86, 112, 120, 124, 177 n.40
  as Jacobean tragedy, 7, 90, 91, 93
  in First Folio, 2
Antony and Cleopatra, critics on
  Belsey, 99, 100
  Dollimore, 95–6, 97
  Frye, 69, 70, 71
  Knights, 61
  Tennenhouse, 90
Aristotle, 4, 31, 60, 174 n.1
Augustan era, 9–16, 17
Austen, Jane, 17
  Mansfield Park, 18
  Pride and Prejudice, 17

Barber, C. L.
  Shakespeare's Festive Comedy, 78
Beat writers, 68
Beckett, Samuel
  Endgame (Fin de Partie), 5, 75
Belsey, Catherine, 82, 83, 101
  The Subject of Tragedy, 7, 97–100
  on *Antony and Cleopatra*, 99, 100
  on *Hamlet*, 98
  on *Macbeth*, 98–9, 100
Berry, Philippa, 100, 119
  Shakespeare's Feminine Endings, 7, 106–11

  on *Hamlet*, 107
  on *Macbeth*, 108–10
  on *Othello*, 107–8
Bible, 52
  1 Corinthians, 139
  Exodus, 158
  New Testament, 158–9, 160
  Old Testament, 102, 103, 158–9
  Romans, 158
  Ten Commandments, 88
  typology, 109
Blake, William, 17
Bradley, A. C., 29, 39, 41, 51, 54, 57, 72, 119
  Shakespearean Tragedy, 3, 4, 5, 7, 31–7, 59, 174 n.1, n.2, 174–5 n.21
  on *Hamlet*, 33, 36–7
  on *King Lear*, 33, 34–5, 59
  on *Macbeth*, 33, 36–7, 59
  on *Othello*, 23, 33–4, 37
Brandes, George, 26, 72
  William Shakespeare, 5, 28–9, 42, 175 n.3
  on *Hamlet*, 28–9
  on *King Lear*, 29
  on *Macbeth*, 28–9
  on *Othello*, 29
Brook, Peter
  and Kott, 72–3
Brooks, Cleanth, 50, 64–5
  'The Naked Babe and the Cloak of Manliness', 6, 65–7
  The Well Wrought Urn, 65
  on *Macbeth*, 65–6, 133
Bunnètt, F. E., 27
Burke, Kenneth
  Language as Symbolic Action, 183 n.46
Burrow, Colin, 4
Byron, George Gordon, Lord
  Don Juan, 17

Cambridge Companion to Shakespearean Tragedy, 4
Campbell, Lily B., 37
Campbell, Oscar James, 67, 179 n.83
Catholicism, 8, 88, 93, 160, 165

Cavell, Stanley, 136
  *Disowning Knowledge in Seven Plays of
    Shakespeare*, 8, 137–41
  on *King Lear*, 138
  on *Othello*, 138–41
Cervantes, Miguel de
  Don Quixote, 122–3
character-centred criticism, 6, 11, 12–13,
    14, 19, 21, 22, 23–4, 27, 31–7, 47, 66,
    89, 113–14, 116, 117, 118, 124, 130
  alternatives to, 6, 20–1, 25, 27–8, 43–4,
    48–50, 54, 58, 63, 69, 73, 74, 76–7,
    78, 81, 104–5
  objections to, 32, 37, 38, 44, 51, 52, 53,
    57, 60–1
characters, analyses of
  Antony, 38
  Cordelia, 21–2
  Coriolanus, 38
  Desdemona, 33–4, 91
  Gertrude, 39, 45
  Hamlet, 20, 22, 33, 36–7, 38, 41
  Iago, 22–3, 24, 34, 36, 73, 91, 125
  Lady Macbeth, 43
  Macbeth, 36
  Ophelia, 45
  Othello, 37, 38, 73, 169
  Polonius, 15
Charles II, King, 9
Cholmeley, Sir Richard, 87
Christianity, 37, 110, 131, 139, 156–60
Cicero, 150
'citizen-saint', 155–6, 160
Civil War, English, 94
'close reading', 7, 56, 65, 101, 110, 124
cognitive science, 150, 151, 154
Coleridge, Samuel Taylor, 5, 17, 18, 38, 41,
    57, 73, 137
  'Lectures upon Shakespeare and Other
    Dramatists', 23
  Literary Remains, 23
  'Notes' on Shakespeare, 23
  on *Hamlet*, 23, 24, 27
  on *King Lear*, 24–5
  on *Macbeth*, 24
  on *Othello*, 22, 24, 125
'combined parent concept', 47
The Comedy of Errors, 166
Conrad, Joseph
  'Heart of Darkness', 30
  The Secret Agent, 30
Cooke, Katherine
  A. C. Bradley and His Influence, 59

Coriolanus, 3, 7, 22, 24, 112, 113
  in First Folio, 2
Coriolanus, critics on
  Adelman, 104
  Dennis, 12
  Dollimore, 95, 96–7
  Edwards, 117–19, 183 n.48, n.49
  Egan, 128
  Estok, 133–6
  Frye, 69
cultural materialism, 82, 83, 131
Cymbeline, 32
  and *King Lear*, 27–8
  as 'late romance', 3
  in First Folio, 2

Dailreader, Celia R.
  Shakespeare and Race, 120
Daily Mail, 58
deconstruction, 7, 83, 101, 137
Degree, 76–7
Dennis, John, 5, 15
  'On the Genius and Writings of
    Shakespeare', 11–13
  on *Coriolanus*, 12
  on *Hamlet*, 13
  on *Julius Caesar*, 12, 13
  on *King Lear*, 13
  on *Macbeth*, 13
  on *Othello*, 13
De Quincey, Thomas
  Confessions of an English Opium Eater,
    17–18
  *On Murder Considered as One of the Fine
    Arts*, 18
Derrida, Jacques, 82, 136
  'Plato's Pharmacy', 81
  Specters of Marx, 8, 141–6
  on *Hamlet*, 141–6
Descartes, René
  Meditations on First Philosophy, 137
desire, 6, 32, 91
  in *Coriolanus*, 117–18
  in *Hamlet*, 6, 41–2, 45–7, 48–50, 102,
    107
  in *King Lear*, 92
  in *Othello*, 91, 103–4
  in *Titus Andronicus*, 125
  'mimetic desire', 7, 75–7
Dewar-Watson, Sarah
  *Tragedy: A Reader's Guide to Essential
    Criticism*, 4
'dissociation of sensibility', 57, 154

Dollimore, Jonathan, 82, 100
    Radical Tragedy, 7, 94–7, 128
    on *Antony and Cleopatra*, 95–6
    on *Coriolanus*, 95, 96–7, 134
    on *King Lear*, 94–5
'double time', 108–9
Dowden, Edward, 29
    *Shakespere: A Critical Study of His Mind and
        Art*, 5, 26–7
    on *Hamlet*, 26, 27
    on *King Lear*, 27
    on *Macbeth*, 27
    on *Othello*, 27
    on *Romeo and Juliet*, 26
Dryden, John, 5, 12, 17, 57
    'The Grounds of Criticism in Tragedy',
        11
Duffy, John J., 38

Eagleton, Terry, 128
Easthope, Antony
    British Post-Structuralism since 1968, 180
        n.68
ecology, 1, 7–8, 119, 120, 127–36
    and *Coriolanus*, 128, 133–4
    and *King Lear*, 128–32
'ecophobia', 132–3, 134–6
Edwards, Jason, 100
    '"Tell Me Not Wherein I Seem
        Unnatural"', 7, 117–19
    on *Coriolanus*, 117–19, 183 n.48, n.49
Egan, Gabriel, 119
    Green Shakespeare, 8, 127–32
    on *Coriolanus*, 128
    on *King Lear*, 128–32
Eliot, T. S., 20, 30, 57, 102
    'Hamlet and His Problems', 5–6, 10, 37,
        38–9, 42, 152
    'The Metaphysical Poets', 57, 178 n.30
    The Waste Land, 30
    on *Antony and Cleopatra*, 38
    on *Coriolanus*, 38
    on *Hamlet*, 38, 39
    on *Macbeth*, 39
    on *Othello*, 10, 38
Elizabeth I, Queen, 42, 90
Elizabethan era, 100
empiricism, 149–50
Engels, Friedrich
    The Communist Manifesto, 142
English Literature, as academic discipline,
        30, 31
Erasmus, Desiderius, 150

Estok, Simon C., 119
    Ecocriticism and Shakespeare, 8, 132–6
ethics, 53, 97, 136, 149, 150–4, 156
    and *Hamlet*, 151–4
    and *Julius Caesar*, 150–1
    and *King Lear*, 21
ethnicity, 1, 7–8, 24, 119, 120
    in *Antony and Cleopatra*, 120
    in *The Merchant of Venice*, 120
    in *Othello*, 19, 24, 33–4, 120, 121–4
    in *Titus Andronicus*, 120, 124–7
Everett, Barbara, 119
    'Spanish Othello', 7–8, 120–4
    on *Othello*, 123

fathers, 40, 84, 175 n.3
    in *Hamlet*, 6, 20, 29, 41, 42, 45, 46–7,
        48, 54, 69, 73, 102–3, 143, 144, 152,
        161–2, 163, 164
    in *Julius Caesar*, 47, 114, 151
    in *King Lear*, 74, 84–5, 87, 88, 92, 105–6,
        129, 130, 166, 167
    in *Macbeth*, 42–3, 44
    in *Othello*, 138
    in *Titus Andronicus*, 126–7
feminism, 7, 50, 71, 83, 99, 100, 101, 116, 133
Fernie, Ewan
    Spiritual Shakespeares, 168–9
    on *Hamlet*, 168–9
First World War, 30
form, 6, 30, 31, 39
    'spatial form', 6, 52
Foucault, Michel, 83
    Surveiller et punir [*Discipline and Punish*], 90–1
Freud, Sigmund, 101
    The Interpretation of Dreams, 6, 40–2
    'Some Character-Types Met With in
        Psychoanalytic Work', 6, 42–4
    on *Hamlet*, 40–2
    on *Macbeth*, 42–4
    on *Timon of Athens*, 42
Frye, Northrop
    Anatomy of Criticism, 68
    *Fools of Time: Studies in Shakespearean
        Tragedy*, 6–7, 68–72
    on *Antony and Cleopatra*, 69, 70, 71
    on *Coriolanus*, 69
    on *Hamlet*, 69
    on *Julius Caesar*, 69
    on *King Lear*, 69, 71
    on *Macbeth*, 69
    on *Othello*, 69, 71
    on *Romeo and Juliet*, 69, 70

on *Timon of Athens*, 69
on *Titus Andronicus*, 70
on *Troilus and Cressida*, 69, 70

Gardner, Helen, 179 n.83
Gennep, Arnold van
   Les Rites de Passage [*Rites of Passage*], 79–80
Gervinus, G. G., 26, 29, 72
   Shakespeare Commentaries, 27–8
   on *Hamlet*, 27
   on *King Lear*, 27, 28
   on *Macbeth*, 27
   on *Othello*, 27
   on *Timon of Athens*, 27
Girard, René, 82
   A Theatre of Envy, 7, 75–8
   Violence and the Sacred, 78
   on *Hamlet*, 76, 144
   on *Julius Caesar*, 76–8
   on *King Lear*, 76
   on *Troilus and Cressida*, 76
Goethe, Johann Wolfgang von, 20, 41
   Die Leiden des jungen Werthers [*The
      Sufferings of Young Werther*], 38
Goldberg, Jonathan, 117
   'The Anus in *Coriolanus*', 183 n.46
Greenblatt, Stephen, 2, 82, 97, 100, 154,
     168–9
   Hamlet in Purgatory, 89, 160–5
   Shakespeare and the Exorcists, 84–90
   Shakespearean Negotiations, 7, 84, 165
   on *Hamlet*, 160–5
   on *King Lear*, 84–9, 93

Halpern, Richard
   Shakespeare among the Moderns, 156
Hamlet, 3, 5, 8, 24, 40, 86, 167, 169, 176–7
   n.39
   as Elizabethan tragedy, 7, 90
   film (1948), 44
   ghost, 20, 46, 48, 141–6, 151–3, 160–5
   in First Folio, 2
   textual issues, 2
   Ur-Hamlet, 2
Hamlet, critics on
   Adelman, 101–3
   Belsey, 98
   Berry, 107
   Bradley, 33
   Brandes, 28–9
   Coleridge, 24
   Dennis, 13
   Derrida, 141–6

Dowden, 26
Eliot, 38–9
Fernie, 168–9
Frye, 69
Gervinus, 27
Greenblatt, 160–5
Hazlitt, 22, 57
Knight, 54–5
Knights, 60–1
Kott, 73, 75, 111
Lacan, 48–50
Nuttall, 146, 148–50
Schlegel, 19–21
Spurgeon, 62–3, 64
Tennenhouse, 90
Wehrs, 151–4
Hamlet, soliloquies and speeches
   'How all occasions', 2, 161
   'O that this too too', 102–3
   'There is a willow', 107
   ''Tis not alone my inky cloak', 98
   'To be, or not to be', 20, 29
Hammill, Donald
   Political Theology and Early Modernity, 155
Harsnett, Samuel
   *A Declaration of Egregious Popish
      Impostures*, 84–9, 165–7
Hazlitt, William, 18
   Characters of Shakespeare's Plays, 5, 22–3
   Lectures on the Spirit of the Age, 18
   on *Hamlet*, 22
   on *King Lear*, 22, 23
   on *Macbeth*, 22
   on *Othello*, 22–3
Hegel, G. W. F., 4, 31, 137, 174, ch. 4, n.2
Hendricks, Margo
   Shakespeare and Race, 120, 123
Henry V, 31, 132
Henry VI 2, 176 n.27
history, 1, 12, 13, 69, 71, 72, 74, 78, 93,
     97–8, 101, 111, 122, 160, 169, 170
   British (legendary), 84
   Elizabethan and Jacobean, 37
   Roman, 12, 77
   Spanish, 122
   Venetian, 160
history of ideas, 37, 110–11
history plays, 14, 60
Holinshed, Raphael, 52
Homer
   Odyssey, 71
humanism, 74, 96, 97–8, 101, 130, 131,
     156–7

imagery, 6, 7, 11, 16, 29, 35, 44, 51–67
  in *Hamlet*, 62–3
  in *King Lear*, 35, 62–3
  in *Macbeth*, 36, 55–6, 58, 59, 64, 65–6
  in *Othello*, 55–6, 63
  in *Romeo and Juliet*, 62
'intentional fallacy', 52
Islam, 121, 122, 156–8, 159–60

Jacobean era, 90, 91, 106, 111, 121
James I, King, 42, 90, 109, 111, 121
Jarry, Alfred
  Ubu Roi [*Ubu the King*], 30
Jekels, Ludwig, 43
Johnson, Samuel, 5, 9, 18, 57
  Preface, 'The Plays of William
    Shakespeare', 13–16
  on *Antony and Cleopatra*, 14
  on *Hamlet*, 15
  on *King Lear*, 13, 23
  on *Othello*, 15
Jones, Ernest, 61
  Hamlet and Oedipus, 6, 40, 44–8
  on *Hamlet*, 44–7, 48, 49
  on *Julius Caesar*, 47–8
Jonson, Ben, 9, 10
Joyce, James, 30
  Ulysses, 30
Judaism, 156–7, 160
Julius Caesar, 22, 31–2, 53, 81, 146
  in First Folio, 2
Julius Caesar, critics on
  Dennis, 12, 13
  Frye, 69
  Jones, 47–8
  Kahn, 112, 113–16

Kahn, Coppélia, 100
  *Man's Estate: Masculine Identity in
    Shakespeare*, 112
  *Roman Shakespeare: Warriors, Wounds and
    Women*, 7, 111–16
  on *Julius Caesar*, 113–16
Kantorowicz, Ernst
  The King's Two Bodies, 144, 156
King Lear, 3, 25, 49, 72, 169
  and *Cymbeline*, 27–8
  as Jacobean tragedy, 7, 90, 91, 92–3
  'Dover Cliff' scene, 74, 85–6, 130, 166–7
  ending, 23, 29, 88–9, 94–5, 167
  in First Folio, 2
  textual issues, 1–2
King Lear, critics on

Adelman, 104–6
Bradley, 33, 34–5, 59
Cavell, 138
Coleridge, 24–5, 28
Dennis, 13
Dollimore, 94–5
Dowden, 27, 57
Egan, 128–32
Frye, 69
Gervinus, 27
Greenblatt, 84–9
Hazlitt, 22, 23
Knight, 6, 54, 55, 56
Knights, 61
Kott, 5
Lamb, 23
Schlegel, 21–2
Spurgeon, 62–3, 64
Tennenhouse, 90, 94–5
Traub, 169
Woods, 165–7
Knight, G. Wilson, 35, 50, 62, 65
  The Imperial Theme, 57, 62
  *The Wheel of Fire: Interpretations of
    Shakespearean Tragedy*, 6, 51–6, 57, 62
  on *Hamlet*, 52, 54–5, 149
  on *King Lear*, 53, 54, 55
  on *Macbeth*, 52, 53, 55–6
  on *Othello*, 53, 55–6
Knights, L. C., 6, 37, 62
  'How Many Children Had Lady
    Macbeth?', 6, 56–61, 63, 65, 81
  'Prince Hamlet', 60–1, 63
  on *Hamlet*, 60–1
  on *King Lear*, 61
  on *Macbeth*, 58–60, 61
  on *Othello*, 61
Kolakoswki, Leszek, 75
Kolin, Philip C., 126
Kott, Jan, 5, 29
  and Peter Brook, 72
  Shakespeare Our Contemporary, 7, 72–5,
    111
  on *Hamlet*, 73–4, 75
  on *King Lear*, 74–5
  on *Macbeth*, 74
  on *Othello*, 73–4, 75

Lacan, Jacques, 83
  'Sept Leçons sur *Hamlet*' ['Seven Lessons
    on *Hamlet*'], 6, 40, 48–50, 176 n.39
Lamb, Charles
  'On the Tragedies of Shakespeare', 23

Leavis, F. R., 37, 51, 56, 57, 58, 60, 61, 65,
    67, 68
  'Literary Criticism and Philosophy', 177
    n.26
Leonardo da Vinci
  'Mona Lisa', 38
Liebler, Naomi Conn
  *Shakespeare's Festive Tragedy: The Ritual
    Foundations of Genre*, 7, 78–82, 107
  on *Coriolanus*, 79
  on *King Lear*, 79–80
  on *Macbeth*, 79–82
Life of Lazarillo de Tormes, 123
liminality, 79–80
Longinus, 11
Loomba, Ania, 119
  Shakespeare, Race and Colonialism, 8,
    124–7
  on *Titus Andronicus*, 124–7
Lucian, 150
Lupton, Julia Reinhard, 154, 155–60,
    168–9
  Citizen-Saints, 8
  Political Theology and Early Modernity, 155
  on *Othello*, 156–60

Macbeth, 3, 5, 32, 40, 86, 146, 169, 175 n.6
  as Jacobean tragedy, 7, 90, 91–2
  babes imagery, 66
  Banquo's ghost, 36, 86, 92, 121
  cloaking imagery, 65–6
  clothes imagery, 6, 64, 65–6
  in First Folio, 2
  Malcolm–Macduff scene, 58–9, 81–2
  textual issues, 2
  'Tomorrow and tomorrow' soliloquy,
    36–7, 59
Macbeth, critics on
  Adelman, 104
  Belsey, 98–9, 100
  Berry, 108–10, 111
  Bradley, 33, 36–7, 59, 82
  Brandes, 28–9
  Brooks, 65–7
  Coleridge, 24
  Dennis, 13
  Dowden, 27
  Eliot, 39
  Estok, 133
  Frye, 69
  Gervinus, 27
  Hazlitt, 22
  Knight, 54, 55–6

Knights, 56–61
Schlegel, 21
Spurgeon, 64
Tennenhouse, 90
MacCallum, Sir Mungo William
  *Shakespeare's Roman Plays and Their
    Background*, 3
Marx, Karl
  The Communist Manifesto, 142
Marxism, 83, 141, 145
Mary Queen of Scots, 42, 109, 111
Mason, H. A.
  Shakespeare's Tragedies of Love, 3
materialist criticism, 155, 168
McAlindon, Tom
  'What is a Shakespearean Tragedy?', 4,
    171 n.5
McCombie, Frank
  'Garlands in *Hamlet* and *King Lear*',
    131–2
McElroy, Bernard
  Shakespeare's Mature Tragedies, 3
Measure for Measure, 3
Menander, 123
Menon, Madhavi, 100
  Shakesqueer, 7, 116–19
The Merchant of Venice, 120
Meres, Francis
  Palladis Tamia: Wit's Treasury, 169
Middleton, Thomas, 2
A Midsummer Night's Dream, 24, 53, 72–3
Milton, John, 17
  'L'Allegro', 9–10
mimesis, 75
Modernism, 30–1
Molina, Tirso de
  El Burlador de Sevilla [*The Trickster of
    Seville*], 123
moral physiology, 150–4
mothers, 7, 40, 41, 70, 101–2, 109, 111
  in *Antony and Cleopatra*, 70, 99
  in *Coriolanus*, 113, 135
  in *Hamlet*, 6, 38, 39, 41, 45–7, 48, 62, 98,
    102–3, 153, 161, 162, 163, 164
  in *Julius Caesar*, 47, 114–15, 151
  in *King Lear*, 104–6, 129
  in *Macbeth*, 42–3, 44, 109, 111,
    182 n.14
  in *Othello*, 103–4
  in *Titus Andronicus*, 126, 127
Muir, Kenneth
  Shakespeare's Tragic Sequence, 4, 171,
    Introduction, n.5

Nashe, Thomas, 123
neuroscience, 8
New Criticism, 6, 52, 65, 67, 68
New Historicism, 7, 82, 83, 89–90, 117
Nietzsche, Friedrich
  The Birth of Tragedy, 4
Nuttall, A. D.
  Shakespeare the Thinker, 8, 136, 146–50
  on *Hamlet*, 148–50
  on *Julius Caesar*, 146–9

'objective correlative', 5–6, 38–9, 102
'ocularcentrism', 107–8
Oedipus complex, 40, 45, 47, 50
Oedipus legend, 40–1, 66
Olivier, Laurence, 44
On the Sublime, 11
Othello, 3, 5, 7–8, 24, 49, 120, 124–5, 167,
    177 n.40
  as Jacobean tragedy, 7, 90, 91
  comic aspects, 122–3, 139
  ethnicity, 19, 24, 33–4, 120, 121–4
  handkerchief, 10, 103–4, 107–8, 139–40,
    182 n.26
  in First Folio, 2
  'ocularcentrism', 107–8
  'Soft you' speech, 159–60
  textual issues, 2
  willow song, 2, 140
Othello, critics on
  Adelman, 103–4
  Berry, 107–8
  Bradley, 33
  Cavell, 138–41
  Coleridge, 24
  Dennis, 13
  Dowden, 27
  Everett, 7, 120, 121–4
  Frye, 69, 71
  Hazlitt, 22–3
  Knight, 55–6
  Knights, 61
  Lupton, 156
  Schlegel, 19
  Spurgeon, 64
  Tennenhouse, 90, 91
Ovid, 52
Owen, Wilfred, 31

Paganism, 156–7, 159
Paget, Sir James, 45, 176 n.15
Paster, Gail Kern
  The Body Embarrassed, 183 n.46

patriarchy, 71, 90, 91–3, 99, 100, 106, 127
Peele, George, 2
Pericles, 3, 87
'pharmakos', 79
philosophy, 4, 6, 8, 24, 53, 54, 56, 60, 63,
    70, 78, 82, 111, 136, 137–52
  and Bradley, 31
  and *Hamlet*, 22, 63, 141–6, 148–50
  and *Julius Caesar*, 146–8
  and *King Lear*, 75, 138
  and *Macbeth*, 58, 59
  and *Othello*, 73, 138–41
Picasso, Pablo
  Les Demoiselles d'Avignon, 30
Pirandello, Luigi, 30
Plutarch, 47, 52, 113
'poetic(al) justice', 12–13, 20, 89
Poland, 72
'political theology', 155, 156, 160
Pope, Alexander, 9, 17
Porter, Cole
  'Brush Up Your Shakespeare', *Kiss Me,
    Kate*, 183 n.46
postcolonial criticism/theory, 120, 124
postmodernism, 82, 101
poststructuralism, 83, 101, 137
  British poststructuralism, 82, 83
Pound, Ezra, 30
power/knowledge, 83
'presentism', 111, 117, 120, 132, 168–9
Protestantism, 89, 160, 164–5, 166
psychoanalysis, 6, 7, 39, 40–50, 61, 77, 83,
    101, 104, 106, 112, 114, 116, 137, 154
purgatory, 8, 89, 160, 163, 164–5

queer theory, 116–19

Radcliffe, Ann
  The Mysteries of Udolpho, 17
Rank, Otto, 47
The Rape of Lucrece, 112
Reformation, 8, 89, 97, 155, 160, 165
relativism, 149
religion, 8, 24, 64, 89, 154, 155–67
'religious turn', 154, 155
Restoration, 5, 9, 11
'return of the repressed', 104–6, 114, 115,
    154
Richard II, 14
Robertson, J. M., 38, 42
Romantic era, 5, 17–25, 26, 38, 54
Romeo and Juliet, 3, 22, 24, 32, 167
  in First Folio, 2

Romeo and Juliet, critics on
  Dowden, 26
  Frye, 69, 70
  Schlegel, 19
  Spurgeon, 62
Rose, Jacqueline
  'Hamlet – the "Mona Lisa" of Literature',
    152
Rymer, Thomas, 5, 14–15, 29, 57, 89, 103
  A Short View of Tragedy, 10
  The Tragedies of the Last Age Considered,
    12–13
  poetic(al) and historical justice, 12–13
  T. S. Eliot on, 10, 57
  on *Othello*, 10, 108

St James, 121
St Paul, 139, 158
Sanderson, Robert
  Sermons, 108
Sassoon, Siegfried, 31
scapegoating, 7, 76, 77
scepticism, 8, 20–1, 137–41, 149–50, 155
Schlegel, August von, 26, 27, 72
  Lectures on Dramatic Art and Literature, 5,
    18–22
  on *Hamlet*, 19–21, 26, 27
  on *King Lear*, 21–2, 23
  on *Othello*, 19
  on *Romeo and Juliet*, 19
Schmitt, Carl, 155
  Political Theology, 156
science, 169
Scott, Sir Walter, 17
Shakespeare, William, life, 42, 61, 62, 175
    n.3
Shakespeare, William, Roman plays, 3, 7,
    12, 22, 111–16
Shakespeare, William, Tragedies
  absurd aspects, 71, 72, 75
  and ancient comedy, 123
  and ancient tragedy, 21, 22
  and Elizabethan tragedy, 7, 90, 93
  and Jacobean tragedy, 90, 91, 92, 93–4, 100
  archetypal aspects, 69, 71, 72
  as 'dramatic poems', 6, 57, 58, 59
  'big four', 3, 5, 22, 29, 33
  chance, 32
  characteristics, 22, 119, 167, 170
  classification, 2–3
  comic aspects, 122–3, 139
  definitions, 3–4, 31–3, 60, 63, 64, 69–72,
    75

domesticity, 169
'early tragedies', 3
gender, 1, 7, 69, 72, 91, 97, 100, 101,
    112, 116
genre, 2, 4, 7 12, 68, 90, 124, 165–6,
    170
homosexuality, 116, 117, 119, 133
language, 1, 5, 9, 12, 15, 16, 24, 35, 36,
    37, 46, 48–9, 55–6, 57, 95, 138, 145,
    147, 168
'mature tragedies', 3
patterns, 6, 26–7, 150
sexuality, 1, 7, 35, 42, 93, 96, 100, 101,
    124, 126, 133, 149
sources, 84–9
spirituality, 168–9
structure, 21, 22, 24, 69, 71, 72, 102–3,
    138, 141, 170
subjectivity, 7, 83, 96, 100, 101, 151,
    153, 154
supernatural, 32, 86, 88
total theory, 3–4, 7
'tragedies of love', 3
'tragedy of isolation', 7, 69
'tragedy of order', 7, 69
'tragedy of passion', 7, 69
tragic trait, 32–3
Shelley, Percy Bysshe, 17
Shuger, Debora
  *Political Theologies in Shakespeare's
    England*, 156
Sidney, Sir Philip
  Arcadia as source for *King Lear*, 84–5
Sinfield, Alan, 117
Sophocles, 41
  Antigone, 21–2
  Oedipus at Colonus, 40
  Oedipus Rex, 41
  Oedipus Tyrannos, 40
Sousa, Geraldo U. de
  At Home in Shakespeare's Tragedies, 169
Southey, Robert, 17
Spain, 121–2
Spinoza, Baruch
  Theological-Political Tractatus, 156
Spurgeon, Caroline, 35, 44, 50, 67
  Shakespeare's Imagery and What It Tells Us,
    6, 61–5, 66
  on *Hamlet*, 62–3
  on *King Lear*, 62–3
  on *Macbeth*, 64–5
  on *Othello*, 63
  on Romeo and Juliet, 62

Stallybrass, Peter
  'Shakespeare, the Individual and the
    Text', 134
Standage, Tom
  *Writing on the Wall: Social Media – The First
    2,000 Years*, 169–70, 187 n.11
Stoicism, 8, 146–9, 150
Stoll, E. E., 42
Stravinsky, Igor
  Le Sacre du Printemps [*Rite of Spring*], 30
Swift, Jonathan, 9
Swinburne, Algernon Charles, 173 n.1
  A Study of Shakespeare, 26

Tate, Nahum
  revised *King Lear* (1681), 13, 23, 130
Taylor, Gary, 1
The Tempest, 3, 53
Tennenhouse, Leonard, 97, 100, 111
  *Power on Display: The Politics of
    Shakespeare's Genres*, 7, 90–4
  on *Antony and Cleopatra*, 90, 91, 93
  on *Hamlet*, 90
  on *King Lear*, 90, 91, 92–3, 94–5, 106
  on *Macbeth*, 90, 91–2
  on *Othello*, 90, 91
Tennyson, Alfred Lord
  Lancelot and Elaine, Idylls of the King, 34,
    174–5 n.21
Tieck, Ludwig, 18
Timon of Athens, 3, 22, 35, 53, 62
  in First Folio, 2
Timon of Athens, critics on
  Freud, 42
  Frye, 69
  Gervinus, 27
Titus Andronicus, 3, 29, 70, 112, 117, 120
  in first folio, 2
  Peele co-author, 2
Titus Andronicus, critics on
  Estok, 133
  Loomba, 124–7
tragedia di fin lieto [tragedy-with-comic-
    ending], 89
tragedy, definitions of, 3, 4, 5
Traub, Valerie
  'The Nature of Norms in Early Modern
    England', 169
  on *King Lear*, 169

Tredell, Nicolas
  Shakespeare: Macbeth: *A Reader's Guide to
    Essential Criticism*, 179 n.83, 182 n.14,
    183 n.35
Troilus and Cressida, 3, 32, 69, 76, 177 n.39
  in First Folio, 2, 174, ch. 4, n.6
Turner, Victor, 82
  The Ritual Process, 80
Twelfth Night, 166

Vickers, Sir Brian
  Shakespeare, Co-Author, 2
  Shakespeare: Coriolanus, 96–7
Victorian era, 5, 25, 26–9, 34, 117,
    173 n.1
Virgil, 52
'visor effect', 143
Voltaire, 14–15
  on *Hamlet*, 15

Walpole, Horace
  The Castle of Otranto, 17
War Poets, 31
Wehrs, Donald, 136
  'Moral Physiology, Ethical Prototypes',
    8, 150–4
  on *Hamlet*, 151–4
  on *Julius Caesar*, 150–1
Wells, Stanley, 1
  Shakespeare and Race, 120
Wentersdorf, Karl P.
  '*Hamlet*: Ophelia's Long Purples', 176–7
    n.39
Williams, Raymond
  Keywords, 134
Wilson, John Dover, 50
The Winter's Tale, 3, 24
Woods, Gillian, 154, 168–9
  Shakespeare: Romeo and Juliet: *A Reader's
    Guide to Essential Criticism*, 172–3 n.7
  Shakespeare's Unreformed Fictions, 8,
    165–7
Woolf, Virginia, 30
  Mrs Dalloway, 30
Wordsworth, William, 17

Yeats, W. B.
  'Lapis Lazuli', 170
Yorke, Sir John and Lady Julyan, 87